DEVELOPMENTAL ASPECTS IN LEARNING TO WRITE

STUDIES IN WRITING

VOLUME 8

Series Editor:

Gert Rijlaarsdam, *University of Amsterdam, The Netherlands*

Editorial Board:

Linda Allal, *University of Geneva, Switzerland*
Eric Espéret, *University of Poitiers, France*
David Galbraith, *Staffordshire University, UK*
Joachim Grabowski, *University of Heidelberg, Germany*
Lucia Mason, *University of Padova, Italy*
Marta Milian, *Universitat Autonoma Barcelona, Spain*
Sarah Ransdell, *Florida Atlantic University, USA*
Liliana Tolchinsky, *University of Barcelona, Spain*
Mark Torrance, *University of Derby, UK*
Annie Piolat, *University of Aix-en-Provence, France*
Païvi Tynjala, *University of Jyväskylä, Finland*
Carel van Wijk, *Tilburg University, The Netherlands*

Kluwer Academic Publishers continues to publish the international book series Studies in Writing, founded by Amsterdam University Press. The intended readers are all those interested in the foundations of writing and learning and teaching processes in written composition. The series aims at multiple perspectives of writing, education and texts. Therefore authors and readers come from various fields of research, from curriculum development and from teacher training. Fields of research covered are cognitive, socio-cognitive and developmental psychology, psycholinguistics, text linguistics, curriculum development, instructional science. The series aim to cover theoretical issues, supported by empirical research, quantitative as well as qualitative, representing a wide range of nationalities. The series provides a forum with research from established researchers, with contributions of young researchers.

Developmental Aspects in Learning to Write

Edited by

Liliana Tolchinsky
Associate Professor Department of Linguistics,
University of Barcelona, Spain

KLUWER ACADEMIC PUBLISHERS
DORDRECHT / BOSTON / LONDON

A C.I.P. Catalogue record for this book is available from the Library of Congress.

ISBN 0-7923-6979-3 (HB)

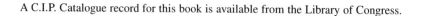

Published by Kluwer Academic Publishers,
P.O. Box 17, 3300 AA Dordrecht, The Netherlands.

Sold and distributed in North, Central and South America
by Kluwer Academic Publishers,
101 Philip Drive, Norwell, MA 02061, U.S.A.

In all other countries, sold and distributed
by Kluwer Academic Publishers,
P.O. Box 322, 3300 AH Dordrecht, The Netherlands.

Printed on acid-free paper

Printed in the Netherlands

TABLE OF CONTENTS

vi

INTRODUCTION

Developmental Perspectives on Writing

LILIANA TOLCHINSKY

University of Barcelona, Spain

The advent of the sixties is considered a crucial moment for the discovery of writing as an object worthy of intellectual inquiry (Havelock, 1986). A number of books, which came out in that decade, set the stage for this turn-to-writing. One of them was the *Preface to Plato* by Eric Havelock. This book, published in 1963, was to become a milestone in the discovery of literacy as a field of research (Bockheimer, 1998). Havelock (1986) referred to three more works that came out at the same time, and Bockheimer suggested adding other publications; for example *La pensée sauvage* by Levi Strauss (1962); *The consequences of literacy* by Jack Goody and Ian Watt (1963) and *La geste et la parole* by Laroi - Gourham (1964/65).

The authors of these books were anthropologists, philosophers and sociologists who coincided in highlighting the significance of writing for human development and, more specifically, for language development. They maintained that many institutions, ideas, beliefs, opinions and convictions of the Western world were a by-product of an 'alphabetized mind'. Writing was for them one of the pillars of subjectivity, responsible for the rise of consciousness, for our conception of words and for our notion of true and false. Amazingly linguists, psycholinguists, psychologists and educators did not participate in the turn-to-writing. The first[1], did not give any atten-

---

[1] *There were some exceptions to this generalization. For example, Vacheck from the Prague Circle who wrote an important work about the need to consider written language as a functional variety of language (Vackeck, 1932/1988), and Vygotsky, by then a Soviet psychologist who was the first to acknowledge the importance of looking at the 'prehistory of written languages' meaning the early development of writing in the child. Moreover the study of written discourse never ceased to be the focus for philology and literature studies*

1

L. Tolchinsky (ed.), Developmental Aspects in Learning to Write, 1–11.
© 2001 *Kluwer Academic Publishers. Printed in the Netherlands.*

tion to writing, while for educators writing was just an instrumental visual-motor ability that had to be taught step by step at school.

The situation has greatly changed. Nowadays the study of writing has become a multidisciplinary endeavor that establishes a 'double bind' (Pontecorvo, 1997) with specialists looking at writing from anthropological, philosophical or sociological perspectives on the one hand and within linguistic and psycholinguistic frameworks on the other. As a consequence, studies of writing generally take into account insights from theoretical linguistics and psycholinguistics. And, conversely, many linguists (*e.g.*, Scholes, 1993; Linnel, 1982) recognize the role of writing not only in determining basic linguistic constructs and shaping our native intuitions of language but also in enabling the very existence of linguistics. In Bugarski's words, 'Basic linguistic constructs like phoneme, morpheme, word, sentence, grammar, languages and so on are all largely, and variously determined by the written mode of linguistic expression. This is true not only in the trivial sense that without writing there would never have been any linguistics, and hence any linguistics constructs in the first place. It is also true in the deeper sense: such concepts owe much in their genesis and development, to specific features of written as against spoken language' (Bugarski, 1993:15).

Increasingly, psycholinguists tend to explore language development in the light of literacy. They are particularly interested in the route that children take in making 'linguistic literacy' part of their cognitive abilities and in the effect of literacy on language and development. Within this perspective, literacy is viewed as one thread of linguistic knowledge which is characterized by the availability of multiple linguistic resources, and by the ability to take control of one's own linguistic knowledge and to view language from numerous perspectives (Ravid & Tolchinsky, in press).

Developmental psychologists have also begun to recognize notational knowledge in general and writing in particular as a domain of development as is the case with mathematical or physical knowledge (Karmiloff Smith, 1992). Moreover, even within the domain of cognitive science, writing and other symbolic systems are conceived of as a 'manipulation of the environment that transforms problem-spaces for the human brain' (Clark, 1999: 252). In other words, symbolic systems are not only communicative tools but also intervening factors which transform the dynamics of mental computation.

The chapters in this volume are a new contribution to the growing body of research in the study of writing gradually reflected in the *Studies on Writing Series*. It is a contribution from a developmental, cross-linguistic and cross-writing systems perspective which covers developmental changes in a variety of aspects involved in learning to write from preschool up to university level. It provides information about the knowledge dimensions encoded in three different writing systems – the Roman alphabetical system, the Hebrew system and the Chinese system – in the context of six different languages.

1 MEANINGS OF DEVELOPMENT

In its most general sense the goal of a developmental approach to writing is to discover the particular ways in which knowledge of writing evolves with time. We should remember, however that this developing knowledge is unavoidably intertwined with school literacy. In the societies in which the authors in this book have gathered their data and in the age ranges they have considered, the passing of time involves increasing experience with writing mainly at school. Therefore, what we obtain in most chapters is a description and explanation of the changes occurring in particular knowledge components of writing as a result of an increasing writing experience.

An additional sense in which development is used in this book relates to an increased semiotic repertoire. This option is represented in this volume by the position of Gunther Kress as quoted in *Scott's* chapter. According to this view, 'development' must be seen as in 'intimate connection with the possibilities of systems of representation'; that is, 'development' is linked to the individual's 'semiotic repertoire' (*i.e.* the particular resources of, for example, language, drawing, or gesture, which the individual has available for representing and communicating her meanings). Within this view development means an increasing use of representational means, and, consequently, developmental growth implies an increase in the proficient deployment of a growing range of symbolic resources. This is the kind of development which Scott is looking for when she observes how students gain experience with a particular genre and a new writing instrument. Her chapter focuses on text production by university students writing academic essays and theses. Although at this level conventions of writing have been mastered, many of Scott's subjects are occupied with the specificity of written English because they are students who use English as an additional language. Moreover, most of them are also occupied in discovering the use of computers to word process their essays or theses.

Scott's aim was to identify postgraduate students' perceptions of the possibilities English offers for the writing of academic argument and to explore how these students accommodate to a new medium which is likely to affect their written expression and communication. In this chapter we learn that development can be seen as a change in the students' perceptions of the semiotic possibilities of written language and in their use of the word-processor's properties and facilities not simply as editing tools but as semiotic resources. Thus, she introduces a core issue in writing, which is relevant at all ages: the influence of the writing instrument, in this case an instrument that enables the writer to perform many operations which have an effect not only on the processing of writing–in terms of velocity or efficiency – but also on the kinds of meanings being expressed.

Finally, another sense of development approached in the book concerns the reorganization and restructuring of writing activities as a result of changing social conditions. In *Lacasa, Martin and Reina*'s chapter development is viewed as an indicator of the modifications in the social organization of the class and in the group hierarchical structure, in the presence or absence of the teacher.

Taking the different perspectives of development offered in the book as a whole we can appreciate the many factors that might influence changes in writing conceptions and performance: time, increasing experience, school literacy, semiotic amplification, writing instruments and social environment. The above are just part of a long list of contexts involved in the development of writing.

2   KNOWLEDGE DIMENSIONS OF WRITING

The term writing entails multiple meanings. It refers to a cultural practice, fulfilling different functions, to the notational system used in these practices and also to the discursive genres resulting from that practice. In the first sense, we talk about writing for mnemonic, magic, religious, poetic or referential functions.

In the second sense we talk about writing systems (*e.g.*, cuneiform, alphabetic, etc) for referring to the different system of graphic signs that are used and in the third sense we talk, for example, about nonfiction writing, business writing, or careless writing. For that latter sense we use the term writings or written language. The practice of writing in multiple circumstances leads to a variety of discursive products characterized by lexical, grammatical and rhetorical devices that are conditioned, though not exclusively, by the medium. In some linguistic communities, once the discursive genres initially associated with the written medium became rooted in those of the community they became detached from the medium and 'circulated' medium-free according to the communicative circumstances. We can find written versions of casual conversations and we can hear elaborated and formal 'written language' in an oral lecture. In other communities not only the discursive style but also the syntactic and lexical features of the language remained attached to the medium (Ibrahim, 1994) implying a marked diglossia between written and spoken language.

Consequently, in some communities it might not be a requisite for the individual to learn to write in order to gain access to the 'language in writing' and to the different genres of written prose because they circulate by other means, whereas in other communities, probably those with a marked diglossia it might be a condition.

The various senses of writing are dealt with in this volume but with differing weight. Lacasa, Martin and Reina's explored the development of writing as an activity without dwelling specifically either on the features of writing as notational system or on the features of written texts. Their aim was to explore in an open-ended fashion how children compose a text as they work in small groups, by paying special attention to how collaboration with each other is integrated with adult roles. Their work is more concerned with the ways children reason with language and the ways in which the social organization of the class affects their discursive behavior than with analyzing the particularities of written products and writing process.

Sandbank, on the other hand, analyzed the production of written texts both from the perspectives of discursive unfolding and the conventions of the writing system. Her chapter deals with the development of text writing in Hebrew during the transition from preschool to primary school. She assumes that a full command of the conventions of the writing system is not a condition for writing different discursive genres and so she asked the children to re-write a story and to describe one of the elements in the story. She observed the way children write and read their own texts, the way they produce a graphic separation between words, and the modifications they produce in their texts while writing, reading and revising them. She found that the nature of the particular discursive genre influences the three aspects. From her study it is clear that we do not learn to read, to write or to revise in a genre-free way, rather the processes and conventions of writing are strongly influenced by the discursive mode. On this basis she suggests that 'the distinction between knowledge of the writing system and knowledge of written language could not be maintained so clearly from the point of view of the child writer who has not yet mastered conventional writing' (Sandbank, this volume).

Many of the dimensions of knowledge encoded in the conventions of writing systems are dwelt on in the different chapters in the book but also with differing weight and differing approaches. The writing systems included in the book differ along two dimensions of knowledge: the repertoire of individual signs and the links to the units and levels of the language these signs represent but all of them relate to meaning through language. One of the main issues concerning the development of writing has, indeed, been to disclose whether and how children grasp the relationships between the signs of writing and language. In this respect, *Pontecorvo and Rossi* raised a fundamental question in their chapter: 'Are children at some moments in their early literacy development sensitive to the content of what they represent through writing?'

A number of studies have shown that children look for ways to reflect differences in content in their written productions. For example, when requested to produce diminutives – which in Italian and Spanish are formed with suffixes that generate words always longer than the base word although the object referred to is smaller – some children increase or diminish the number of graphic marks according to the size of the object and not according to the length of the word (Pontecorvo, 1997). A similar trend was found when preschoolers were asked to write pairs of words in which the longer word represent the smaller object and the shorter word represents the larger one. Some children try to adapt the number of graphic marks to the size of the referent. Although there is some doubt about the generality of this phenomenon, there is no doubt that children are concerned with the content of what they are writing even before they look for ways to reflect in their written production the sound pattern of the words.

The aim of the study which Pontecorvo and Rossi report in their chapter was to investigate the hypothesis that, before they are systematically taught writing, preliterate children work out the written representations of absence, negation, impossibility and falsity. These semantic cases were selected because of the potential cognitive conflict that they can create. For example there is a potential conflict between them and the use of letters to represent something which does not have the status of a concrete referent or of an existing event. The authors found that some responses to the semantic cases correlated with the level of writing development whereas others correlated neither with level of writing nor with age. The conclusions raised in this chapter are in line with those suggested in Sandbank's chapter. In each study children were required to write different units – sentences in Pontecorvo and Rossi's study, texts in Sandbank's study. The constraints of content also differed in the two studies – conflicting semantic cases in Pontecorvo and Rossi's study, discursive genres in Sandbank's study. Nevertheless the two studies showed how children's way of writing is sensitive to content and how much the development of the conventions of writing is related to the 'kind of stuff' children are attempting to write.

The rest of the studies dwelt more directly on the dimensions of knowledge encoded in the writing systems. Except for Chinese, the languages in which the studies presented in the book have been carried out, use alphabetic systems of writing (the Roman and the Hebrew system). Alphabetic systems have a relatively closed set of signs including letters and diacritics. Although the precise number of letters and diacritics and their linguistic correlates is language specific, the total number of each has been subject to relatively small variation from their inception to their current use if compared to the Chinese system

As explained in Chan and Nunes' chapter, in Chinese, there are eight types of basic stroke that conventionally combine in stroke-patterns to form the different characters. A character may consist of one stroke-pattern or a number of stroke-patterns. It is interesting to note that, in contrast to the alphabetic writing system, the number of characters in the Chinese system has been subject to strong variation. 'By the twelfth century AD it had soared to 23,000 and to as many as 43,000 in the eighteenth century... whereas most present day publications are supposed to represent 90 per cent of their content with the one thousand most frequent characters' (Coulmas, 1990: 106-107).

Chan and Nunes' study showed that Chinese children, apparently in an untutored way, recognize early the orthographic pattern of strokes; that is, they recognize those patterns that are permissible in Chinese in spite of not necessarily being Chinese characters. The authors showed as well how children's writing of their own names is distinguished at an early stage from drawing, and displays the superordinate and ordinate features of Chinese. The findings presented by Chan and Nunes are very interesting from many perspectives. First, they confirm once more that children are active learners – in the domain of writing as in other domains of knowledge – Their learning path is not a mere reflection of the steps followed by formal teaching. Second, this finding shows the important role of categorical perception in guiding children's learning of the features of writing. Starting with the pioneer study by Ferreiro and Teberosky (1979), studies in different languages have shown that children distinguish writing from other notational means very early and establish certain criteria for separating readable from non-readable strings and units (for a review see Tolchinsky, 1990). Chan and Nunes's study is a new contribution in this area of research. Indeed, recognizing patterns of strokes seems to be the best way of guiding children through the tremendous number of characters they must learn on their way to literacy.

As for the linguistic correlates of the writing elements, alphabetic systems represent phonological (rather than semantic) units as the basic components of the writing system (Coulmas, 1990). Alphabetic systems vary in the specific way in which they represent phonological components. For example, Hebrew over-represents consonants and under-represents vowels whereas in Roman systems consonants and vowels are represented in a more even way. However, graphic signs do not reflect only phonology. Morphological, syntactic and lexical information is also represented by direct graphic means. This dimension of alphabetic systems has been called the ideographic dimension (Blanche-Benveniste & Chervel, 1974) because information is provided directly and not by a linkage of the sign to sounds. Thus *helped* and *frightened* have an identically spelt *-ed* ending despite their differing sounds, /t/ and /d/ respectively. Endings such as *-ed* or *-ing* have morphological meaning as does the *--s* on the end of nouns. The same spellings can be subject to different interpretations and still have the same meaning while the selection of letters does not respond to phonographic explanations. And therefore the term ideographic is introduced. The ideographic is another dimension of knowledge that is becoming increasingly explored in developmental studies on writing. Previous research on the development of written morphology looks for the extent to which children need to be aware of grammatical relations in order to spell them correctly (*e.g.*, Levin, Ravid, & Rappaport, (in press), Nunes, Bryant, & Bindman, 1997).

The authors in this volume have dealt with a different sub-domain of written morphology: the written representation of plurals which in many cases is discrepant with phonetic realization. The fundamental hypothesis, which was confirmed both in the study by *Fayol and Totereau* and in the study by *Rijlaarsdam, Van Dort-Slijper and Couzijn*, is the fundamental role of experience with writing in the implementation of this knowledge.

Fayol and Totereau's main goal is to explore the learning and implementation of French written morphology for noun and adjective number (*–s*) on the one hand, and for verbs (*-nt*) on the other. This domain of written morphology is particularly interesting because the reference to oral language is of little use to learners. They must discover the specific markers of the written system and their meaning: *–s* for nouns and adjectives, *–nt* for verbs. Once this discovery has been made, then children have to automate the implementation of inflections. This automation needs regular and frequent practice in writing. Furthermore, the authors indicate that 'the existence of all these difficulties allows us to understand why France has elaborated and perpetuated the learning of grammar up until the ninth grade. Indeed children, teenagers and adults need to have an explicit grammar able to guide the detection and the correction of errors.' (Fayol & Totereau, this volume). The chapter is very interesting not only for the specific findings it presents, for example, the stages the subjects go through in their understanding of the rules and their difficulties in generalizing to every category of words and then their difficulty in automating the rules. It is also interesting because it presents evidence against the widespread conception of alphabetic systems as representing just sounds. In the case of written morphology it is clear that reliance on pronunciation is of no help. An additional point of interest is that the chapter opens the debate as to whether explicit teaching of grammar is the way to overcome the mistakes the subjects produced or whether a more effective writing practice should be recommended.

Rijlaarsdam, Van Dort-Slijper and Couzijn also focus on the domain of written morphology. They report two studies concerning the acquisition of the written morphology of adjectives and they show the influencing effect of adjacent elements in the application of spelling rules, in this case the effect of nouns on adjectives. Viewed from the perspective of correct spelling and morphology this would be a case of 'distracting influence' or 'miscue'. Nevertheless it can also be taken to illustrate parsing processes in writing. One of the main issues for the understanding of writing process relates to the unit of processing. In other words, what are 'the chunks' in which writers produce their texts? Do the 'chunks' correlate with any syntactic unit? Is there a strictly personal way of 'chunking' when writing? We believe that the kind of mistakes produced by writers while writing can be an interesting clue to follow in order to discover how different parts are connected in order to produce a message. In this case the influence of nouns on adjectives in defining the morphological spelling of the latter may indicate that writers are linking them in a way that differs from the way in which nouns and verbs are linked. In order to answer this question it would be necessary to compare morphological spelling mistakes in different parts of the sentence. In any case, this sounds like a very promising area of research.

In addition to phonology and morphology, alphabetic orthographies express suprasegmental, syntactic, semantic and pragmatic information in the form of additional non-alphabetic devices including punctuation marks. One of the main conventions in the domain of punctuation concerns the creation of blanks to indicate separation between words. Words are relatively easy to define in graphic terms – groups of letters separated by blanks on both sides – but to find stable linguistic correlates of this definition is rather tricky.

The above is another dimension of knowledge explored in the volume, and it concerns the separation between words. This convention is approached both in Sandbank's and in *Tolchinsky and Cintas*'s chapter. The latter chose to explore those cases in which subjects perform differently from group performance. Although they focused on Spanish speaking children from preschool up to third grade they reviewed data from other languages as well. Using this approach they were able to unveil the many factors that may be involved in children's decisions to create a blank. The syntactic category of the elements children are attempting to write, the syntactic domain in which elements are included, the length of the text, the immediate previous experience with other written texts, the kind of font privileged at school and the context of elicitation are some of the factors that may be involved in word-separation.

As it is well known, until the generalized use of printing, separation between words was very unstable, depending on the scribe and the way of reading. The results included in this chapter recall the pre-printing uses of writing when the separation between words was unstable, depending on the scribe and the way of reading. Another conclusion reached in the chapter concerns the notion of words as constructed through writing. Children approach the learning process with some intuitive prototypes as to what should be written separately – mainly nouns, proper names and some verbs – and only through interaction with the conventions of writing do they construct a notion of 'graphic word' that is language specific.

The two chapters (Sandbank's and Tolchinsky & Cintas's) show the extent to which, in the first stages of learning this convention is affected by discursive, syntactic and contextual factors. Moreover, the two chapters suggest that the notion of word is obtained by interacting with written texts rather than being constructed outside the writing system and applied later on.

3   WRITING AS A SOURCE OF KNOWLEDGE

Although the authors in the volume do not draw on any one sense of development and have explored different components of knowledge, they all believe that writing is a source of knowledge and they all consider symbolic systems to be intrinsically linked to the changes they observe in the different domains they have studied. That belief is not new. It has appeared in many different forms, ranging from the old, well known aphorism 'we learn to write by writing' to the more sophisticated forms expressed, for example, by the notion of a 'virtuous loop' suggested by Clark (1999). In its basic forms the claim is that with writing, as with any symbolic system, there is a particular interaction between users and artifacts so that both are affected and mutually influenced.

None of the conventions dealt with in the book – phonographic conventions in Hebrew, stroke patterns in Chinese, word separation in Hebrew or Spanish, spelling of plural markings in French or Dutch – can be learned outside the written system. However, sometimes the knowledge encoded in the system is just one among other sources of knowledge whereas at other times it is the only source. Written morphology would be an example of the first kind, for in this case, writing is one among other sources of knowledge. In this case it is linguistic knowledge that interacts with the conventions of writing so that the conventions are better understood and the linguistic knowledge is altered. 'Practice of writing must take place in order to ensure the transition from the knowledge of markers to their implementation' (Fayol and Totereau, this volume) but knowledge of markers is indeed part of the subject's linguistic knowledge.

The acquisition of writing conventions is an example of writing as a unique source of knowledge. There is no way to acquire the conventions of a particular system except by discovering them in the system. If we reflect on this point, the evidence currently gathered about the precocity of children's sensitivity to most conventions of particular writing systems (*e.g.*, Chan & Nunes, this volume) acquires crucial relevance. This evidence demonstrates that very early on and long before being used as a tool for communication, writing is a problem space for the child, at least in the cultural environments that have been explored so far.

The 'discovery' of early writing development is not only important in itself, as a demonstration of children's precocious engagement with writing and as a demonstration of the active role of the subject in building her /his knowledge in every domain. This discovery has implications for understanding child development in general. It compels psychologists and psycholinguists to take it into account in evaluating other aspects of knowledge, in particular linguistic knowledge. If the conventions of writing are part of children's knowledge from so early on, they form a basis on which to construct future knowledge. Therefore, the influence of written language on the changes in phonological, morphological or syntactic representations cannot be disregarded. Writing is not only a source of knowledge of its own conventions but also of the different units and levels of language that are encoded in writing systems.

4   DEVELOPMENTAL RESEARCH AND EDUCATIONAL IMPLICATION

Taking a developmental approach to writing has many implications for education as well. In the first place it provides teachers and curriculum planners with the voice of the students. The kind of performance and justifications of the subjects in any of the domains that have been studied developmentally provide educators with useful information. This information can help them to understand the possible reasons underlying a particular difficulty, to be aware of the different logic that may underlie unconventional performance and to acknowledge views about a particular content that may be at odds with teaching methods.

Secondly, the developmental approach is useful for the purpose of clarifying the role of errors in the learning processes. Most research on the development of writing uses as raw data the 'errors' or the subjects' unconventional responses to the writing tasks designed or observed by the experimenter. Some of these errors unveil an implicit knowledge that is important for teachers to be aware of. After the pioneer work of Read (1973) on invented spelling, psychologists and teachers began to relate to children's mistakes or unconventional spelling not just as errors that must be corrected, but as steps in the process of learning. Moreover, they began to appreciate the extent to which some of these errors express children's implicit knowledge about phonology. Read's early insight into the importance of 'invented spelling' to tapping children's intuitions on phonology has now been extended to morphology, syntax and text construction. Some of these extensions are displayed in this volume. Five chapters in the book (Pontecorvo & Rossi; Sandbank; Totereau & Fayol; Rijlaarsdam, Van Dort-Slijper, & Couzijn and Tolchinsky & Cintas) show writing as a primary locus where children reveal their implicit conceptions and knowledge about syntax, morphology or discursive genres. This finding has tremendous educational implications, not only for the design of activities but also for evaluating children's linguistic knowledge and for recognizing the importance of their interaction with writing to the improvement of their grammar and spelling.

A third aspect of great educational impact relates to the role of the social organization of the classroom and its effect on writing tasks. The way writing tasks are organized, the role assumed by teachers and classmates seem to have far reaching consequences both in the process of text-production and in the quality of texts produced (Camps & Milian, 2000). This volume offers only one specific piece of research on this aspect, but the ground has been prepared for new research on writing processes within educational environments.

To sum up, the reader will find in this book different perspectives on development and on the meanings of writing supported by the results of empirical studies on various dimensions of knowledge encoded in three different writing systems and six languages. This research is framed by a conviction shared by every author: the idea that written language and participation in writing activities are a source of knowledge that triggers development in any sense of the term. The different chapters in the book will also show that this conviction has crucial implications for developmental psychologists and educators.

AUTHORS' NOTE

Many thanks to Clotilde Pontecorvo for her help throughout the review process of the chapters included in the book. Special Thanks to Gert Rijlaarsdam for his constant support, personal involvement and dedicated effort throughout the processes of editing and beyond.

ABSENCE, NEGATION, IMPOSSIBILITY AND FALSITY IN CHILDREN'S FIRST WRITING

CLOTILDE PONTECORVO & FRANCA ROSSI

University of Rome 'La Sapienza', Italy

Abstract. The study aims at investigating the hypotheses that preliterate children work out, before the systematic teaching of writing, about the written representation of negation, absence, impossibility, and falsity. This problematic area has been previously investigated by Ferreiro (1981; 1997) and by Olson (1996). The present study focuses on a whole range of tasks concerning written representation, that were presented to 62 preliterate children, attending kindergarten and having an age between 4 yrs. 8 mth. and 6 yrs. 5 mth. The children were given a complex interview, including tasks that concerned children's skill in representing negation, quantifiers and absence, and the written representation of impossible and false statements. Some of these tasks may create representational problems in children, since a contrast between reality and writing was purposively created. We expected a relationship between children's writing development (that we measured independently) and their answers, at least in the two first tasks.
The results showed a difference between children who are at different levels of writing development: those whose writings were in the first phases are often available to «write» everything. Those who wrote in ways that are closer to the conventional system of writing, showed limited refusal to write absence, while they often refused to write statements that are impossible and false and verbally argued about them. There is also a difference in the role of writing development as concerns this field of representation. A consistent group of children (who wrote in a syllabic and/or alphabetic way) refused to write down phrases that described falsity and impossibility, while they were available to write about negation and absence. This proved that they did not require overcoming an objectivistic view (in which an object must be present to be written down) but rather they have to cope with an attributed truth value to any writing. Thus we do not share the position of Olson (1996) who stated that children cannot write absence or negation because they think that writing concerns an existing object and not a word. This could be true only at a very initial level of writing development and can explain only some results in the first two tasks of our interview, concerning negation and absence. As concerns the other two tasks of writing about impossibility and falsity, the difficulty encountered by children who wrote at a syllabic and/or alphabetical level and who have surely overcome any objectivistic view of writing, seems to have to do with the necessary truth value of what you write. This latter aspect deserves further studies.
Key words: early writing, levels of writing, Italian, representation of content, representation of negation, impossibility, falsity.

1 INTRODUCTION

Research on how children, before beginning any schooling aimed at literacy acquisition, develop their ideas and hypotheses concerning the structure and function of the system of the writing of their own language now has a history of more than twenty

13

L. Tolchinsky (ed.), Developmental Aspects in Learning to Write, 13–31.
© 2001 *Kluwer Academic Publishers. Printed in the Netherlands.*

years (Ferreiro & Teberosky, 1979/1982). A large number of studies have been carried out in different languages and in different cultural contexts (Goodman, 1990; Tolchinsky, 1991; Pontecorvo, Orsolini, Resnick, & Burge, 1996). Many different languages and cultures have been investigated, including languages whose systems of writing are not based on the Roman alphabet, such as Hebrew (Tolchinsky, 1988; Sandbank, this volume), or do use ideograms, such as Chinese (Chan & Nunes, this volume) and Japanese (Kato, Ueda, Ozaki, Mukaigawa, 1999). An interesting comparative study between Spanish speaking and Hebrew speaking children was carried out by Tolchinsky and Teberosky (1997) about children at different levels of writing development, comparing how they manage different ways of phonemic segmentation while they write single words that are phonetically similar in the two languages, although they have to be written in two completely different writing systems.

Regarding this research field, many studies have looked at how children construe the principles of a system of writing. It was considered central to study the interplay between children's hypotheses about the writing system and the conventional rules of correspondence between phonemes and graphemes or between oral and written forms in the specific languages they are trying to represent in writing. In other words, most researchers have been interested in the way in which children's original hypotheses meet or clash with the effective rules of the writing system. Formal principles are developed autonomously by children before the beginning of phonetization, and they concern the need for minimal quantity, internal variety and combinations of marks, so that a word can be read or written.

Apart from the widely tested sensitivity to formal principles, are children in some moments of their early literacy development sensitive to the referential meaning of what they represent through writing? There has been a range of answers to this question. Regarding semantic versus formal aspects of writing, one of us studied (Pontecorvo & Zucchermaglio, 1988) early modes of writing differentiation in young preschool children. The children were requested to produce diminutives (in Italian they are formed by using suffixes that generate words that are always longer that the base word although the object referred to is smaller) and plurals (that, although representing a more numerous set, do not vary in length, but only change in the final vowel in spoken and written Italian). We wanted to check whether they produced differentiations and kept some similar elements. We found that about one third of the children's writings could be considered examples of a kind of semantic phase, in which they tried to keep the similarities of the semantic field of the base word in diminutives and plurals and varied the dimensions of the marks used in the first case or used repeated marks for the plurals (for instance, for writing 'cats' children repeated twice the sequences of marks used for 'cat') (Pontecorvo & Zucchermaglio, 1988).

Figure 1. Anna Maria, age 5 yrs., 7 mth.

Tolchinsky (1988; 1991) claimed that children face the problem of the relationships between form and content all along their development toward the conventional way of the writing system of their culture and language. In her 1988 paper she studied preschoolers conceptions about the representational meaning of writing via their written notation of pairs of sentences that presented a range of different syntactic and semantic relationships: identity, total difference, redundancy, entailment and inconsistency. The results showed an increasing differentiation in sentences as children grew older, reflecting the different relationships between sentences related to the congruence of the pairs of sentences that were presented. Preschoolers seem to work about the metalinguistic sensitivity that writing is conventional and they are progressing toward the idea that the relationship between signifier and signified is arbitrary, although Tolchinsky (1988) speaks of 'an Aristotelian period in children's conception of the representational meaning of writing.' (Tolchinsky, 1988: 396). In her subsequent 1991 paper, Tolchinsky brought examples of Israeli children's writings that are still in a prephonetization phase (*i.e.* they still write without phonetic reference to the spoken words) and show a range of use of referential elements: some children seem to refer to the schematic shape of the object by a single sign, some others use the prototypical color of the referent, others prefer to use the number (or the size) of the signs for representing the different size of the referents. In children's further developments, 'referentialization and phonetization appear as alternative principles regulating written representation. This claim becomes especially clear when observing the writing process itself.' (Tolchinsky, 1991: 94).

Other studies, carried out in other languages have noted that young children do not write all the words when they are asked to write down sentences dictated to them. Most young children do not write marks for articles, qualifiers, or even verbs when asked to write full sentences. They only consider the characters and the objects referred to. Another indication of their being content-sensitive, in which only referents, expressed in full nouns, have a reality that can be marked in writings.

Another dimension that was studied (Pontecorvo, 1995) concerned the iconicity emerging in children's first writings. We found that preschool children were sensitive to the type (or genre) of texts we asked them to write down, and this was shown in the differences in the graphic layout they produced. Most of the Italian preschool children that were interviewed distinguished text segmentation and layout in writing different texts such as writing about their favourite toys (set down mostly as a kind of list), writing a sentence spoken by the experimenter or writing a well-known nursery rhyme (see figure 2).

Figure 2. Writings of different text genres in preschool children.

Something similar was found in slightly older Israeli children who used a different layout for writing a narrative versus a descriptive text (Sandbank, this volume).

2   QUESTIONS ADDRESSED IN THE STUDY

The sensitivity of children to the referential meaning of the sentences they are requested to write can be tackled in different ways. Within the problematic framework in which children's attempts to represent referential content in their writings have been studied, we wanted to explore how young preliterate children face the problem of writing statements that represented absence, negation, impossibility and falsity. This study directly concerns the issue of to what extent young preschool children are sensitive to the meaning of the sentence when they are asked to write something that can create cognitive conflict because it has to do with absence, negation, impossibility and falsity.

We drew the specific questions from an important forerunner study by Ferreiro (1981, 1997). More recently Olson (1996) took up the topic by focusing on how and why young children can refuse to write absence and negation. His conclusion was that children at an early age could not mark anything for absence or negation, because they presumed that writing concerns an object and not a word, and an object must be present: if it is not, the phrase cannot be written. Since we considered that these conclusions were not fully justified, we decided to explore a larger problematic set. Particularly, while exploring a larger set of related tasks that have to do with writing phrases concerning diverse semantic aspects, we assume that it is not an objectivistic view (as Olson said) that is at stake, but rather the progressing child conception of written language (that is different from the fully literate one) in which in writing perhaps the truth value has to be taken into account.

First, it seemed to us that it was important to distinguish clearly between statements concerning absence and those concerning negation, since absence can be verbally expressed without a negative phrase and negation is not necessarily linked to absence. Thus it is better not to overlap these two issues. Moreover, we also wanted to add the request to write what is clearly impossible or false. To this aim we identified different tasks in order to tackle different features of the problem and to interview preschool children at different ages.

Negation was intertwined to absence when children were asked (as in the Olson' study of 1996) to write down something for 'no pigs'. For these reasons we avoid the use of negation, when we asked to write down the absence, and we preferred an expression with 'zero'. In a study concerning the representation of zero, Tolchinsky (in press) found that, by asking children to throw a dice and to mark the number of dots, when the dice showed an empty face, the children left an empty space to represent absence. These answers were rightly called analogical. In this case the children were asked to represent in writing a state of the world, corresponding to an absence of marks, not a linguistic sentence about the world, that has only a linguistic appearance, as we did.

Given the previous assumption, we wanted to interview also children who were beginning to look for syllabic or alphabetic correspondences when writing, so that we could control which tasks were still problematic for them. Thus we decided to include both a larger range of ages, all within the preschool period, and different features of this field of investigation. We included not only absence and negation (as Olson did) but also impossibility and falsity (as in Ferreiro, 1981, 1997). So our research paradigm is larger and more similar to the one used by Ferreiro in her original study (1981).

The study aims at investigating the ideas that preliterate children work out, before the systematic teaching of writing, about the written representation of negation, absence, impossibility, and falsity. In defining our research field, we defined and distinguished four settings.

Negation statement. This is a statement which negates something and that can have different forms. A statement can be in a negative form, inasmuch as negation is used to predicate what the referent is not, with a linguistic statement about 'what x is not': A problem that typically haunted the presocratic philosopher Parmenide in 5th century B.C. (Untersteiner, 1959) in his search for the absolute Being, of whom you can say only what IS, because it is impossible that He is NOT something. But a negation can also be used in a more pragmatic way: we can inform others that there are no more places for the movie to be had or fruits to be eaten. In theses cases the negation only has a pragmatic meaning and not a logical one.

Absence statement. This is a statement concerning something that is not present, or that can be a null or a zero quantity. This was the situation studied by Olson (1996), but he combined negation and absence by asking very young children to mark in sequence: two pigs, one pig and no pig. He found that children were willing to carry out the two first requests but refused to write when they were faced with the last one.

Impossibility statement. This is a statement concerning an impossible event, an event that is against the law of nature or of common sense or completely beyond the usual experiences of children in our culture.

Falsity statement. This is a statement which purposively contradicts or is in sharp contrast with the way in which the world appears usually or is represented to the child.

Preliterate children can encounter particular problems in trying to write down marks that represent the above quoted semantic domains, because in all cases, there is something conflictual about reporting statements on those events in writing.

We assume that the possible difficulties have to do with written language and not generally with language from what we know about children's language development. Very young children are soon able to use negation as an oppositive move (Volterra, 1972); in the preschool phase, they are even able to formulate and to distinguish different types of falsities, such as lies, mistakes and jokes (Bombi & Marotti, 1998). Thus, basing our work on what other researchers have found, we were looking at the ensemble of difficulties children could meet in tackling the task *to write* the above statements.

A factor that should be considered when asking children to face these tasks of writing is the level of development of their usual writings, that is only partially related to age, as it was shown in previous studies. In fact one issue, that is not yet clear-cut, concerns the possible relationships between such a general level and the representational level in the four difficult semantic domains we wanted to explore in this study.

We also suppose that in all these types of request the level of conceptualization of writing is implied (as measured according to the theory and methodology, developed by Ferreiro and Teberosky, 1979/1982). Indeed, in the study carried out by Olson (1996), the children interviewed were between 3 and 4 years of age and no information about their level of development in writing was provided. We can suppose that they were at the very beginning of their writing development, in which they only begun to differentiate between drawing and writing. However, this differentiation is the onset of a long way toward conventional writing. One third of the children were reported to say that they could not write it because 'there are no pigs'. Olson concluded that this resembles the behavior of those ancient populations whose use of ideographic writings forbids them to represent a never happened event, revealing that for them writings represent things and not linguist objects. These populations (he reports) had no marks for negation. However, we do not want to enter into the argument about the analogy between early writings of young children and ancient populations, since many different itineraries have been traced for diverse populations and systems of writing. We prefer to look at the problem from the point of view of the developing child in our literate cultures. In this respect Ferreiro rightly claimed that coming back to history in order to understand present-day child literacy development 'does not imply, of course, any temptation to assimilate one line of development to the other' (Ferreiro, 1994: 126). Some kind of development has taken place in history, even though the so-called 'evolutionary theory of the development of writing' is now rejected with good historical and archeological findings (as Michalowsky (1994) clearly stated). The links that can be found between the two histories concern the need to fight both against the presumed derivation of writing from drawing (the graphic continuity does not imply a conceptual one) and the 'alphabetic supremacism', to which the pshychological look to children's development has to add the avoidance of the risk to look at children's evolution from the adult-centric point of view of an already literate adult (which is really the main obstacle for the research in this field). However children's writings are related from the very beginning to language, but not to the adult-conceptual object called 'language' (heavily impregnated with the written form itself) as Ferreiro, 1994, stated: 120), and as also Olson has shown in his important book (Olson, 1994).

The general expectations of the present study are the following:

1) We expect that our diverse requests may create some conflicts in children given that they have to write down phrases that semantically or pragmatically have no clear referents.

2) Assuming the level of writing development as an independent variable, we expect different behaviors according to the different tasks:

•   in particular we expect positive relationships between levels of writing development and answers in writing negative statements and phrases with quantifiers, including the null quantifier (zero) that is absence, because those tasks could well correspond to the evolution of general written language conceptions in children and children could have previous experiences with similar types of referents;

•   on the other hand, we do not expect strong relationships between levels of writing development and answers to the request to write down impossible and false statements, and it is unlike that these tasks are part of the children's usual writing experiences. Thus we assume that a certain level of writing development is not a sufficient condition to overcome the conflicts that can be raised by the representation of impossibility and falsity.

In other words, while the refusal to write about absence could be related to early children's assumption (also considered by Ferreiro, 1981, 1997) that equates 'no quantity' to 'no letters', the refusal to write impossible or false phrases could appear also in children who write and read looking for some correspondences between graphemes, syllables and/or phonemes.

3   METHODOLOGY AND PROCEDURE

The participants in the study were 62 Italian children attending kindergarten's centres. They were living in two small towns of Southern Italy (subgroup A: 30 subjects, subgroup B: 32 subjects), both groups aged between 4 yrs. 8 mth. and 6 yrs 5 mth. Their social class, as measured through the educational level and work of the parents, was in both cases medium-low. The level of writing development was also checked, as mentioned above.

The children were administered a rather complex individual interview, including the four tasks and lasting about twenty minutes. Each task required writing down one sentence, as specified in the following.

As for the first task (the representation of negation), two forms of negation were used with two different subgroups of children: subgroup A of 30 children was addressed a request concerning the written representation of the negative phrase 'there are no pears', presented as a caption to a drawing, representing a tree full of apples. Subgroup B of 32 children was presented with a more pragmatically realistic task, because they were informed that 'there were no more cookies in the shop near the kindergarten' and that the shopkeeper needed help to write a notice for mothers and children. They were asked to produce this notice in writing.

The second task concerned children's skill in representing quantifiers until absence: the children were asked to write down 'one pear, two pears, three pears' (without any image); then they were asked to write down that 'there were zero pears' to see whether they could represent the null quantifier, not accompanied by a negation.

The third task concerned the written representation of impossibility. First, the child was asked to write down the phrase 'children and cats are flying' which is considered to be as an impossible statement: if she refused to write, she was asked a second time to write the same phrase, after being shown an image in which some children and cats are represented as flying.

The fourth task concerned the written representation of falsity: there is a picture in which some birds are flying and there is a child who is reported to say that 'the birds are not flying': the children were asked to write down this sentence (that is a false one).

We are aware that it is highly critical how the questions about these problematic tasks are proposed to children. For example, the first question, as it was proposed to the first group, in which they were shown a picture of an apple tree and were asked to write down the phrase 'there are no pears', involved the use of a negation to say something about an existing object. In other words we are predicating what an existing object is not: it is a linguistic comment which is true in a negative sense, because the apple tree is really not any other fruit tree. It is a negative predicate that does not touch the presence of the object, but its formulation is not an usual one. On the other hand the more pragmatic request, proposed to the second group, involves writing a negative statement about the lack of something, in our case the cookies in the shop.

A problematic issue can also concern the request to represent a null quantifier, *i.e.* to write down the absence of an object. This request is perhaps differently decoded by the child, whether it is or it is not preceded by an analogous request concerning the writing of one, two or three objects. It is also different to ask them to write that 'there are no cats' or 'zero cats'. Moreover, coming to the task of producing a written mark for absence, if nothing is equated to zero and there are no objects in a void set, there are perhaps no good reasons for using letters when referring to a phrase which expresses an absence.

The situation is different when the children were asked to write down phrases that can be positive or negative but that refer to states of things that are impossible or false. That is what we studied by asking the children the third and fourth task of our interview. With the third, the children were asked to write down that 'children and dogs can fly', so they had to write down something that is usually considered impossible. But if they refuse to write, they were shown an image corresponding to the requested phrase. With the fourth question the children were asked to write down the phrase 'birds don't fly', as an expression of a child who was looking (in an image that is shown at the same time) at birds flying; in this case they had to write down a phrase which is clearly false, but produced by another speaker.

4   ANALYSIS AND DISCUSSION OF THE RESULTS

4.1 Levels of writing development

Table 1. Subjects distribution in the different levels of writing development.

	Age			
Writing Level	4 yrs. 6 mth. 4 yrs. 11 mth.	5 yrs 5 yrs. 5 mth.	5 yrs. 6 mth. 6 yrs. 6 mth.	Total
Presyllabic initial	4	6	8	29 %
Presylabic advanced	6	9	5	32 %
Syllabic initial	-	2	-	3 %
Syllabic advanced	-	2	-	3 %
Syllabic alphabetic	-	4	5	14 %
Alphabetic	2	4	5	19 %
Total	12	27	23	100 %

$r = .348$; $p < .005$.

All 62 children were interviewed at first with a general task in order to establish their level of writing conceptualization. The analysis of children's ways of writing and reading of ten words of different length permitted the division of the sample into six main subgroups (see table 1) according to the different levels of writing development as established by Ferreiro and Teberosky (1979/1982). To make the above table readable we clarify the definition of the different levels.

Presyllabic initial writings	Those writings in which there is only an initial differentiation between drawing and writing.
Presyllabic advanced writings	Those writings present a variety of letters and/or pseudo-letters, following the formal principles of minimum quantity and of internal variation.
Initial syllabic writings	Children read these writings in a syllabic way, even though they may write down more marks than syllables.
Advanced syllabic writings	A number of marks correspond almost precisely to the number of syllables in the written word.
Syllabic-alphabetic writings	Writing in which in the same word both a syllabic hypothesis and a correspondence between phonemes and graphemes is looked for
Alphabetical writings	Writings in which there is search of correspondence between phonemes and graphemes in writing letters, although the writings are not yet fully conventional

The coding of the written products and of the subsequent readings was done always by two independent judges at first; the third judge was used in the few cases when there were disagreements. It resulted that our subjects are not distributed with the same proportion on all the levels of writing, as we expected on the basis of previous studies: the intermediate levels are much less represented in the writings we collected, particularly the syllabic ones. One possible reason for these unexpected findings could be that these children are all coming from low-middle class families from two small Italian towns where the preschool services are not generally sensitive to this aspect of children's development. It could be that in some cases, in the last year before primary schooling (this is the mean age of our subjects), there had been perhaps a direct educational intervention of the families that pushed the children from their pre-phonetic ideas of writing toward conventional writing, without letting them develop autonomously their syllabic hypotheses.

However two data are evident: 1) the 62 children are distributed in all the six levels of development; 2) this distribution is somewhat correlated with age, but not strongly. This could be produced by the 27 children whose age range is between 5 yrs. and 5 yrs. 5 mth. that are distributed in all the levels of writing development.

In the following presentation of results, we will refer to the above six subgroups, that were resumed in table 1. We will present and discuss the results for each single task that we proposed to the children. At the end we will try to put together the main results, in order to have a general intrasubject information across the tasks.

4.2 Writing negation

30 children of Subgroup A, who were interviewed about writing negation by asking to write 'what something is not', were presented with a drawing (representing a tree full of apples), and were asked to write a correct predicate that was expressed with a negative phrase ('there are no pears'). The task's results are correlated with the level of writing development ($r = .545$; $p < .005$). The results are presented in table 2.

Table 2. Subjects distribution in the different types of answers in the two negation tasks.

	Justification when refuse to write		Writing in some way	Total
Task	No	Yes		
Saying what something is not.	-	6	24	30
Announcing that there is no more of something.	1	-	31	32
Total	1	6	55	62

Types of answers

$\chi^2 = 7.71$; df = 2; $p < .05$.

Six children out of 30 refused to write because they said that 'you cannot write what is not there' and that letters can be used only if there is something there. One of them said: 'You cannot write it because there are no pears on the tree, there are just apples'.

The other children interviewed tried to write something in some form, even the eleven children whose writings were still at a presyllabic level.

With a different request, the 32 children of Subgroup B were asked to write negation to announce that there was nothing left of something. The children were asked to help the shopkeeper to write a notice that could tell mothers and children that 'there are no more cookies'. Also this task resulted correlated with the level of writing development ($r = .502$; $p < .005$). Only one child refused to write it without justification; the other 31 children wrote something. However seven out of 31 did not use negation and declared they would write a different (positive) phrase, such as 'the cookies are finished' while four children wrote negative phrases that were related but not exactly corresponding to the request. The remaining 20 children wrote the notice in some way: 13 declared that they put the negation at the very beginning of the phrase such as 'No sweets' or 'No more cookies' that looks more like a notice, while seven wrote and read the phrase we asked for without specific comments.

In comparing the two similar but different requests addressed to two comparable groups of children, for age and levels of writing development, a difference can be noted. In the first request the explicit refusal (although limited) of using letters to mark 'what something is not' emerged; children had to write a statement that, although being true, only has a linguistic existence (and a very rare occurrence in everyday life). On the other hand, in the second request, although seven children avoided the negative expression, they all wrote something, perhaps because negation was used to express an absence that was pragmatically informative.

The distribution of the answers of the two different groups to the question concerning the writing of negation is different and also the application of the chi square test proved this difference as being statistically significant ($\chi^2 = 7.71$; df = 2; p. <.05). We attribute the differences to the task and not to the group, because we checked that this is the only setting in which the two groups behaved differently.

4.3 Writing of quantifiers until writing of absence

Writing of quantifiers is the type of task that depended on writing development ($\chi^2 = 69.6$; df = 15; p <.01). In marking increasing quantities, we distinguished three types of answers (see figure 3 and table 3) of which we report some examples in the following. Only an initial presyllabic child refused to complete this task. From table 3 it appears that (1) writings that use a string of characters for representing 'one pear' and repeat the same string of characters for increasing quantities (20 children); (2) writings that try to represent quantity, by varying the order of the letters used, adding more characters for two and three pears or another similar string for 'three pears', or initiating the string with the presence of the name of the number (25 children); (3) alphabetic writings with the almost conventional name or the figure of the number (16 children).

Table 3. Subjects distribution in the different types of writings in the quantifiers task.

Writing Level	Refusal to write	Writings with a repeated element	Writings representing quantifiers marks with variations	Almost conventional numbers	Total
			Types of answers		
Presyllabic initial	1	13	4	-	18
Presyllabic advanced		4	16	-	20
Syllabic initial	-		2	-	2
Syllabic advanced	-		2	-	2
Syllabic alphabetic		2	1	6	9
Alphabetic		1	-	10	11
Total	1	20	25	16	62

$\chi^2 = 69.9$; df = 15; p < .01.

ANI'RAR	= 1 pear	
ANI'RAR ANI'RAR	= 2 pears	Rosaria (5 yrs. 5 mth.)
ANI'RAR ANI'RAR ANI'RAR	= 3 pears	
A AA MMI	= 1 pear = 2 pears = 3 pears	Luca (4 yrs. 8 mth.)
UNOPERA DUEOIAR TEOIR	= 1 pear = 2 pears = 3 pears	Francesca (5 yrs. 4 mth.)

Figure 3. Rosaria, Luca, and Francesca writing numbers.

Table 4. Subjects distribution in the different types of writings in the absence task.

		Types of answers		
	Refuse to write	Writing in someway		Total
		Not aware of meaning	Aware of the meaning of zero	
Writing level				
Presyllabic initial	2	10	6	18
Presyllabic advanced		12	8	20
Syllabic initial		1	1	2
Syllabic advanced			2	2
Syllabic alphabetic			9	9
Alphabetic		1	10	11
Total	2	24	36	62

χ^2 23.42; df = 10; p <.05.

Writing of absence is a type of task that resulted to be related, even though not strongly, with writing development (χ^2 23.42; df = 10; p <.05). However only two children (whose writings are presyllabic) said that it was not possible to write 'zero pears' and refused to write by saying that the pears were not there. 24 Children (out of 60), although not aware of the correct meaning of 'zero', wrote something which was 'a round number' or said 'that there are many'.

Of the thirty-six children who were aware that zero means nothing and said it verbally, the written productions were largely different. Ten children, whose writings were at an alphabetic level, represented 'zero' with a figure. Some of the other children, that knew the meaning of zero, needed to refer verbally to the causal event that produced the absence of quantity, and said that they had written, for instance, that 'someone has eaten them'. It seems to us that this task did not give clear-cut results, apart from the low number of refusals. We conclude that this semantic domain should be further investigated with other tasks and with younger children.

4.4 Writing an impossible statement

The last two tasks – proposed to all 62 children – concerned the area of writing phrases that refer to impossible and false events of the world, and were the more problematic tasks even for children who wrote looking for correspondence between graphemes and phonemes.

An interesting result of the impossible statement task was that the different answers were distributed across all the levels of writing development and did not show any relationships with this latter ($\chi^2 = 10.091$; df = 10; n.s.).

First the children were asked the following question: 'Could you write the phrase: "children and dogs fly"?' If the child said 'no', she was given a picture 'taken from a book' showing a girl and a dog flying. Then they were addressed again the request to write.

Table 5. Subjects distribution in the different types of answers when writing the impossible phrase.

Writing Level	Types of children's answers			
	'The phrase cannot be written in anyway'	'It is possible to write the phrase with the picture'	Responding (in someway) at the first question	Total
Presyllabic initial	3	3	12	18
Presyllabic advanced	4	2	14	20
Syllabic initial	-	-	2	2
Syllabic advanced	-	1	1	2
Syllabic alphabetic	5	1	3	9
Alphabetic	2	2	7	11
Total	14	9	39	62

Table 5 shows three categories of children's responses:
- Fourteen children (23%) said that this phrase cannot be written because it says something that does not exist in reality;
- Nine children said that it is possible to write it down only if there is the picture, because the phrase can be taken from a tale. One said:

> 'With the picture, yes, because there is a dog and a child who are flying'.

Another one said:

> 'Here you can write it, because in the picture the girl and the dog are flying. But, if there was no picture, you cannot write it.'

- 39 children wrote something when addressed the first question, without expressing any difficulty verbally.

4.5 Writing a false statement

Also in this task the answers were distributed across all levels of writing development and did not depend on the latter ($\chi^2 = 9.841$; df = 10; n.s.). The linear correlation between the answers to the task about impossibility and to the one about falsity is statistically significant: r = .433 (p<.005).

The children were addressed the task in the following way. The interviewer showed a picture in which there are birds flying and in which there is a child who says (it is written like in comics): '"The birds are not flying". Is it possible to write down this sentence?' If the child said no, she/he was asked why.

Table 6. Subject's distribution in the different types of answers when writing the false phrase.

	Types of answers			
Writing Level	The phrase cannot be written because it is false	Children wrote and attributed to the picture the responsibility of the answer	Children accepted to write	Total
Presyllabic initial	7	1	10	18
Presyllabic advanced	5	1	14	20
Syllabic Initial	-	1	1	2
Syllabic Advanced	-	1	1	2
Syllabic alphabetic	2	1	6	9
Alphabetic	3	1	7	11
Total	17	6	39	62

The answers produced by the children can be divided into three main categories, similar to the ones of the previous task:

- Seventeen children (27%) said that they would not write it because the sentence was false and contradictory with the illustration (that represented flying birds). It cannot be written. A presyllabic girl (Savery: 5 yrs. 6 mth.) said:

    'What the child said cannot be written because birds are flying and if they don't fly, they fall'.

    In this way, she expressed the constraining necessity of flying for birds.
- Six children (10%) attributed to the child (represented in the illustration) the responsibility of the phrase and wrote something like: 'the child says that the birds are not flying, but instead they are'. Some children modified the phrase, saying that: 'birds that are flying'. A syllabic child (Alessio: 5 yrs. 7 mth.) said:

    'No, because birds have wings; without the child, it cannot be written'.

    He cumulated two factors: both a factual datum and the position of the speaker.
- 39 children (63%) accepted to write down the phrase. One of these 37 children is a presyllabic child who answered to the last two tasks in the same way: in both cases, he said that he could write it because he *knows* how to write.

4.6 'Can't write this'

In this section, we focussed our attention on the answers of refusing to write that we got in all the four tasks. We got 40 answers of refusal to write throughout all the tasks, with rather different motivations, as we presented above. There is not an homogenous distribution of the refusal answers in the different tasks: the refusal answers were mainly activated by our requests to write phrases about impossibility and falsity.

The distribution of the refusal answers is presented in table 7, corresponding with the levels of writing development.

No child refused to write in all the four tasks. In the tasks of writing the representation of negation and of absence, only one child is refusing to write in both tasks. We cannot identify any trend, given that only two children out of 62 refused to write about absence.

On the other hand, as we already noted in comparing the results of the two last tasks (that are highly correlated), 11 out of 14 children (79%) who refused to write the impossible phrase were also refusing to write the false one. So it really seems that the refusals to write in the two tasks had a similar basis, although they are distributed in all the levels of writing development that are represented in the children we interviewed.

Table 7. Subjects that refused to write in the four tasks.

			Task		
Writing Level	Negation	Absence	Impossibility	Falsity	Total
Presyllabic initial	3	2	3	7	15
Presyllabic advanced	3	-	4	5	12
Syllabic Initial	1	-	-	-	1
Syllabic Advanced		-	-	-	
Syllabic alphabetic		-	5	2	7
Alphabetic		-	2	3	5
Total	7	2	14	17	40

5   CONCLUSIONS

As we hypothesised at the beginning of this study, the field of children's written representation of statements concerning negation, absence, impossibility and falsity is a rather differentiated domain. However, the writing requests we proposed to the children have in common a possible conflict in using letters for representing something which does not have the status of a concrete referent or of an existing event.
We have shown that the answers were rather articulated. From what we found, it is possible to group the first two tasks together (negative statements and statements including quantifiers until absence), because they both depended on the levels of writing development. In other words, answering to writing tasks of negative phrases or about quantifiers until absence (including zero which is more difficult to be understood) resulted to be related with the general development of writing representations. However the statistically significant difference between the two negative forms confirmed that the pragmatically more informative statement was much more acceptable by children than the only logical one.
    The last two tasks of our study show completely different results. Firstly, answers are neither related with the level of writing development, nor with age (subjects are distributed along a range of almost two years of age). Moreover, the well motivated refusal to write a phrase which is false appears a little less in children whose writings are not yet phonetically sensitive (38%) and a little more in children who look for some correspondence between graphemes and phonemes and/or syllables (45%). It is almost the same in the answers to write what is considered impossible. About one fourth of the children, independently of their levels of writing development (see table 5 and 6), refused to write down phrases which described falsity and impossibility.

Our study concerned children whose mean age was 5 yrs. 2 mth. and who had all overcome the first phase of differentiation between drawing and writing in their written productions (Ferreiro & Teberosky, 1979/1982). Children's explicit worries seem to have more to do with the truth value of what they are asked to write (tackled with the third and fourth task), since also writing phrases that describe impossible events resulted in writing down falsity that they mainly want to avoid. Something which is more similar to the value of written documents in the life experience of illiterate adults (as Ferreiro, 1981, rightly noted). Ferreiro reports that illiterate adults refused to write falsity, probably because they knew very well that identity and ownership must be 'proved' by written documents. A concrete social evidence that writing should have to express the truth. This assumption is completely different from the refusal to write because there are no objects present. In a sense our results are more similar to those collected by Ferreiro (1981 and 1997) and our interpretation is closer to hers, while they conflict with the hypotheses advanced by Olson (1996) who attributed the refusals to write negation and/or absence to a supposed 'objectivistic view of writing' that we could not find in the children we interviewed.

However our study still had a mainly exploratory flavor. We found that the field is clearly a composite one. It is worthwhile to study it further in order to clarify many open questions within the different tasks, investigated in the present study.

An interesting direction to be explored better is the whole domain of 'negation'. We explored only two aspects of it, but, given the different results we have already obtained, many others could be studied by using possibly the same participants. For instance, since negation can be used with the function of denying a qualification, a location, an intention, a taste, a will, (and also an existence or a presence), these aspects should be carefully distinguished, also by varying the linguistic formulation of the negative statement (*i.e.* the exact location of the negation in the negative phrase). Another interesting field to be investigated better is the one of absence that also can be the result of many diverse activities: not only by reducing the numerosity of a set until a void, but also by referring to the absence of someone or of something from a particular context, giving the task with different vignettes. Moreover, there could also be diverse children's ideas about writing different types of impossibility: is there something more radically impossible than something else? It could also be a relevant problem that of studying whether children refuse to write down 'lies' that always have a falsity value, but often also a 'moral' implication of hiding something from someone, of wanting to deceive another person. It would also be possible to check whether there is an added factor by some social marking (adults versus children's peers or siblings; parents, teachers versus generic adults). Is it the same with jokes that seem to have a different status? The exploration of the problematic area that was investigated in this study can find many new further directions. One may be also that of comparing verbal written representations with other ones (*i.e.* figurative ones). Another direction could also be that of studying how children react to real answers given by other children to this representational field, with the aim of finding out further explanations children can give to the spoken and written answers of their peers.

It must be reminded that the distinction between what can be written and what cannot (as well as what can be read and what cannot) is a critical one in children's writing development and accompanies all the early development of children's writing (as it has been proved by many researchers, as in Ferreiro, 1994). Thus the explanation cannot be the one that was claimed by Olson (1996) as a general one who stated that children couldn't write absence or negation because they think that writing concerns an existing object and not a word. When children begin to differentiate between drawing and writing, their itinerary to represent language in writing has just begun. Obviously they represent what is language for them (that is not the same than for us). For this reason we stressed that tasks we used in our study could also be problematic for those children who since long think that language had to be written down, since in their writings they are looking for diverse correspondences between what is said and what is marked.

AUTHORS' NOTE

The research was thought and carried out together by the two authors with a 1996 MURST grant given to C. Piperno Pontecorvo: Clotilde Pontecorvo has written the introduction and the conclusions, whereas Franca Rossi has done the statistical analyses and written all the other paragraphs.

The authors want to acknowledge the work done by Dr. E. Perrella and R. Formillo (graduate students at the University of Rome) who helped substantially in collecting part of the data used in this article.

The careful suggestions of three reviewers, that we want to thank here, were very useful to revise our chapter: however we assume full responsibility for any left shortcoming.

EXPLICIT TEACHING AND IMPLICIT LEARNING OF CHINESE CHARACTERS

LILY CHAN* & TEREZINHA NUNES**

*Hong Kong Institute of Education, Hong Kong, ** Oxford Brookes University, England

Abstract. To read and write Chinese require an ability to recognise more than 1,000 basic graphic units. Very few studies have looked into the perceptual learning process of these graphic units at the initial stage when young children are being introduced to the script. Two tasks were developed to tap children's understanding of graphic properties of written Chinese. In the name writing task, we investigated whether preschool children, aged 3-5, (1) would differentiate drawing from writing, (2) used a correspondence between character and syllable in their writing, (3) used multiple units within one character or across characters, and (4) respected some of the supra-segmented properties of written Chinese. In the graphic acceptability task, we examined if 5-9 years old children could make orthographic judgements based on positioning and graphic properties of the stroke-patterns. Our results indicated that preschool children could already demonstrate some knowledge of the properties of graphic units in Chinese by using strokes or made-up stroke-patterns in their name writing. Five and six-year-olds rejected words with illegal graphic features and seven- and eight-years-olds distinguished nonwords from pseudowords based on illegal position of stroke-patterns. We conclude that Chinese children implicitly learn graphic properties of the writing system which are crucial in the learning process, the possibility to shift perceptual learning of graphic properties of written Chinese from implicit learning to explicit teaching deserves further investigation.

The aim of this chapter is to analyze children's developing knowledge of the graphic units that are related to speech units in Chinese and the difference between what children are explicitly taught and what they learn implicitly about these graphic units. The term 'implicit' is used here to indicate that both Chinese children and adults are usually unaware of those formal characteristics of their script that are analyzed in this paper (see, for example, Berry & Dienes, 1993, for a conceptualization of implicit learning). In the introductory section, we consider briefly the development of children's recognition of graphic units in alphabetic scripts and explain some of the difficulties in the identification of graphic units in written Chinese. In the second section, the basic approach to the teaching of these units in Hong Kong is succinctly presented. The third section contains results of investigations about Chinese children's knowledge of graphic units in written Chinese. In the final section, we consider implications of these results for the teaching of written Chinese and examine the connection between explicit teaching and implicit learning in a more general way.

Keywords: Chinese characters, children's writing, preschool children, perceptual learning, strokes, stroke patterns, implicit learning.

L. Tolchinsky (ed.), Developmental Aspects in Learning to Write, 33–53.

1   THE DEVELOPMENT OF RECOGNITION OF GRAPHIC UNITS

The study of reading and spelling has been dominated by investigations on one kind of writing system, the alphabetic (Perfetti, 1997). Graphic units in alphabetic languages can be letters or groups of letters that correspond to multilevel units in phonology and morphology (Perfetti, 1997). Alphabetic systems contain a restricted number of characters, usually fewer than 60 even if one considers lower and upper case letters. Most people would agree that it is necessary for readers to be able to identify visual characters in reading – and some visual analysis tasks given to children at age four predict progress in reading ten months later after a few months of reading instruction (Ho & Bryant, 1999). However, the task of learning to read in alphabetic languages is relatively simple in comparison to learning to read in Chinese. The number of characters needed to write any word in alphabetic systems is so small that it would be perfectly possible for children to be explicitly taught and learn each of these forms by rote. In contrast, this is unlikely to be the case in written Chinese, which contains more than 1,000 basic graphic units. One could easily be lead to the conclusion that visual learning of characters in alphabetic and Chinese scripts are rather different: the mastery of the alphabet could be based on rote learning whereas the same would not be possible in the case of Chinese graphic units. Yet, the evidence that we review here suggests that both learners of alphabetic and of Chinese scripts undergo a process of perceptual learning of the characteristics of writing before entering school. In neither case the children are taught explicitly all the graphic principles of their script (although they may be taught some) but many children display knowledge of these principles in research situations or when pretending to write.

Investigations of children's perceptual learning of graphic units in alphabetic scripts have been carried out for more than two decades. Lavine (1977) investigated perceptual learning processes related to the identification of reading using a classification method. She asked preschool children attending nursery schools and kindergartens in the age range 3 to 6.5 to separate a set of cards into those that had writing on them and those that did not. The designs on the cards were composed by units which were either pictographic, or non-pictographic; some of the non-pictographic units shared perceptual features with Roman letters but were not Roman letters and some were conventional Roman letters either printed or in handwriting. These units were presented singly or in strings; the strings were either composed by the same unit repeated a few times or by different units. Finally, the displays were presented in linear or non-linear arrangements. Lavine distinguished between supra-segmental features of the script, that is, features that describe the organization of the units, such as linearity, multiplicity (*i.e.*, use of more than one unit) and variety (*i.e.*, use of different units) and characteristics of the units themselves, both similarity/nonsimilarity to Roman letters and belonging/not belonging to the set of Roman letters.

Lavine observed that the supra-segmental properties of linearity and variety of units were used as a criterion by the children at all three age levels to distinguish between writing and non-writing. Multiplicity was a significant property only for 3-

year-olds; the 4- and 5-year-olds did not use it and consistently identified single letters as writing (c.f. Ferreiro & Teberosky, 1983). The 3- and 4-year-olds used general similarity to Roman letters as a criterion for judging a display as writing but 5-year-olds were more discriminating. For example, a sharp decrease in the acceptability of displays as examples of writing was observed only amongst 5-year-olds when the linear strings contained a series of single strokes [- | \ - ~]. Such displays were considered as writing by approximately 70% of the 3-year-olds, 47% of the 4-year-olds and only 23% of the 5-year-olds. In contrast, letter-like strings with varied characters composed by more than one stroke were judged as writing by over 70% of the 3- and 4-year-olds and over 60% of the 5-year-olds, although these did not contain conventional letters. These results indicate that there is some form of perceptual learning taking place between the ages of three and five years.

Although none of the children could read, they did not lack letter knowledge entirely: 27% of the 3-year-olds, 47% of the 4-year-olds, and 67% of the 5-year-olds were able to name at least two of the three letters displayed (A, B and E). Lavine suggests that, as children learn more letters, they start to use the presence or absence of conventional units (both letters and numbers) as the most important criterion in their judgments of acceptability of designs as writing. For example, both 4- and 5-year-olds judged the single letters A, E and B as writing more than 80% of the time but rejected a triangle, which is a letter-like design (it contains more than one stroke and only strokes which are actually used in Roman letters): only 7% of the 4-year-olds and no 5-year-old judged the triangle as writing. In contrast, 47% of the 3-year-olds accepted the triangle as writing, thus seeing it as more acceptable than the older children did (but still less acceptable than the single letters, for which the lowest level of acceptability was 73%). The 5-year-old children had both greater knowledge of the features of writing and more letter knowledge than the younger children. It is possible that this perceptual learning helps children identify instances of writing in their environment, thereby facilitating letter learning. However, the significance of this connection cannot be interpreted because of the nature of the design: it is not possible to know whether better knowledge of the characteristics of the script facilitates letter learning or vice-versa. Nevertheless, the study shows unambiguously that there is some perceptual learning of the general features of Roman letters during the pre-school years.

A comparison between alphabetic and Chinese writing suggests that the role of perceptual learning may be much more significant in learning written Chinese, where rote learning of the basic graphic units is not easily accomplished. We describe briefly the levels of organization of graphic units in Chinese before presenting evidence on children's perceptual learning.

There are five principal levels for the description of graphic elements in written Chinese: stroke, stroke-pattern, character, word and sentence. A stroke is the smallest graphic unit in Chinese. There are only a few basic strokes in Chinese; the most common ones are dots, lines, and hooks (Figure 1) which can be used in different orientations and combinations. Strokes are quite different from letters because they do not have functions in and of themselves and the identification of the strokes in a character is not as easy as counting letters in an English word. The segmentation of individual strokes in Chinese characters is not always directly visible, and often it is a matter of writing conventions. Because strokes have no function, they may not appear to be meaningful graphic units to Western eye. However, they clearly are units from the Chinese perspective; Chinese dictionaries organize the characters by the number of strokes they contain.

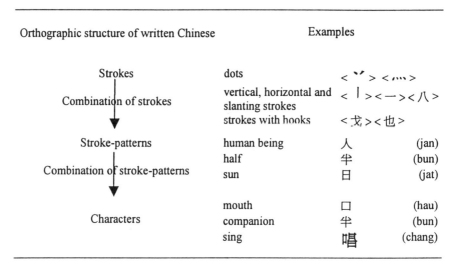

Figure 1. Examples of stokes, stroke-patterns and characteristics of written Chinese. Notes: * this section consists of a simple character 口 [hau], and two compound characters 半 [bun], 唱 [chang]. **Pronunciation: Cantonese.

Strokes are conventionally combined in *stroke-patterns*. Unlike strokes, most stroke-patterns are pronounceable and have their own meaning. Figure 1 shows three stroke-patterns:

人 consists of two strokes, pronounced as [jan] and means *human being*;

半 consists of five strokes, it is pronounced as [bun] and it means *half*;

日 consists of four strokes, pronounced as [jat] and means *sun*.

Chen & Allport (1995) proposed that stroke-patterns should be considered the basic graphic units of Chinese, rather than strokes or characters, because stroke-patterns are related to speech units in terms of phonology and meaning. Stroke-patterns are the elements that form compound characters.

A character may consist of one or more stroke-patterns. A simple character consists of one stroke-pattern, and a compound character consists of two or more stroke-patterns. Only less than 10% of the characters are simple characters; the remaining

90% are compound characters. In Figure 1, there is a simple character *mouth*, and two compound characters *companion* and *sing*. Because characters occupy a fixed area, stroke-patterns appear in writing in different sizes depending on how many are present in the same character. In Figure 1, the size of the stroke-pattern □ is different in the characters *mouth* and *sing*.

A Chinese word is composed of characters. *There is a one-to-one correspondence between a character and a syllable*: a one-character-word consists of one syllable, a two-character-word consists of two syllables, and a three-character-word consists of three syllables. Liu, Chuang and Wang (1975) identified a total of 40,032 Chinese words; of these, about 65% were two character words. Hoosain (1992) suggests that two character words are similar to English nominal compounds (such as motorcycle, raincoat etc) but much more frequent than the latter. *Each two-character word has its own meaning but the constituent characters have independent meaning too*, even if they only appear in that word (Taft & Zhu, 1995). Although two-character words are more frequent than single character words, according to Liu, Chuang and Wang (1975) the identification of single characters is essential in learning written Chinese.

Similarly to alphabetic writing, Chinese graphic units are organized according to supra-segmental principles. Alphabetic letters are organized linearly forming words and words are also organized linearly following the same direction (in English from left to right). In contrast, there are two forms of supra-segmental organization in the Chinese script.

First, there is the intra-character organization of stroke-patterns to form one character. Characters are written within a square area. Within this square area, stroke patterns are organized usually in a horizontal or vertical arrangement. Figure 1 shows the character 唱 which contains three stroke patterns; the left side contains □ and 昌 and the right side consists of two identical stroke-patterns 昌 being arranged vertically. The vast majority of characters in Chinese is categorized as 'ideophonetic compounds', that is, characters that contain a set of stroke-patterns which give a clue to their meaning and another set which gives a clue to the pronunciation of the characters. It is the location of a stroke pattern within a character that indicates its function either as a phonological component or a semantic radical.

Some stroke patterns have only one of these functions and consequently appear in fixed locations across different characters. Placing these stroke-patterns in a different location would not be a simple 'orthographic' error, comparable to misspelling a word (*e.g.*, writing 'bak' for 'bake'), but a 'graphic' error (*c.f.* Moreira & Pontecorvo, 1996), because the pattern produced is not a possible exemplar in written Chinese (similar to writing an unpronounceable letter string such as 'abk'). Other stroke patterns can have either function. Their function is then defined by their position: for example, when they appear on the right they convey phonological information but when they appear on the left they convey semantic information. The latter type of stroke pattern can appear in different positions across characters.

The second form of supra-segmental organization applies across characters. Chinese is written linearly, like alphabetic scripts, but the linear arrangement can be from top to bottom starting on the top-right corner of the page or from left to right starting on the top-left corner of the page. These two linear arrangements are perceptually quite distinct even to a non-Chinese reader but directionality must be learned.

Characters are evenly spaced in text with no extra space between words. Readers have to segment character strings into words for comprehension. Commas indicate clause and phrase boundaries, and sentence boundaries are marked by full stops. Interrogation and exclamation marks are used with similar functions as in alphabetic writing.

As indicated earlier on, the syllable is the most important phonological unit in written Chinese and is represented by a character. The relationship between the writing units and phonology is made less transparent by the large number of homophones (i.e. words which differ in meaning but sound the same), if tone is not considered. In the XIN HUA dictionary, 52 distinct characters can be found under the syllable [jiao]. Most individual characters usually have no more than ten homophones. The relationship between the phonological components and the pronunciation of the characters varies across characters. Pronunciation of a character can be achieved either by derivation (when the pronunciation of the phonological component on its own and in compound characters is the same) or by analogy (when the phonological component on its own is not pronounced in the same way as it is pronounced when it is used in compound words, although pronunciation is consistent across compound words). The predictive accuracy of the pronunciation of a character from that of its phonological component is about 39%, ignoring pronunciation on the basis of analogy (Zhou, 1980).

However, reading characters is not as unpredictable as this would suggest because Chinese writing is not based only of phonology: characters contain lexical information and this reduces considerably the ambiguity of reading on the basis of the phonological component taken by itself. The lexical information is conveyed by the semantic radical. The degree of semantic information provided by semantic radicals varies, but in general they are helpful in deriving partial meaning of the characters (Fang & Wu, 1989). In spite of the possibility of variations that weaken the connection between the isolated components and the reading of the characters, studies of Chinese adult readers (Chen, Allport, & Marshall, 1996, Flores d'Arcais, 1992; Flores d' Arcais, Saito, & Kawakami, 1995; Seidenberg, 1985; Zhu, 1987) have demonstrated that adults rely on the semantic radicals to identify the meaning of words and the phonological components for pronunciation.

In short, written Chinese involves two types of supra-segmental properties: a within character-organization, connected to the functions of components in ideophonetic characters, and the linear organization of characters. Each character corresponds to a syllable and has its own meaning, even if it is part of a two-character word. The clues to character pronunciation and meaning are obtained from knowledge of stroke patterns and their functions within characters. We suggest that a careful analysis of how children come to understand the organization of stroke-patterns within a character will contribute to our understanding of the cognitive processes implicated in the development of Chinese children's recognition of the basic graphic units of written Chinese.

We now turn to the way children are explicitly taught reading and writing in the initial phases of literacy instruction in Hong Kong. We will try to show that the explicit teaching that pupils receive does not directly address the basic graphics units and their organization within a character.

2   EXPLICIT TEACHING OF WRITTEN CHINESE AND ITS DIFFICULTIES

It is common belief that learning written Chinese is a laborious process that demands hard work and practice. In Hong Kong, there is a tendency to begin the teaching of written Chinese at an early age. At the age of four children are already required to write and practice some simple characters. Teaching emphasizes the sequence of strokes in writing the character and the size of the characters. Accuracy and precision are expected right from the start.

The idea that learning to write is a complicated process and demands excessive attention from adults is deeply rooted in parents' and teachers' views. A standard teaching procedure of a character to a group of children is as follows.

Teacher: 'Children, look at the character on the board, what is it?'
Children: 'Sky' [天].
Teacher: 'You are right, now, take your pointing finger and follow me.
              horizontal stroke   ‾
              horizontal stroke   二
              long slanting stroke to the left   ヂ
              long slanting stroke to the right'   天

The children are then expected to follow the teacher, write in the air with their pointing fingers, and chant with the teacher three to four times. Throughout the preschool and early primary school years, children are also required to memorize new characters by laboriously copying the same character many, many times and practicing dictation in class. It is assumed that children learn all the Chinese characters in this way, memorizing each character laboriously by practicing its constituent strokes; stroke-patterns and their rules of composition are not considered in this common sense view of literacy learning.

There are two problems with this view of the learning process: the first relates to the assumptions it makes about children's literacy learning and the second relates to the evidence that we will present later on showing that children come to recognize and use stroke-patterns as graphic units.

Research on literacy learning in alphabetic languages has shown that children are not passive reproducers of the instruction that they receive but are active in constructing their understanding of the world even in the absence of instruction (for a review, see Teale & Sulzby, 1986). As illustrated in Lavine's study, children learn some supra-segmental features of writing before they are taught and learn all the Roman letters. It has already been documented that preschool children attempt to understand the written language that surrounds them, formulate hypotheses about how speech and written language are related, search for regularities and test their predictions (Ferreiro & Teberosky, 1982). There is some evidence that also Chinese children are active in understanding the world of literacy around them. Lee (1989) adapted Goodman's Print Awareness Tasks (Goodman, 1984) to Chinese and applied them to children in Taiwan. This study showed that about 30% of the 3-year-olds could read environmental print when it is embedded in context. By age six, this proportion reached 60%. Thus Chinese children begin to learn about written language early and do not wait until formally taught to start learning written Chinese.

In the section that follows, we describe children's learning of the structure and organization of graphic units in Chinese. We refer to this learning as 'implicit' in view of the fact that the type of knowledge that we documented in children through these studies is not explicitly taught either by parents or teachers, and that it is unlikely that the children can explain it verbally.

3   IMPLICIT LEARNING

Implicit learning is characterised as a non-selective process in which learners take information from the environment with little awareness of underlying structures or abstract rules (Gomez, 1997). There is learning that is undoubtedly implicit: learners of artificial grammars, sequential positions and control in complex systems tasks can succeed in transfer tasks in the absence of the ability to report how they make decisions in these tasks. Bryant, Nunes and Snaith (2000) showed that 8-9-year-old children learn a sophisticated rule (which past verbs are spelled as 'ed' at the end and which are not) that their teachers do not teach them because they do not know it themselves. The children's knowledge of this rule is entirely implicit but nonetheless effective.

We investigated how the characteristics of written Chinese are implicitly learned by children in the initial stages of literacy learning using two methods, a Name Writing Task and a task of judgment of graphic acceptability. In the Name Writing Task we analyzed the graphic features of the children's written productions (c.f. Hildreth, 1936) and the connection they establish between the graphic units and speech (c.f. Ferreiro & Teberosky, 1982). In the Task of Graphic Acceptability we analyzed the characteristics which render a design acceptable as writing from the children's perspective (c.f. Lavine, 1977).

3.1 The Name Writing Task

Writing one's own name has always been regarded as an important landmark in children's early literacy development. Ferreiro and Teberosky (1983) suggested that 'it is a model of writing, the first stable written string and the prototype of all subsequent writing'. Hildreth (1936) conducted the first study in name writing, and observed that between the ages of three and six, children were eager to write their names on their drawings and their ability to write their own names improved steadily during this period without any direct instruction in writing. Name writing has been studied in various alphabetic languages including English (Scarlett, 1989), Spanish (Ferreiro & Teberosky, 1982), and Hebrew (Tolchinsky-Landsman & Levin, 1985).

Ferreiro and Teberosky (1982) were interested in looking at the idiosyncratic correspondence children could relate while they were writing. Children were asked to write and then read their own names. If a child did not know how to write, movable letters were supplied to encourage the child to form his own name. The child's own writing was segmented into different parts to see if the child could relate the phonetic correspondence into his own name. Their studies in children's writing came up with a detailed account of children's interpretation of the written system, and identification of five developmental levels of writing where children progress from establishing their basic writing model to gradually attending to syllable, and then proceed to letter sound correspondence. Scarlett (1989) followed Ferreiro's work closely in investigating English children's knowledge of written language before receiving formal teaching instruction in school. Seventy-five children, aged from 4 to 6 years, were asked to write their names, various other words and a sentence in a decontextualized situation. Results confirmed that children evolve through developmental levels in their understanding of writing. Children are more advanced in writing their own names than other unfamiliar words. Tolchinsky-Landsman & Levin (1985) investigated Hebrew speaking children's conceptualization of the writing system. Forty-two Israeli children, age 3 to 5, were asked to draw, write their names and some utterances, such as 'a house', 'a child playing with a ball', 'a red flower'. They found that children progress from making global correspondences between what they write and the designated object, to an understanding that each letter corresponds to a sound unit smaller than a syllable. It is now widely accepted that, in order to learn an alphabetic script, children must understand how the alphabet works and learn letter-sound correspondences.

As mentioned earlier on, in Chinese each character corresponds to a syllable. It is expected that children can understand and apply this syllabic rule in their writing at an early age. What may be difficult for the Chinese children is the complicated within-character graphic structure, about which children are not taught explicitly.

Chan and Louie (1992) investigated whether, when writing their names, preschool children will: (1) differentiate drawing from writing; (2) use a correspondence between character and syllable in their writing; (3) use multiple units within one character or across characters; and (4) respect some of the supra-segmental properties of written Chinese. Most of the Chinese names in Hong Kong consist of three characters and correspond to three syllables respectively. Only a small percentage of names is written with two or four characters. This allows for an analysis of correspondences between number of syllables in the name and number of graphic units as well as the use of linear arrangement of graphic units.

We asked sixty preschool children to draw a picture of self and write their names. There were twenty children in each of three age groups. The mean age for each age group was 3 years 1 month; 4 years 0 month; and 5 years 0 month. All the children attended nurseries or kindergartens. There was no formal teaching of writing for the 3-year-olds; they were encouraged to draw and did some pre-writing exercises (holding a pencil in a 'proper' way; practicing horizontal and vertical strokes in the correct direction for writing). At the age of four the children were guided to write some simple characters with simple stroke-patterns. The five-year-olds had been exposed to formal writing instruction for a whole year, during which they are required to do writing exercises daily.

3.1.1   Differentiation between drawing and writing

Children's ability to differentiate drawing from writing was analyzed by judging their drawing of self and name writing as 'same' or 'different' according to their representation. The two researchers (Chan & Louie) carried out the judgements independently. In order to make this judgment, the researchers considered only the overall similarity of the two productions but did not include criteria such as type and number of elements or their spatial arrangement. Agreement between the judges was obtained in 97% of the cases. In the two cases where there was disagreement, classification was obtained by consensus after discussion.

Figure 2. Example of children's name writing (*) and drawing: Chan (4 yrs. 1 mth.).

There were five 3-year-olds, four 4-year-olds and two 5-year-olds who produced similar scribbles for both the drawing and writing. These productions were judged as not differentiating between drawing and writing and were excluded from further analyses. Figure 2 shows Chan's production (4 yrs. 1 mth.) illustrating how she differentiates between drawing and writing; linearity can already be identified in her writing.

3.1.2 Character-syllable correspondence

All the children in the study had names that are written with three characters. Table 1 presents the number of characters that the children used to write their names. Approximately one third of the total number of children used three characters in writing their names. Although quite a few children could not produce the characters in their names correctly, they still used three units for their names. Although it is possible that children would have learned that names have three characters and thus use three without consideration for the number of spoken units, observations of the process of production demonstrated that this was not the case. Only the children who used the number of syllables as a guide to their production used three characters for their names.

Table 1. Number of children using one, two, three, and more than three characters in name writing task[1].

Number of characters	Age 3 yrs.	Age 4 yrs.	Age 5 yrs.
1	8	9	7
2	3	1	3
3	3	6	8
> 3	1	0	0
Total	15	17	18

3.1.3 Supra-segmental graphic features

This analysis includes both within-unit and across units features. The children's productions were assessed regarding whether they respected the features of linearity, regularity of blanks and constricted size across the units (see Figure 3). The produc-

---

[1] Children who did not make a distinction between drawing and writing are excluded from this table. The same holds for tables 2 and 3.

tions were also judged in terms of the multiplicity of strokes used either within or across graphic units. Table 2 presents the number of children whose writing exhibited each of these graphic features. Many children's writing could not be examined for graphic features that only apply across units because they only contained one unit. An age effect was found across all the features. Most of the children who used various graphic units in writing their names placed the characters in a horizontal linear arrangement. Older children used more strokes and stroke-patterns in their writing and still produced characters of approximately the same size and within a square area.

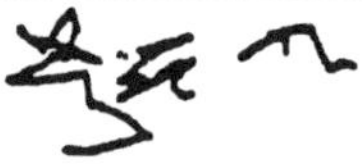	Kay (3 yrs. 1 mth)	Nill	Scribbles
	Chan (3 yrs. 8 mth)	Presence of units	Presence of strokes
	Lo (4 yrs. 8 mth)	Presence of units	Presence of stroke-patterns
	Cheung (4 yrs. 4 mth.)	Presence of units	Presence of stroke-patterns
	Wong (5 yrs. 0 mth.)	Linearity Presence of units Constricted size	Presence of strokes
	Lai (5 yrs. 3 mth.)	Linearity Regularity of blanks Presence of units Constricted size	Presence of correct characters

Figure 3. Name Writing Task among 3-, 4-, and 5-years-old children.

Table 2. Number of children demonstrating knowledge of supra-segmental graphic properties in writing.

Properties	Age groups		
	3 yrs.	4 yrs.	5 yrs.
Linearity of units	4	10	13
Presence of units	4	11	14
Regularity of blanks	4	6	10
Constricted size	4	6	10
Total	2	7	12

3.1.4   Graphic units used and their features

The children's writings were classified into one of the following four categories that describe the type of unit used: (1) scribbles (writing which is not formed by strokes but is distinct from pictures); (2) presence of strokes (conventional or not) without use of stroke-patterns; (3) presence of stroke-patterns (the child combines strokes into stroke patterns instead of using isolated strokes as in the previous category); and (4) correct writing. The classification of the production in these categories was carried out independently by two judges and disagreements were resolved through discussion and consensus. Table 3 presents the number of children using these graphic features in their name writing.

Table 3. Number of children demonstrating knowledge of graphic features in writing.

Categories	Age groups		
	3 yrs.	4 yrs.	5 yrs.
Scribbles	11	3	0
Presence of strokes	1	4	5
Presence of stroke-patterns	2	3	4
Correct characters	1	7	9
Total	15	17	18

Scribbles are characterized by a single slash, joined writing, irregular lines and patches of similar marks; they show little resemblance to written Chinese even if they are distinct from drawing in appearance (Figure 3). About 28% of the children who differentiated between drawing and writing used scribbles when writing their names.

Children's productions were classified as use of strokes if they wrote strokes in isolation, not combined into more complex units. For example, Wong (5 yrs. 0 mth.) used vertical and crooked strokes to write his name. An unconventional (or illegal) stroke, a circle, was also included (Figure 3). About 20% of the children used strokes in their name writing.

Some children (18%) used more than one stroke in each unit, combining the strokes into more complex designs, thereby creating units like stroke-patterns. Cheung (4 yrs. 4 mth.), for example, seems to have recognized that most Chinese characters are not formed by single strokes but complicated patterns placed in a square shaped unit; her name was composed with these complex units (see Figure 3). Although her units were not conventional stroke-patterns, her production is not completely arbitrary: she followed a symmetry rule in creating the character by expanding the visual unit on the left to balance the set of complicated units on the right.

About 50% of 5-year-olds used correct characters in their names but only 35% wrote their names correctly. Lai (5 yrs. 3 mth.) has a name that consists of three characters, all quite complicated. All the characters (see Figure 3) are in square shaped areas and separated by blanks.

This analysis demonstrated that the children do not move from lack of knowledge to complete knowledge of particular characters, as one would expect if their learning were determined exclusively by the teaching processes that they are exposed to. Only 35% of the 5-year-olds wrote their names correctly but this does not mean that the remaining children did not know anything about written Chinese. If we consider that those children who used strokes or made-up stroke-patterns were demonstrating some knowledge of the properties of graphic units in Chinese, we conclude that 72% of the total number of children who differentiated writing from drawing produced forms that revealed some implicit knowledge of the graphic features of written Chinese although they could not write their names correctly. One third of the children used at least implicitly a syllable-to-character correspondence and those who used several graphic units in their writing recognized the use of linear arrangement of units. Thus there is evidence that preschool children have some understanding of the graphic properties of units in Chinese, their arrangement, and possibly their connection with speech units.

We turn now to a more complex property of written Chinese, the organization of stroke-patterns within characters, which will be investigated by means of a task of graphic acceptability.

3.1.5 The Graphic Acceptability Task

Research on alphabetic systems suggests that judgements of the acceptability of letter strings reflect children's understanding of principles used in generating written words in their language. Many studies have been carried out and it is not our aim here to review them; our aim is to consider how such studies can be constructed, what they tell us about children's knowledge of their written language, and whether such tasks can give useful information to teachers.

These studies were pioneered by Gibson and her colleagues in the US and carried out initially with adults and later on with children. The initial studies involved a learning paradigm: the participants were presented with the stimuli at very short exposure times and were asked to recall them in writing. It was assumed that learning would be easier if the stimuli were in agreement with the orthography of the language and were pronounceable. Gibson and her colleagues generated pronounceable and unpronounceable letter-strings and presented these to adult subjects, who had to reproduce them in writing afterwards. The same consonant clusters were used in generating the pronounceable and the unpronounceable letter strings by shifting their position with respect to the vowels; for example, 'land' is pronounceable and 'ndasl' is unpronounceable. Adults learn pronounceable letter strings more effectively than unpronounceable ones (Gibson, Pick, Osser, & Hammond, 1962).

Research with children using the same paradigm (Gibson, Osser, & Pick, 1963) showed that the level of literacy knowledge interacts with the use of graphic structure in the learning task. First graders learned pronounceable three-letter strings significantly better than unpronounceable ones but had great difficulty in reproducing longer strings of letters irrespective of their structure. Third graders were able to reproduce both pronounceable and unpronounceable three-letter strings efficiently and learned longer pronounceable strings significantly better than unpronounceable ones of comparable length. These results suggest that there is an implicit learning of what is an acceptable within-word organization, which relates to the children's competence in literacy and facilitates further learning (Gibson & Levine, 1975).

The significance of children's implicit knowledge of the graphic acceptability of letter strings as words was demonstrated by Rosinski and Wheeler (1972) and Golinkoff (1974). Rosinski and Wheeler designed a task where children were shown pairs of letter strings and asked to judge which one 'was more like a real word'. None of the letter strings were real words and thus the children could not use specific word-knowledge in this task. Their judgments would have to be based on within-string structure. One of the strings in the pair was pronounceable and the other one was not. A response was scored as correct if the child chose the pronounceable string. The first-grade children performed as a group at chance level whereas third and fifth grade children performed significantly better than chance. Golinkoff replicated these results and related the scores in this judgment task to scores in a reading test given to the children later, at the end of the year. A significant correlation ($\underline{r}$ = .50) was observed, suggesting that children who later become better readers have earlier on learned more about the within-word structure in their language. This study supports the idea that children learn much about graphic structure on their own because they were not taught about pronounceability explicitly. Unfortunately, the design of this study does not allow for an analysis of cause and effect because the proper controls were not used (such as partialling out the effects of age, intelligence and reading level at the first assessment). Thus we cannot know whether this implicit knowledge is an important factor in promoting further the children's reading and spelling development or whether it is a consequence of the children's specific knowledge at the time of the first assessment.

Types of characters

Example 1. Pseudo characters with correct positioning of stroke-patterns

Example 2. Non-words with illegal position of stroke-patterns

Example 3. Non-words with illegal graphic features

Figure 4. Examples of pseudo-words and non-words in Graphic Acceptability Task.

We designed a task to examine children's ability to make judgements regarding the acceptability of graphic patterns as characters considering different aspects of written Chinese (Chan & Nunes, 1998). As in the studies by Rosinski and Wheeler (1972) and Golinkoff (1974), none of the stimuli were real words and thus the children could not use word-specific knowledge to solve the task. Three types of stimuli were used: (1) *non-words with illegal graphic components* (elements that are not strokes in Chinese, such as circles) *or with legal components used inappropriately* (such as stimuli containing five dots, which violate the restriction regarding the maximum number of repetitions of the same stroke); (2) *pseudo-words* (stimuli that were not conventional words but were composed of conventional stroke-patterns in their legal positions within the characters); and (3) *non-words with* conventional stroke-patterns placed in *illegal positions.* Examples of these stimuli are presented in Figure 4.

The pseudo-words used were all one-character stimuli. Thus they can be compared to meaningless syllables in alphabetic scripts in so far as they would be pronounced in the same way by competent adult readers but would not be a word in the language. However, they would not be completely meaningless, as they contained a semantic radical, a necessary pseudo-component for generating a pseudo-word. In this sense, they can be compared to a derived word in English, such as 'unclimb'; although the morphological cues to interpret 'unclimb' are much more precise than those that would be offered by a semantic radical in isolation. The non-words also contained semantic radicals and phonological components but they cannot be treated in the same way because, since the position of these elements was incorrect, they would not be performing their usual functions.

Hong Kong children are explicitly taught the strokes used in characters. Thus we expect that the children will use this knowledge and be able to judge as unacceptable units that contain illegal strokes. However, they are not taught the rules of composition nor the positional rules for stroke patterns. If the children can systematically judge pseudo-words as acceptable and reject non-words that contain illegal compositions or stroke patterns in illegal position, we can conclude that the children have acquired knowledge of these formal constraints in the absence of explicit teaching. There is evidence that Chinese adults are sensitive to positional rules (Chen & Allport, 1995) but there is no work on children's sensitivity to these aspects of Chinese characters. We hypothesize that age and years of instruction (which cannot be differentiated in this study) interact with the type of judgment that the children make in the task. Younger children and those with less instruction are more likely to recognize that the use of illegal strokes renders a pattern unacceptable than the violation of composition rules or the placement of a stroke-pattern in an illegal position. The latter, subtler principles may be just as important for older children as the simpler ones.

Participants in the study were 100 children in the age range 5 to 9 years. There were 20 children in each age group, with equal numbers of boys and girls. The children in each age group were approximately of the same age (plus or minus one month) with at least ten months difference between the age groups. We included older children in this study because we expected the level of knowledge of characters to be related to knowledge of different aspects of the within-character structure. According to the 'Syllabus for the Teaching of Chinese in Primary Schools', 5-year-olds are expected to read ten to 20 characters; 6-year-olds are expected to read around 100 characters; from this age onwards children are expected to learn about 500 characters in each year of primary school.

In our version of the Graphic Acceptability Task, the children were invited to 'be a teacher' and mark the words supposedly written by a child living in another planet who was trying to learn how to write Chinese. It was necessary to use a play setting in order to engage the children in the task because the children might have refused to judge stimuli that they did not know. There were altogether 30 stimuli, 10 pseudo-words and 20 non-words. Pseudo-words were constructed by substitution of one unit from real characters to form a non-existing combination of graphic units. The stroke-patterns (*i.e.* the semantic radicals and the phonological components) were always in their legitimate positions. The non-words were of two types; equal numbers of each type were used. One type was constructed by generating a pseudo-word in the same manner as described above and then changing the positions of the stoke-patterns. The second type was created by substituting legal with illegal graphic properties in pseudo-words (Figure 4). The order of pseudo-words and non-words was randomized for presentation. They were then written on three pages. Each child received one set of pages to 'mark'.

Figure 5 presents the percentage of children accepting the different types of stimuli as words by age groups. Children of all age groups accepted *pseudo-words* (71%) more than *non-words with illegal positioning of stroke-patterns* (39%) and in turn, *accepted non-words with illegal position of stroke-patterns* more than *non-words with illegal graphic features* (25%). One score was given to positive responses to each item. A mixed ANOVA was conducted with the response to orthographic acceptability effect in the three types of stimuli as a within factor, and age as a between factor. There was a significant age effect, $F(4, 95) = 4.05$, p<.05, a significant orthographic acceptability effect $F(2, 190) = 135.96$, p<.001 and a significant age by orthographic acceptability effect, $F(9, 190) = 3.14$, p<.05. Older children responded differently as compared to younger children, especially in accepting 'nonwords with illegal positions' as 'words', and a downward trend could be traced. In spite of this, at all age levels, children judged more pseudo-words than non-words as acceptable. Younger children (5 and 6 years of age) judged words with illegal graphic features as the least acceptable of the three types of stimuli. They rejected the non-words with legal elements in illegal position less often than the older children but accepted them less often than the pseudo-words. Children in the age range 7 to 9 years distinguished strongly between the two types of non-words and the pseudo-words. We conclude that the Chinese children have some knowledge of the graphic structure of Chinese characters. This knowledge requires them to consider composition rules and the positional organization of stroke-patterns within a character. There are graphic properties of written Chinese about which the children do not receive any instruction. The evidence obtained in this task is compelling because the children could not use specific word knowledge in these judgments: none of the stimuli was a real word.

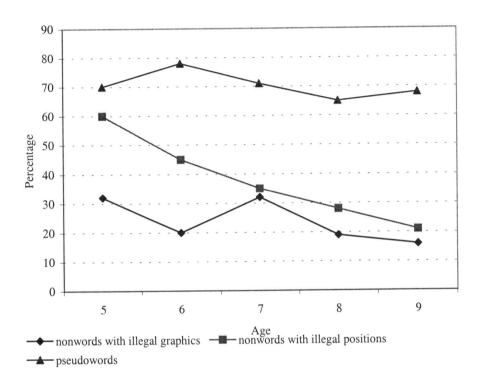

Figure 5. Percentage of graphic ability of pseudo-words and nonwords by age groups.

Our results are analogous to those obtained in English: the children's level of knowledge of the script was associated with their performance in the task of graphic acceptability at the group level. However, without further research we cannot tell whether the implicit knowledge of structure simply develops from the children's knowledge of characters or whether it can be used to further the children's learning.

4   CONCLUSION

The studies considered here on children's implicit knowledge of the properties of their writing system indicate that even quite young children are engaged in actively trying to understand the writing system that is present in their environment. When we invited children to write their names, even the 3-year-old children could make sense of this request and the majority differentiated between drawing and writing. In spite of the fact that all the children in the Name Writing Task were non-readers, they showed much understanding of general properties of writing, although it is unlikely that they had been taught about these properties of writing. Some children also recognized that there are conventions for writing and that they only knew the overall properties of writing, not the specific conventions: they explicitly indicated that what they were writing was not the correct way to write their names but only something like writing. For example, one child remarked about his production: 'It is not my name, I don't know how to write yet, but it looks like it'. Another child knew that his name consisted of three characters, he knew how to write the first and a bit of the second, but he had no idea how to write the third. He was not satisfied writing only two characters for his name. So he put a line next to the second character and a cross above the line to indicate that he knew that there should be one character there but he could not figure out how to do it.

We found that, after children progress beyond scribbles, their writing becomes distinctly Chinese. About one quarter of the 4- and 5-year olds could write some correct characters. The majority of the remaining 4- and 5-year-olds who did not produce correct characters (16 out of 24) used either strokes or stroke patterns in their writing. We hypothesize that this type of exploratory writing may help children focus their attention on the graphic structure of Chinese and develop a sense for what looks more like a character.

Children exposed to Chinese and to alphabetic script learn implicitly important properties of the structure of their script: in an alphabetic script they know whether strings of letters are or are not pronounceable words and in Chinese they know whether the stroke-pattern that gives a clue to meaning is adequately placed in a pseudo-character or not. As Gibson and her colleagues showed, in alphabetic scripts this implicit knowledge predicts children's progress in reading longitudinally and facilitates the learning of novel stimuli that conform to the canonical structure of the script. It is thus reasonable to hypothesize, as Gibson and Levine (1975) did, that this implicit knowledge is an important process in literacy learning. So far the evidence is ambiguous with respect to the status of this knowledge of structures. It is possible that the implicit learning of the structural properties of the script is a factor in facilitating reading progress but it is also equally possible that it results from progress in literacy learning.

Our hypothesis is that learning general structural properties of the script and learning specific examples are mutually enhancing processes. As children learn more instances of graphic units in their script and their connection to speech units, they form schemas that contain information about basic forms and transformations in the written language (see Franks & Bransford, 1971). We also hypothesize that the learning of specific instances is enhanced when children develop a general schema that can be used for the assimilation of novel instances. In the studies by Gibson and her colleagues, the first grade children, who did not seem to have formed schemas for identifying pronounceability had much difficulty in learning long strings of letters, whether they were pronounceable or not, whereas the third and fifth graders, who had these schemas, learned the pronounceable stimuli efficiently. There is also some evidence for this hypothesis in our previous work on children's use of morphology in spelling in English (Nunes, Bryant, & Bindman, 1997a and 1997b) but further research is clearly needed to examine these hypotheses.

We believe that it is useful for teachers to observe their children's knowledge of the structural properties of their script and try to enhance this knowledge. The tasks of graphic acceptability of pseudo-words, which, as we have seen, can be meaningfully carried out by young children at the start of literacy instruction, seem to reveal the children's grasp of graphic properties of their script. These tasks can easily be transformed into games to be carried out in the classroom by groups of children, who could not only classify the stimuli but also discuss their criteria for doing so. It can be speculated that this use of tasks of graphic acceptability might strengthen the children's awareness of the properties of their script and consequently their ability to assimilate new instances and perhaps even other properties of the script.

To conclude, we suggest that teaching programs should not consider only strokes and characters in the design of instruction; there is also an important role for stroke patterns, the rules of position and the related functions of stroke patterns. There is as yet no evidence to indicate whether these should be taught explicitly or whether it is best to organize materials in a way that children can be asked to study and discover the importance of the position of the stroke-patterns in defining their function. Perhaps if children are invited to explore the various ways of combining stroke-patterns to form characters, they will come to understand the relation between position and linguistic function. Systematically grouping characters that share the same semantic radical or where the pronunciation can be achieved from the phonological component by similar rules (derivation or analogy) may facilitate the development of an explicit understanding of underlying principles in the Chinese writing system and thus further learning.

AUTHOR'S NOTE

Address for correspondence: Lily Chan, School of Early Childhood Education, Hong Kong Institute for Education, 10 Lo Ping Road, Tai Po, New Territories, Hong Kong. E-mail: lchan@ied.edu.hk.

ON THE INTERPLAY OF GENRE AND WRITING CONVENTIONS IN EARLY TEXT WRITING

ANA SANDBANK

Beit Berl College – Israel

Abstract. This chapter concentrates on early text writing. 16 preschoolers and 16 firstgraders, all native Hebrew speakers, were asked to write, read and revise a fairy tale – a narrative – and a description of one of the objects in it. Texts were analysed in terms of grapho-phonemic correspondences, the spaces between words, and the children's own reading of their written text and their modifications of it. With age, children wrote according to grapho-phonemic correspondences the two genres. Blanks between words were more frequent in first grade children. They are likewise more frequent in descriptions than in narratives. The number of modifications increased with age, in narratives more than in descriptions. Both age groups performed modifications on different text levels in both genres, mainly during the revision phase. Findings are examined within the frame of writing development studies and also from the perspective of the researcher analysing the texts.
Keywords: early text writing, genre, writing conventions, grapho-phonemic correspondences, blank spaces, reading of own writing, revision

1   INTRODUCTION

When Maya, an Israeli first grade girl, was asked to write the tale Ammy and Tammy (the Hebrew version of 'Hansel and Gretel'), she wrote it according to grapho-phonemic correspondences although she had not yet mastered the Hebrew orthographic rules. Moreover, her writing was accompanied all along by verbal comments such as those in the following scheme.

Verbal comment	Explanatory comment
'Does Ammy (the name of the protagonist) have an <u>ayin</u> or an <u>aleph</u>?'	Two Hebrew letters that are both possible options for writing phonemic /a/. Here the letter should be <u>ayin</u>.
'How do you write "Tammy"? What letter do I need for /ta/?...'	Hebrew has two letters for phonemic /t/ <u>tet</u> and <u>tav.</u>

L. Tolchinsky (ed.), Developmental Aspects in Learning to Write, 55–75.

'I don't know what I wrote here...'   The words the mother and the father should
                                             be followed by (the words) went to the chil-
                                             dren's room.

'I would like to add'   This is what she replied when she was asked
'...I am thinking now...'   at the end whether she would like to add,
'...I have so many stories in my head'.   change or erase anything.

These comments reflect that, while writing the text, this first grade girl was working
on several levels involved in text production, among which: the grapho-phonemic
correspondences; the story she wanted to write or the story she though she should
write; as well as more local decisions concerning a particular predicate. Her comments likewise point out the fact that children are capable of thinking about the actual writing process. That is, they are capable to 'going meta' (Olson & Bruner,
1996:19).

This chapter concentrates on the development of writing texts in preschool and
firstgrade children. I shall present a study of the writing of narratives and descriptions, which is grounded on previous research on early text writing.

2   EARLY TEXT WRITING RESEARCH

Studies on early text writing are based on a fundamental distinction between two
different meanings of writing. The first refers to writing as a notational system, that
is the process of writing symbols in order to convey a message. The second refers to
writing as a mode of discourse, that is, the production of written, permanent texts in
different genres (Pontecorvo, Orsolini, Burge, & Resnick, 1996; Pontecorvo, 1997).

Based on the above distinction, scholars have adopted two central approaches in
research. The first approach focuses on the text, on genre differentiation and writing
style, and put aside concerns about the conventions of the writing system. Two main
methodologies have been used within this approach: either the child is asked to dic-
tate his/her text to the researcher, or after the child has written his/her text, the researcher rewrites it in conventional writing. These studies have demonstrated that
long before children read and write in a conventional way, they are sensitive to certain grammatical, rhetorical and lexical devices for written language and distinguish
between different genres (Pontecorvo & Morani, 1996; Tolchinsky Landsmann,
1990; Zuccermaglio & Scheuer, 1996).

A second approach looks at how children write texts and explores children's
ways of writing in terms of the conventions of the writing system. In general, studying the development of writing conventions in text production allows researchers to
go beyond the grapho-phonemic correspondences and orthography rules of writing
words. Hence, they can examine conventions such as blank spaces between words,
which are language and script specific, as well as those conventions defined as such
by editors and the literate community, i.e., capitalization, punctuation or layout
(Ferreiro & Pontecorvo, 1996, 1999).

Studying writing development within the latter approach revealed that knowledge of text-specific features such as genre and communicational intentions might affect writing conventions before children master conventional writing – cf. writing letter strings as opposed to writing according to grapho-phonemic correspondences (Sulzby, 1992; Zecker, 1996). Moreover syntactic elements, such as the grammatical category of words have been found to affect separation between words in the young school grade children (Ferreiro & Pontecorvo, 1996). These findings suggest that the distinction between knowledge of the writing system and knowledge of written language that is central to research on writing development cannot be strictly maintained from the point of view of the child writer who has not yet mastered conventional writing. These studies likewise stress the importance of studying writing within a more integrative approach. In other words, to study the ways in which genre and writing conventions interplay not only in writing but also in reading.

Children's early readings of their own written texts provide valuable information about their knowledge of written in contrast to oral discourse, even when their writing is not close to convention. Analysis of young children's reading of their own written texts has led to the assumption that their knowledge concerning genres is more advanced than their mastery of grapho-phonemic correspondences. Thus children's ways of readings have been characterized as better sources for unveiling children's emergent knowledge of the functional aspects of written language than their written products alone (Zecker, 1996).

Reading their own written text not only reflects children's knowledge but also provides the writer with the chance to reflect, to go back to his/her own written text, review their writing and modify the texts (Piolat, 1988; Ravid & Tolchinsky, in press). The modifications children perform during the text production provide a good way to study children's monitoring over their linguistic production at the levels of representational knowledge or awareness, not accessible to verbalization, which has been termed an intermediate level of representational knowledge or awareness. Besides, discourse principles operate strictly on-line, and hence are relevant only at the time when a particular text is being produced, which in turn means that they may not be available to metalinguistic reflection at all (Karmiloff Smith, 1992; Tolchinsky Landsmann & Karmiloff Smith, 1992).

The present study aims to concentrate on the interplay between the writing conventions and the written language from three main perspectives. The first relates to the interplay between writing conventions with genre in writing. The second, to the interplay between the conventions and the text through the ways children read their own written texts, and the third, to the modifications children performed during writing, reading and revising their texts.

The analysis of children's text production from these three perspectives aims at shedding light on general trends in development by discriminating between those writing conventions that are influenced by genre and those that developed across the two genres. It also unveils the ways children relate to their own written product in reading and revising during the whole writing process.

'It has been said that any problem examined in the right way becomes even more complicated' (Goldfajn, 1998: 2).

In line with this insight I here consider not only what was revealed about children's writing, but also what may be involved in the researcher's decisions both about the context of research regarding the characteristics of narratives and descriptions and about each one of the aspects of the text that were analyzed.

3   NARRATIVES AND DESCRIPTIONS

Narratives and descriptions can be classified along two axes: chronological organization and the way the writer relates to his/her subject matter and to his/her reader (Perera, 1984). Narratives are chronologically organized and enable some personal involvement They are composed of two major elements: structural elements making up the backbone of the story and expressed in chronologically ordered referential clauses and evaluative elements of content expressing the narrator's interpretation and perspective on these events (Berman, 1997). In the present research, children were asked to write a fairy-tale. Fairy tales are fictitious and the writer is a concealed presence in the text, so there is a distinction between the implicit narrator and the characters (Todorov, 1977).

Descriptions, in contrast, are not chronologically organized and are impersonal. They consist of different elements related to a common thematic axis, which are grouped according to different dimensions, depending on to the type of the description – an emotional state, a landscape, or an object. Here children were asked to write a description of an object – the house of the witch – that constitutes a text segment in the story. Descriptive text segments may alternate with narrative segments in a particular story. They may appear for defining the framework of one of the sequences in the story either from the perspective of the narrator or from the perspective of a character, suspending the actions related (Adam & Petitjean, 1989). Hence, they differ from the story linguistically.

Before referring to the study let me briefly present the central features of Hebrew orthography.

4   SOME FEATURES OF THE HEBREW WRITING SYSTEM

Hebrew writing system is essentially consonantal: all 22 letters denote consonants. Four of these letters, aleph, hey, waw, and yod, known as 'matres lectionis', designate both semivowels and glottal/pharyngeal segments as well as noting vowels ambiguously and inconsistently (Coulmas, 1990; Ravid, in press). Context helps to decide the correct reading of a group of consonant letters, which may allow for different possibilities.

Since vowels are not noted in all occurrences, Hebrew-speaking children do not have to reach an exhaustive alphabetic writing. Thus, when analyzing children's writing in Hebrew the distinction between syllabic and alphabetic writing is often difficult to define. For example, a young child writes the word *kinor* 'violin' only with consonants KNR this could be categorized as syllabic writing because the vowels /i/ and /o/ should be noted by letters. Yet, if he/she writes the same letters KNR for *kanar* 'violinist' it will be conventional writing, since no letter should stand for the vowel /a/.

Hebrew orthography has also a vocalized variety that coexists with the non-vocalized. The vocalized orthography uses a whole set of diacritics that denote vowels unmistakably and somewhat redundantly. It is common only in children's books, for distinguishing between two possible readings of a word, in foreign words, in Biblical texts and poetry.

Learning the grapho-phonemic correspondences is not enough for conventional writing, since Hebrew has a morphologically motivated orthography (Ravid & Tolchinsky, in press). Firstly, there are surface homophones expressed by two graphemes reflecting historically distinct segments that have been neutralized. For example /t/ derives from a historically emphatic voiceless coronal stop *tet* (written as t), and voiceless coronal stop *tav* (written as T) (Ravid, in press). Thus, the word *taxana* meaning 'mill' is spelled t*H*NH with a root first t (from the root T*H*N 'grind'), and the word *taxana* meaning 'station' is spelled T*H*NH (from the root *H*NY 'stand park')[1]. That is, homophonous units may have different morphological values.

Secondly, three letters (the remains of a larger class of historically spirantizing stops) denote two distinct sounds (*e.g.* the letter K indicates both the phonemes /k/ and /x/). For example, the word for the verb meaning 'write' in the present tense is pronounced *kotev*, and is spelled KWTB and the noun meaning '(a) letter' (in the sense of a missive, not a graphic symbol) is pronounced *mixtav* and is spelled MKTB. Thus, the two words write and letter are spelled with the same consonantal root KTB, but the letter *kav* (written as K) is pronounced /k/ in the word *kotev* 'write' and /x/ in the word *mixtav* (letter).

There are two types of morphological constructions: interdigitated consonantal roots plus affixal patterns and concatenated stem and suffix. The first refers to the typically Semitic root and pattern morphology, involving a combination of a tri or quadri consonantal mapped onto a vocalic pattern. For example, combining the root HLK 'walk' with other patterns yields past tense *halax* 'walked', spelled HLK; present tense *holex* '(he) walks', spelled HWLK; '(a) walk', spelled HLYKH, *hilux*, 'gait', spelled HYLWK. The second type of morphological structure is linear, *i.e.*, a concatenation of a stem (typically a word), a prefix and a suffix, *e.g.* *yeled* 'boy', spelled YLD, *yald-a* 'girl', spelled YLDH, *yeladim* 'boys', spelled YLDIM, *yeladot* 'girls', spelled YLDWT. Unlike content words, most Hebrew grammatical closed class items are usually monosyllabic and morphologically simplex, without an internal derivational structure (Ravid, in press).

Hebrew has no independent words with one single letter. The prepositions in; to, from, as; the definite article the; conjunctions: the connector and, and the relative marker that, which consist of one single letter, are written attached to the next word. For example, the word *bayit* 'house' as well as the construction *u-me-ha-bayit,* spelled WMHBYT 'and-from-the-house', are both written as single words, *i.e.*, a string of letters between blanks.

---

[1] *The letter* H *indicates the phoneme* /x/ *which derives from historical H.*

Hebrew is written with separate characters both in handwriting and in print. Thus, writing involves control on two levels of blank spaces: a small space between one letter and a larger space between words. Rounded letters are used mainly in hand-writing whereas angular letters are used in print. These two varieties of Hebrew script developed from the Hebrew square script: the Sepharadic type (that is, oriental Spanish), characterized by rounded lines, and the Ashkenazic type, which is angular (Coulmas, 1990). That is, when children write, they have to differentiate between small blanks spaces that separate letters and larger blank spaces that separate words.

5   SUBJECTS AND PROCEDURE

The sample includes 16 preschoolers and 16 first graders, with a mean age of 5:4 and 6:4 years respectively at the first months of the school year. The population included an equal number of boys and girls, all of whom were native Hebrew speakers. The children came from a single neighborhood, and their parents were from the low middle and middle class (blue collar workers, technicians, small businessmen, teachers). That is, children who are in the transitional period, in which writing becomes close to convention, and even at the time that formal instruction begins.

Since learning environment has been found to influence writing, it is important to take into account the school practices (Tolchinsky Landsmann, 1990). Preschool children were not engaged in early writing activities. School children were used to write texts – mostly stories – even before they master conventional writing. Consequently, asking from these first graders as I did to write or rewrite a tale was a well-known practice for them.

The fairy tale Ammy and Tammy was read to the children in small groups in order to provide children both with a basis in content, what to write about, and also with the structure and the language that characterize a written text. Approximately one week after the reading, children were asked to write the texts in their own way. Half of the children wrote the narrative first and the description second, whereas the other half wrote the description first. A week elapsed between the two sessions.

Asking children to write a text that had been read to them is based on the assumption that a rewriting situation creates an inter-textual space between the read text and the text the children write and provides children with important linguistic knowledge and forms of expression, which influence the quality of their texts (Pontecorvo, *et al.*, 1996; Zucchermaglio & Scheuer, 1996). Rewriting a text is a constructive process, so that certain aspects of the read text will be preserved, some will be modified, and others ignored.

Each child was asked to write the fairy tale and to describe how the witch's house looked like. This was done in two different sessions. For the writing task every child received a pencil and two blank sheets of paper with a carbon copy sheet between the two, in order to keep a copy of the first original version and compare with the second modified version. After writing, the copy text was removed and the child was asked to read out his/her text and 'if you wish to change, add or delete something, you can do it'. Then, the child was asked to look at the text 'now look at the text you have written, and see if there is something you want to add, delete or change in it'. The following sections outline some of the results obtained in this study.

6   THE GRAPHO-PHONEMIC CORRESPONDENCES

Most preschool children wrote, both texts, with pseudo letters or random Hebrew letters. That is, their writing was constrained by the principle of writing different letters or combining the same letters in different ways in order to convey different utterances. When asked to read, some children mapped globally between letters or pseudo letters to utterances or between letters and the number of phonological segments in the utterance they were attempting to write, *i.e.* they tried to make quantitative correspondences. As possible to see in Table 1, global mapping was more frequent in their narratives than in their descriptions, whereas quantitative mapping was more frequent in their descriptions than in their narratives.

Table 1. Distribution of the categories of grapho-phonemic correspondences by age and genre (n=32).

| | Preschoolers | | First graders | |
Genre Categories	Narratives	Descriptions	Narratives	Descriptions
Systematic	0	1	4	7
Non systematic	2	1	9	6
Quantitative	4	8	2	0
Global	10	6	1	3
Total	16	16	16	16

Most first graders, in contrast, wrote with qualitative grapho-phonemic correspondences. They use letters according to the conventional phonological value. And yet, a distinction was made between systematic and non-systematic qualitative grapho-phonemic correspondences. Writing according to qualitative correspondences was classified as systematic if some words were written according to convention, some words according to conventional phonological value, some words in a syllabic way – a letter for a syllable CV or CVC or for a word segment that should be written by more than one letter – and the entire text could be reconstructed in reading. Writing according to qualitative correspondences was classified as non-systematic if there were also some strings of letters whose meaning could not be reconstructed or when children 'read' words that were not written at all. The distinction between non-systematic and systematic qualitative correspondences involves not only the way children write the whole text, but the extent to which children could reconstruct what they wrote as well as the extent to which the researcher was able to reconstruct the text without relying on what the child said he/she had written. It is important to note that there is a difference between writing according to phonological correspondences and writing according to orthographic rules, which implies deciding between two or more possible letters according to morphology. Differences between genres were not significant.

Thus, writing according to grapho-phonemic correspondences is a general developmental path across genres[2].

7   BLANK SPACES BETWEEN WORDS

Studies on early text production demonstrate that children may omit spaces between words. They draw long strings of letters without any spacing. When children start to create some sort of spacing between strings of letters, they sometimes create spaces in non-conventional ways (Bissex, 1980; Ferreiro & Pontecorvo, 1996). Moreover, preschool children do not seem to perceive blanks as word boundaries when asked to interpret what is written in each one of the written words of a sentence (Ferreiro & Teberosky, 1982).

Most of the school children produced strings of letters separated by blank spaces. In some cases, the strings of letters between spaces corresponded to actual words in the language, but in others, the written strings consisted of units that differ from what is considered a written word in Hebrew. This category includes cases in which children left less blank spaces than convention requires (hyposegmentation) and cases in which prepositions or connectives – i.e., closed class items – that in Hebrew, as described earlier, must be written attached to the open class words – were written separately (hypersegmentation). More than half of the preschool children did not produced spaces between strings of letters. Some of the children did, but it was difficult to identify the reason (see table 2).

Table 2. Distribution of the blank spaces by age and genre (n=32).

| | Preschoolers | | First graders | |
Genre Categories	Narratives	Descriptions	Narratives	Descriptions
Words	1	3	4	9
Hypo-hyper	4	3	8	4
No separation	9	9	2	2
Other	2	1	2	1
Total	16	16	16	16

---

[2] *A series of one way Fisher Exact Tests were carried out comparing 2 (age groups) x 2 (categories of grapho-phonemic correspondences) in (a) conventional in both genres (b) conventional only in narratives (c) conventional only in the description (d) non- systematic grapho-phonemic correspondences in both genres. Only differences in the last condition were significant.*

Most of preschool children did not separate between words neither in narratives nor in descriptions, whereas first graders separated between words in one text at least[3]. Differences between genres were significant (CATMOD (χ^2 (2) = 4.06 p<.05).

One possible explanation for this difference between genres refers to the role of iconicity or *mise en page*, which might have some influence on children's decision to create blanks. Creation of blanks could be motivated by the children's search for a different graphic presentation for distinct genres (*e.g.*, for lists, descriptions, narratives, poetry), rather than by their need for blank spaces between words. A number of children wrote the descriptive text as lists while they wrote their narrative using the full space of the line. A similar tendency was observed when children were asked to write single words as opposed to whole stories (Sulzby, 1986).

For example, Hadar, a 6 year-old girl, wrote the following two texts in Hebrew letters (figure 1). She did not write according to convention, in her descriptive text, a line corresponds either to a single word or to a compound noun; in her narrative text however it is hard to define blank spaces.

The narrative

ami ve tami
Ammy and Tammy

ima amra le^ aba she hem
the mother said to the father that they
xayavim lacet ki ha-yeladim oxlim lahem et ha-kol
have to go out because the children eat everything
ve lahem lo nish'ar klum
and nothing is left to them
ami ve tami sham'u et ze
Ammy and Tammy heard that
aval ha^ horim lo yad'u she hem sham'u et ze
but the parents did not know that they heard that
ami siper le tami she ima sipra le-aba
Ammy told Tammy that his mother told to (the) father
ve hu yac'a le'esof avney xacac
and he went out to pick up pebbles

---

[3]*A series one way Fisher Exact Tests were carried out comparing 2 (age groups) x 2 (word separation) for each one of the following conditions: (a) between words in both genres, (b) only in the narrative (c) only in the description (d) neither in the narrative nor the description. Only differences in the last condition were significant.*

The description of the witch's house

mic kola
cola juice

mic limon
lemon juice

shokolat
chocolate

vafelim
waffle

sukaryia
candy

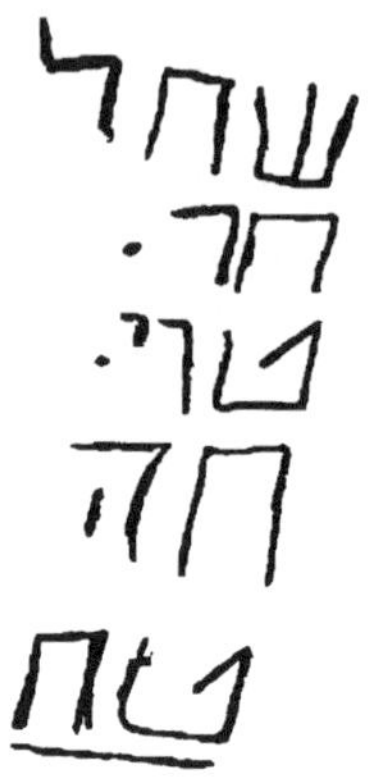

Figure 1. Example of a narrative and a description by Hadar (girl, 6 yrs. 0 mth.)

Children who did not write descriptions as lists still tended to create blank spaces between strings of letters that corresponded to words more frequently in descriptive texts than in narratives.

A second possible explanation refers to children's assumptions about what constitutes a written word. Research has shown that young children assume that nouns are words and are written as such, but that verbs and closed class items are not written independently, or are not written at all (Ferreiro, 1978). These findings may lead to the conclusion that differences between narratives and descriptions have to do with to the lexical category of the words in the two genres. In order to evaluate this alternative explanation, we analyzed the words children read out from their written texts in terms of their lexical class membership.

As seen in Table 3, the ratio of nouns was higher in descriptions than in narratives in the two age groups. The ratio of verbs and closed class items was much higher in narratives than in descriptions. These findings could mean that nouns are written between spaces more often than verbs and closed class items.

However, the tendency of writing nouns between spaces may not appear when the syntactic structure includes other lexical categories. For example, Meytal (6; 9), who wrote according to grapho-phonemic correspondences, did not create blank spaces according to the convention in her narrative text, even between proper nouns, such as Ammy and Tammy. Thus, the blank spaces between strings of letters may be influenced by the kind of syntactic structure (Tolchinsky & Cintas, this volume).

This last explanation seems to be the most appropriate for explaining our results. However, differences in the criteria of spacing between strings of letters have been found within the same text and not only between genres. In a previous work, in which children were asked to write the story 'Little Red Riding Hood', it was found that children created less blank spaces than the convention requires (hyposegmentations) in direct speech than in the narrative discourse, both in Spanish and Italian (Ferreiro & Pontecorvo, 1996). It may be possible that in such cases what is written between spaces is related to those aspects of speech that conventional writing does not depict, *e.g.*, the illocutionary force (Olson, 1994). Hyposegmentation could be a graphic clue indicating how the speaker intends the text to be read or interpreted.

To sum up, before writing becomes conventional, blank spaces between words appear to be influenced by genre. This finding could be related to the graphic layout of the text and its content and structure, and to what children perceive as a word.

Table 3. Distribution of lexical categories by age and genre (n=32)[4].

Categories \ Genre	Preschoolers		First graders	
	Narratives	Descriptions	Narratives	Descriptions
Nouns	34	60	35	64
Prepositions & nouns	9	4	7	7
Verbs	20	5	20	3
Copula	4	6	3	10
Adjectives	3	6	6	4
Closed class	30	19	29	12
Total	100	100	100	100

8 ANALYSIS OF BLANK SPACES: THE RESEARCHER'S PERSPECTIVE

In addition to evaluating why children create blank spaces between strings in the way that they do, researchers need not only to determine whether the child has in fact left a space but also what is written between spaces.

In some cases, it may be difficult for a researcher to know whether the child intended to leave a space or not. This difficulty may be due to children's previous experience with a specific writing style – *e.g.*, small print or cursive. For example, blank spaces according to convention have been found more common among Italian children who have been formally instructed in cursive writing than among Mexican children who were formally instructed in small print writing (Ferreiro & Pontecorvo, 1996).

Since Hebrew is written with separate characters both in print and in cursive, there is no option for connected writing. It is quite possible that controlling the dif-

---

[4] *The values represent the ratio of each category relative to the total number words, in percentages.*

ference between a small blank between letters within a word and a larger blank between words is difficult for young children.

Another consideration concerns the fact that researchers themselves analyze language through what they know about their own specific language. It is possible that
when reading a text written by a child, a researcher expects to find a blank at the end
of a word. In this case, even if it is only a small blank, the researcher will tend to see
it as a blank, while if the same space is within a written word he or she may not notice it.

Once the researcher has defined spaces between a string he/she has to decide
what the child intended to write between the spaces. Again, as soon as children's
writing becomes more conventional they tend to refer to what they have written
when reading out the text, and in such cases the researcher can also interpret what
children wrote between spaces, in most of the cases if not in all of them. In contrast,
when writing is according to certain formal constraints, such as different letters for
different words, neither the child nor the researcher is able to read from what is written on the page. Thus, the only way to access the written units between spaces is the
child's reading of these. However, in some cases there was a divergence between
what a child wrote between spaces and what he/she read.

Eyal, a boy aged 6; 6, wrote as a single string *she-yesh bo harbe* 'which has in it
lots', which should be written, as three separated words in Hebrew. Then he read out
the same segment as *she-ba-xuc* 'that (is) outside', which in Hebrew is one written
word. Thus, defining written words on the basis of what is read disregards what the
child wrote. This example introduces another aspect in early text writing analysis:
the writing reading relationship.

9   READING THEIR OWN WRITTEN TEXTS

The ways young children read their own written texts can be characterized in terms
of the interplay between, on the one hand what they wanted to write and / or what
they remembered to have written on the other hand — the internal text — and what
they actually wrote — the written text.

Table 4. Distribution of reading categories by age and genre (n=32).

	Preschoolers		First-graders	
Genre Categories	Narratives	Descriptions	Narratives	Descriptions
Written text	0	1	8	9
Internal text	2	15	4	1
Matching	14	0	4	6
Total	16	16	16	16

Table 4 shows the distribution of reading categories by age and genre. As seen, some children rely on the internal text. They 'read' the same written marks in more than one way, added or changed in their oral rendering without changing the written product. Some children read relying on what had been written. Then, if they could not reconstruct what was written, they refused to read those segments. Some of them changed their written product in order to be able to read the entire text. Thus they tried to match between the written product and the text they read.

Preschool children reconstructed their texts based mainly on the text they wanted to have written. First grade children, in contrast, relied significantly more on the written text both in narratives and in descriptions[5]. However, this developmental path is far from being a linear one, particularly when writing was in transition to convention. The following examples present three different ways of reading texts, which were written at a similar writing level: non-systematic qualitative correspondences. The first example presents a case of adding to the text only when reading it, without changing the written text.

Limor, a girl aged 6yrs 4 mth., wrote her narrative text in syllabic and alphabetic writing, with some words written according to convention. When she read her text, she added come to take Ammy and Tammy back home after the, in her oral rendering without changing anything in her written text.

Written	Read
Ami ve tami Ammy and Tammy	*ami ve tami* Ammy and Tammy
pa'am ima racta lakaxat et once (the) mother wanted to take	*pa'am ima racta lakaxat et* once the mother wanted to take
Ami ve tami la-ya'ar axar-kax Ammy and Tammy to (the) forest afterwards	*Ami ve tami la-ya'ar axar-kax* Ammy and Tammy to (the) forest afterwards
Ami baxta axarkax aba ami cried afterwards (the) father	*ami baxta axarkax aba* ami cried afterwards (the) father *bah lakaxat et ami ve tami ha-bayita* come to-take Ammy and Tammy back home
Ima meta mother died	*axarey she ima meta* after (the) mother died

Figure 2. Example of a narrative by Limor (girl, 6 yrs. 4 mth.)

---

[5] *A series of one-way Fisher Exact Tests were carried out comparing 2 (age groups) x 2 (relying on written text or the internal text) for each genre. In narratives first grade children were relying significantly more on the written text than preschool children did. The same tendency was found for descriptions.*

The second example presents a case of deleting and modifying text only when reading it, without changing the written text.

Eyal, a boy aged 6 yrs. 6 mth., wrote his descriptive text in syllabic and alphabetic writing, but he could not read everything he wrote. He sometimes changed in his oral rendering what he had written, in one case he did not read a word he had written.

Written	Read
hu nir'a ke-bayit she yesh bo harbe	*ve-nir'a kmo bayit she ba-xuc*
it look like (a) house that has in it (a) lot	and (it) looked' like (a) house that outside
ugiyot ba-gag u-ba-delet	*yesh ba-gag ba-delet*
(of) cookies on the roof and on the door	there are on the roof on the door

Figure 3. Example of a description by Eyal (boy, 6yrs, 6 mth.)

The third example presents a case of modifying the written text. Ziv, a boy aged 6; 2, was able to read parts of the text he had written, and when he could not read he modified the written text. For example, he read *amy* 'Ammy' instead of *im* 'with' — in Hebrew this is also a possible reading. But he could not continue, and hence he decided to modify the text. He went back to the written text and read: 'Ammy found (a) house', and changed accordingly the unreadable line to: 'Ammy found candies'. He continued reading, and where it was written *ha- mexashefa* 'the witch', he read *amy* 'Ammy' while pointing to the first two letters – again this is a possible reading in Hebrew. But again he could not continue, and he decided to modify it, by deleting the rest of the word; he wrote, 'Ammy' continued walking'. He deleted the last line 'the witch saw and (was) angry' – because he couldn't read it – and rewrote it with some changes in grapho-phonemic correspondences.

Interestingly enough, after not being able to read his last line of the text he rewrote the same fragment but with some differences in terms of writing conventions. This may support the idea that texts become stable, in the sense that children reconstruct the same text they wrote even before they can reconstruct them from what they had written (Sulzby, 1996).

The three examples show that differences in reading cannot be explained only as an outcome of children's ways of writing since children may relate to what they have written in different ways even when their writing level is similar in terms of the grapho-phonemic correspondences. In line with findings related to the grapho-phonemic correspondences, differences between genres were not significant. That is, the ways children reconstructed their own written texts were general, across genres.

Reading has been approached as a particular relationship between writer, reader and text. This relationship has been characterized as a wonderful paradox:

'... Only when the writer relinquishes the text, does the text come into existence. ... Only when the able eye makes contact with the marking on the tablet, does the text come to active life' (Manguel, 1996: 179).

This quotation can be understood as a metaphor for the relationship between writing and reading in early text production, once it is approached as a process. Writing development can thus be seen as the process of relinquishing the text, how texts come into existence, and a process by which the eye becomes able to make contact with the written text in order to bring it to active life.

Written	Read	Modified
ami ve tami pizru perurey lexem Ammy and Tammy scattered bread-crumbs	*Ami ve tami pizru perurey lexem* Ammy and Tammy scattered bread-crumbs	
yom exad ha-perurim ne'elmu one day the bread crumbs disappeared	*Yom exad ha-perurim ne'elmu* one day the bread crumbs disappeared	
ami halax ba-ya'ar Ammy walked in the forest	*Ami halax ba-yaar* Ammy walked in the forest	
ve maca bayit im sukaryot and found (a) house with candies	*ve maca bayit ami* Ammy found (a) house Ammy	
		ami maca sukariyot Ammy found candies
ami ve tami axlu et ha-sukariyot Ammy and Tammy ate the candies	*Ami ve tami axlu et ha-sukariyot* Ammy and Tammy ate the candies	
ve zalelu and stuffed themselves	*ve zalelu* And stuffed themselves	
ha-mexashefa ra'ata the witch saw	*ami...* Ammy...	
		lalexet ami himshix Ammy continued *Lalexet* Walking
ve ka'asa and (was) angry		
		ha-mexashefa the witch *ra'ata* saw *ve ka'asa* and (was) angry

Figure 4. Example of a narrative by Ziv (boy, 6yrs. 2 mth.)

Once children have written and read something in their own way, they can reflect on what they have done, the written product itself becomes an object of reflection. In this sense, writing and reading the written text give writers the opportunity to look again, to 're-view' his/her own production. Evidence of this revising process emerges through the modifications children perform in their texts.

10 MODIFICATIONS OF THE WRITTEN TEXT

Every modification children produced by leaving a trace on the paper was considered a token and categorized according to the following criteria: (a) the unit – letters or diacritic marks, a single word, several words, punctuation or graphic marks – that was subject to a modification; (b) the way of modifying – adding, deleting or changing; (c) the location of the modification – within the limits of the written product or outside it; (d) the text level involved in the modification – discourse, writing conventions or graphic aspects; and (e) the phase – writing, reading or revising – during which the modification was produced. Each modification differing from one another in any of these criteria of analysis was considered a type.

The number of modifications increased significantly with age (F (1,30) = 8.37, p<.05) and in narratives compared to descriptions (F (1,30) = 4.62, p<.05). Preschool children performed 58 types in narratives and 54 in descriptions whereas first graders performed 101 types in narratives and 71 modifications in descriptions. Thus, as children's writing became closer to convention, they tended to reflect more on the relations between what they wanted to write and what was written. Yet, both age groups performed significantly more modifications in narratives than in descriptions. Differences in number of modifications can be related to the length of the text, measured by number of words in the narrative (mean= 23 tokens in both groups) compared with descriptions (mean= 9 tokens in preschool and 8 in first graders). Thus in narratives there are more potential contexts for modifying than in descriptions. Besides, the same story can be told or written in many different ways, whereas a list of nouns referring to a specific object is more restricted both in content and structure.

Both preschool and first grade children performed modifications that involved all text levels – the graphic aspects, the conventions, and discourse in the two genres. Preschoolers paid more attention to the graphic aspects of their writing (*e.g.*, the shape of the letters), whereas first graders were more concerned with graphophonemic correspondences and orthographic rules. Yet first graders were still concerned with the graphic aspects of writing although to a lesser extent than the preschoolers did. Both groups made modifications involving the discourse level. Thus there were no significant differences in the number of modifications according to the level of the text involved.

The following examples present two modifications on the discourse level, made by two first graders who wrote at two different levels regarding the conventions of the writing system.

koteret
title

ha-bayit shel ha-mexashefa haya asuy
the witch's house was made
mi-shokolad ve-sukariyot
with chocolate and candies
ha-gag shela haya asuy mi-ec mecupe be-sukariyot
it's roof was made of wood covert by candies
ve ha-dlatot hayu mecupot mi-shokolad
and the doors were covert of chocolate

ha-dlatot hayu mecupot mi-shokolad
the doors were covered by chocolate.

Figure 5. The description of the witch's house: Ariel (boy, 6yrs. 8mth).

Ariel, a boy aged 6yrs. 8mth., wrote his descriptive text using various Hebrew letters, which he joined together without any grapho-phonemic correspondence. When reading this out, he paused and said: 'I forgot that the doors were covered by chocolate'. Then he added at the end of the text: *ha-dlatot hayu mecupot mi-shokolad* 'the doors were covered by chocolate'.

Another such example is provided by Ziv, aged 6yrs. 2mth., who wrote a description of the witch's house in Hebrew letters according to grapho-phonemic correspondences, but not always according to the orthographic rules. He wrote letters that in some cases denote phonological segments according to convention; in others, the letters stand for syllables. During the revision phase, following his first writing and reading, he added an introductory phrase at the top of the text: *ba-bayit hayu* 'in-the-house (there) were'. He also added *ve* 'and' (which conventionally is written as part of the word that it precedes) in two places, before the word *sukariyot* 'candies' and before the word *shokolad* 'chocolates'.

First version

mamtakim
sweeties

sukaryiot
candies

shokoladim
chocolates

al ha-gag
on the roof

hayta aruba
was a chimney

ממטקים

סקריט

שכלדס

אלאגג

אירב

Final version

ami ve tami
Ammy and Tammy
ba-bayit hayu
In the house (there) were

mamtakim
sweeties

ve sukaryiot
and candies

ve shokoladim
and chocolates

al ha-gag
on the roof

hayta aruba
was a chimney

אמבעמ

באביתהי

ממטקים

רסקריט

ושכלדס

אלאגג

אירב

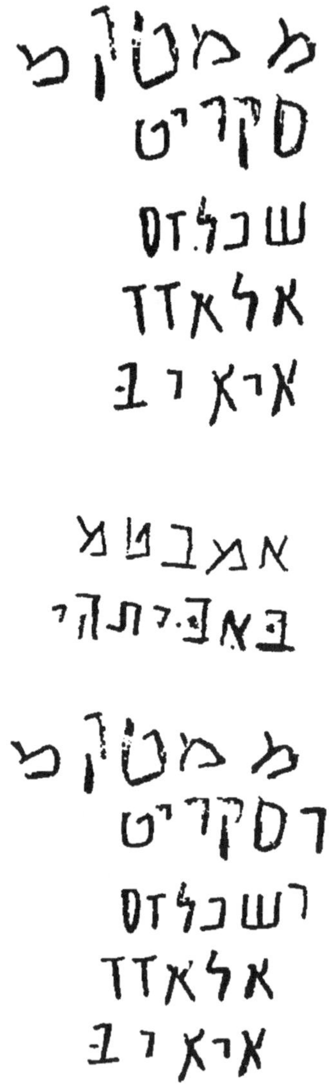

Figure 6. The description of the witch's house: Ziv, (boy, 6yrs. 2mth.).

These last examples suggest that the type of discursive modifications may vary according to how children write in terms of conventions. It is possible that, when children can reconstruct the text based on what is written on the page, they can also reflect both on the more local level of the text, such as lexicon and syntax, as well as at the global level of thematic content and discourse organization. Table 5 displays the distribution of type of modification by age, genre and the level of text involved.

Modifications involving the discourse level were performed mainly during the revision phase in the two age groups, when the children 'returned' to their own written text and read what they had written. There was a significant interaction between phase and text level ($F (2,60) = 10.59$, $p<.01$) and interaction between phase, text level and age group ($F (2,60) = 3.26$, $p<.05$). In other words, young children, who were asked to read and revise their texts, modified their texts in ways that more experienced writers do spontaneously.

Table 5. Distribution of the number of modifications by age, genre and text level (n=32[6]).

| Phase/ Level | Preschoolers | | | | First graders | | | |
| | Narratives | | Descriptions | | Narratives | | Descriptions | |
	Writing	Revising	Writing	Revising	Writing	Revising	Writing	Revising
Discourse	0 (0)	19 (33)	1 (2)	20 (37)	5 (5)	22 (22)	1 (2)	25 (35)
Conventions	1 (2)	9 (15)	0 (0)	9 (17)	14 (14)	22 (22)	7 (10)	15 (21)
Graphic	8 (14)	21 (36)	4 (7)	20 (37)	17 (17)	21 (20)	11 (15)	12 (17)
Total	9 (16)	49 (84)	5 (9)	49 (91)	36 (36)	65 (64)	19 27)	52 (73)

11   MODIFICATIONS IN WRITTEN TEXTS: THE RESEARCHER'S PERSPECTIVE

Asking children to modify the text if they want to do so is conceptually anchored in a Vygotskian approach. It transforms the eliciting situation into a more dynamic one and creates a zone of proximal development, thus extending what children have done to what they are able to do with adult support. Moreover, reading and revising the written text – as I asked them – characterize the writing process of more experienced children (Piolat, 1988).

The differences between the written and the revised text raise an interesting question: which text should be analyzed, the text children wrote without intervention or the revised one? If this question were formulated in relation to a text written by an adult, there would be no doubt that the revised text should be the one to be evaluated. In a way, the first writing of a child is considered the spontaneous writing, *i.e.*, the writing that reflects what children truly know. Such a split between what children do spontaneously and what they are able to do when a researcher asks them to

---

[6] *The values represent total raw numbers, percentages appear in parentheses.*

revise implies a dichotomous view of knowledge. The view that if children write as a result of some kind of intervention, the product does not reflect their own knowledge, but someone else's.

12 CONCLUSION

This chapter has concentrated on the interplay between the conventions of the writing system and the written language from three main perspectives: the development of the conventions of the writing system in writing two texts in different genres, children's ways of reading their own written text and the modifications children performed during writing, reading and revising their text.

The analysis of the grapho-phonemic correspondences conventions has shown a general developmental trend across genres. Genre affected the use of blank spaces between strings. This finding may be related to the analysis involved in each one of the conventions. Grapho-phonemic correspondences involve intra word analysis whereas separations between words involve inter word analysis, which is related to the type of text. Further studies should distinguish between different text variables such as syntactic structures, content, layout, and writing instrument in order to shed light on what influence word separation.

Children's ways of reading their own written text have shown a general trend across genres. However, they could not straightforwardly be related to children's level of writing, especially, when writing became closer to convention but children were not able to read the entire text from what they had written. Thus in some cases the text children read unveiled their knowledge about genre, but in some cases it was the written which did. These findings challenge in some way the assumption that the analysis of written texts can be conducted exclusively on what has been written, and stress the importance of considering in text analysis the ways children read and revise.

The analysis of children's modifications suggest that going back to their written text depends, on the one hand, on the degree of conventionality of writing and, on the other, it is influenced by genre. In other words, genre affects not only the written product but also the writing process. A more qualitative analysis shows that changes with age in the text levels involved in children's modifications can be better described as a process of widening children's monitoring activity rather than a shift from one text level to another. This tendency was found across the two genres. Changes seem to appear within the text levels, *i.e.* the way children modify the discourse level may be different before and after children master writing conventions. Similarly, the ways children relate to the graphic aspects or to the conventions may vary with age.

Changes in the text level involved may be related to the children's stands in relation to their written product. While writing young children are concerned with the graphic aspects and the conventions, but after the text is written they are able to reflect on the discourse. Thus, in order to understand more about revision processes it may be important to analyze text production in more than one single session.

Analogously to the claim that the 'choice of pedagogy inevitably communicates a conception of the learner' (Olson & Bruner, 1996:23), every choice in research communicates a conception of the learner. By learner I refer to both children as well as to the researcher who studies them. This suggests three main arguments that should be taken in further research:

First, writing development is a multifaceted process that involves acquisition of the language used in written texts along with an understanding and mastery of the notational system. Therefore, children's writing development should be studied in settings that can capture the full complexity of writing (Sandbank, 1999). Thus, the analysis of each one of the aspects of writing should be done without 'loosing' the text as a whole.

Second, studying writing in the transitional period – from preschool to school – may contribute to a deeper understanding concerning the relations between literacy development before schooling and when children are exposed to formal education.

Third, research should not be restricted to the question of how writing changes with age and genre, but also focus on changes that occur at the time of writing, since children can learn from their own production and not only from the environment (Veneziano, 1992).

To sum up, this chapter started with an example of a young child reflecting on her own writing, and it ends stressing the importance of having the actual researchers reflect on their own decisions regarding the context of research and the criteria used for analyzing children's early text writing.

AUTHOR'S NOTE

This chapter is based on the thesis submitted for M.A. Degree of Tel Aviv University: The Development of Text Writing in Preschoolers and First graders: The Writing Process and the Written product. This work was conducted under the supervision of Dr Liliana Tolchinsky Landsmann and Prof. Iris Levin. Part of this chapter was presented at the E.A.R.L.I Conference held at Aix-en-Provence, in 1993; at SIG Writing Conference held at Barcelona, 1996. Thanks are extended to Dr. Liliana Tolchinsky Landsmann, and to Dr Tal Goldfajn-Benhamou for their most helpful comments on a previous version of the manuscript.

THE DEVELOPMENT OF GRAPHIC WORDS IN WRITTEN SPANISH

WHAT CAN BE LEARNT FROM COUNTEREXAMPLES?

LILIANA TOLCHINSKY* & CONCHA CINTAS**

*University of Barcelona, Spain, **Autonoma University of Madrid, Spain

Abstract. This chapter focuses on the development of graphic words in early writing. Its aim is to gain a deeper understanding of children's motives for leaving or not blank spaces between letters or strings of letters. Previous studies in different languages have found four aspects that seem to influence children's decision for creating blanks: (1) Type of text, which affects external text boundaries from very early on; 2) Syntactic category of words and syntactic context, which affect internal chunking of graphic marks within the boundaries of a text; (3) Kind of handwriting (linked cursive vs. separate print), which may facilitate or hinder children's identification of graphic words, and (4) Length of texts, which seems also to affect children's separation of strings of marks.
A closer analysis of individual cases revealed, that some of them resist generalization; these cases appear as a sort of counterexample to the observed regularities. We have decided to look both at the observed regularities and at the counterexamples. The idea is to use them to call attention to the many aspects that may affect children's decision to create blanks and may be blurred when focusing just on the regularities.
Key words: separation between words, punctuation, early writing, Spanish, word category, text layout.

1   INTRODUCTION

Languages with alphabetical systems represent phonological rather than semantic units as the basic components of their writing system (Coulmas, 1989). An additional dimension of meaning of these systems relates to the morphological and semantic levels of language rather than to the phonological level. For example, in English, the letter <S> represents the consonant /s/, but in addition to this when this letter appears at the end of a string it also represents the plural marking. Similarly can be said for capital letters, in addition to their phonological meaning, when written at the beginning of a string, they indicate that the string is a proper name or the beginning of a sentence. Sometimes the morphological meaning of graphic elements is spread over more than one string constituting 'discontinuous morphograms' like it is

L. Tolchinsky (ed.), Developmental Aspects in Learning to Write, 77–95.

the case for number agreement (Fayol & Totereau, this volume, Reichler Beguelin, 1992, Rijlaarsdam, van Dort-Slijper, & Couzijn, this volume).

Besides learning to process the phonological and morphological information in graphemes, linguistically literate individuals have to learn about another component of alphabetic orthographies, the punctuation system. This system expresses suprasegmental, syntactic, semantic and pragmatic information in the form of nonalphanumeric devices (Nunberg, 1990). Punctuation marks are taken here in their broadest sense, including fonts and emphasis markers and blank spaces for text segmentation and marking of word boundaries. Although strictly speaking blank spaces are not a *punctum*, they are part of the punctuation system. One of the functions of these blank spaces is to indicate the boundaries of graphic words. That is, they function to indicate the beginning and the end of strings of elements that, according to the convention of the writing system in question are considered words. Without blank spaces texts may appear as containing just one level of units, the presence of spaces indicates by graphic means the existence of two levels of units. The graphic marking of words frees the reader from the burden of looking for the two-level hierarchical organization of the message while reading and guides the reader in using both the phonological and morphosyntactic information required for recovering the sense of the message. The presence of a blank space helps, for example, to find more easily the end of the string, the place where morphological markers may stand, and facilitates, therefore the inferential processes related to number or gender marking of the following strings.

Indeed, the presence of blanks increases legibility and, historically, had contributed to a democratization of literacy by making reading a task not reserved to specialists (Sirat, 1994). The existence of these signs (blanks), that represent by absence together with the rest of graphic marks is another prove of what Catach (1989) called the *mixité des ecritures*. That is, the fact that no writing system is strictly 'phonographic' but rather includes 'ideographic' dimensions of meaning (Blanche Benveniste & Chervel, 1974).

In order to learn how to write children must grasp this 'mixed' character of the writing system; they must grasp both the phonographic and the ideographic dimensions of meaning. Most research on early writing has been devoted to the development of children's understanding of the 'phonographic' dimension, specifically to children's discovery of the alphabetic principle in different languages (*e.g.*, Ferreiro, 1988; Tolchinsky Landsmann & Levin, 1986). A number of studies have also dealt with children's understanding of the ideographic dimension of writing system. For example, some studies have explored the process by which children learn to identify, disambiguate and spell correctly the English marker for past tense which is orthographically stable <ed> (Nunes, Bryant, & Bindman, 1997). Other studies have investigated the extent to which children use morphological cues in learning to spell in a highly synthetic language with a morphologically motivated orthography like Hebrew as compared to languages with sparse morphology and a relatively transparent orthography like Dutch (Gillis & Ravid, 1999).

This chapter focuses on the ideographic dimension of writing but not in relation to spelling of words but in relation to separation of words. Our goal is to gain a deeper understanding of children's motives for leaving or not blank spaces between letters or strings of letters. Previous studies in different languages have found four aspects that seem to influence children's decision for creating blanks: (1) Type of text, which affects external text boundaries from very early on; 2) Syntactic category of words and syntactic context, which affect internal chunking of graphic marks within the boundaries of a text; (3) Kind of handwriting (linked cursive vs. separate print), which may facilitate or hinder children's identification of graphic words and,(4) Length of texts, which seems also to affect children's separation of strings of marks.

A closer analysis of individual cases revealed that some of them resist generalization; they appear as a sort of counterexample to the observed regularities. By definition, counterexamples serve to refute an assertion or claim but, in developmental research, as in any other kind of research, they may serve also to question the processes under scrutiny by highlighting factors or dimensions that were not seen on a general observation. For that reason, we have decided to look both at the observed regularities and at the counterexamples. The idea is to use them to call attention to the many aspects that may affect children's decision to create blanks and may be blurred when focusing just on the regularities.

The structure of the chapter is as follows. First, we introduce a short characterization of the notion of graphic words in alphabetic systems, which is our object of inquiry. Then we look at the development of graphic words in children's writing by reviewing previous research showing the extent to which type of text, syntactic category of words, kind of handwriting and text length affect children's decision to create blanks. This review will take into account both the general developmental trends and the counterexamples that controvert these trends. Finally, we discuss the implications of our approach for grasping multiple processes involved in learning to write and suggest that the developmental study of writing enables to access the learner implicit linguistic knowledge.

2   THE NOTION OF GRAPHIC WORD

Graphic words are easy to define: one letter or a string of letters with blanks spaces on both sides. The problem starts when we try to look for correlates to this definition beyond the limits of a writing system. Literate people usually say that strings of letters separated by blanks are words. In order to say so, they resort to a practical intuitive criterion which is useful and very strong. For the word, despite the difficulty we have for its definition, is a unit that 'imposes itself on our soul' (*car le mot, malgré la difficulté qu'on a à le définir, est une unité qui s'impose à l'esprit,...* (Saussure, 1916: 154). To that practical intuitive knowledge, linguists have opposed different definitions. But, words in common with many other linguistic constructs elude clearcut definitional criteria outside writing.

First, because the notion of graphic word is language dependent. In Eskimo no element, except proper names appear isolated; in English, prepositions and articles are written with blanks on both sides, whereas in Hebrew most of the prepositions and the only existing article are written as prefixes bound to the content word. Even in languages of the same family like Spanish and Italian, both Romance languages, the same elements 'to' 'the' would be written separately in Spanish *a la playa* 'to the beach' but all together *alla spiaggia* in Italian.

A second source of difficulty for establishing correlates beyond the limits of a writing system is that the notion of graphic words in Latin systems covers a range of units having different morphological status. In Spanish a graphic word may represent a single morphemes (*fin* 'end'); clauses *damelo* 'give it to me'; complex lexical constituents including more that one morpheme (*agricultura* 'agriculture') and, a sort of 'infra-morpheme' (Reichler Beguelin, 1992) which means as part of a formulae (like in Spanish *a fuer de sano* or in French *au fur et à mesure*) but not in isolation, are written with blanks on both sides. In short, there is not a unique morphological correlate to graphic words beyond the writing system of a particular language. Therefore, it is difficult to see what exactly does a speaker mean when saying that blanks separate between words.

In the history of writing the separation of letters into graphic words developed very gradually. Most early scripts – Egyptian hieroglyphs, Sumerian cuneiform, Sanskrit – had no such divisions. In the Greek tradition, the same language was known through three different writing systems the Minoic and Chipriotic syllabary and the Alphabetic system derived from the Phoenician. Articulation in graphic words was taken more seriously by the syllabaries than by the alphabetic system. Indeed early alphabetic writers were so occupied with phonographic correspondences that any other correspondence was secondary. When flattering the advances of the Greek Alphabetic system it is hardly mentioned the great burden the system imposed on the reader who had first to vocalize in order to understand. Further development of separation was indeed triggered by the development of silent reading.

In the Roman tradition, punctuation of words is found already among the Etruscans, it increases during the classic period, but almost disappears during the 2nd century probably by the influence of Greek texts that were written *scriptio continua*. Early Christian monks often knew by heart the texts they were transcribing, so they may not need any visual aid. However, in order to help poor readers they use to divide the text into lines of sense to help them to find their way in the texts (Manguel, 1995; Parkes, 1992, Reichler Béguelin, 1990). The avatars of punctuation continue by a constant interplay between reader's need for cues followed by the introduction of such cues in the texts which in turn increasingly facilitate reading-by-eye (silently) which in turn increases the need of visual aids. By the ninth century, silent reading was probably common enough to require scribes to be silent in the monastic scriptorium and to *separate* each word from its encroaching neighbors to simplify the perusal of a text... 'Irish scribes began isolating not only parts of speech but also the grammatical constituents within a sentence, and introduce many of the punctuation marks we use today....' (Manguel, 1995). Despite this general development, writing everything attached, *scriptio continua,* was widely practiced up to the 10th century and still evident in the Renaissance epoch (Blanche Benveniste, 1997: 38) and it was only with the advent of printing that a generalized presence of graphic words became relatively stable.

3 THE DEVELOPMENT OF GRAPHIC WORDS AND SOME COUNTEREXAMPLES

Researchers interested in unveiling the development of graphic words use a diversity of approaches both naturalistic and very controlled. Whatever the approach was, studies have shown that *scriptio continua* is the most frequent way of writing in the earliest stages of learning to write. Then the graphic space available to the child is the only limit for his/her writing. Three to 4-year olds attempting to write a word or a short sentence may start at any point on the page and stop at its edge, no matter how big or small the page is, there are not self-imposed limits to their writing. Indeed, preschoolers' earliest written productions look like linear, discontinuous, unconstrained patterns of wavy lines. They write very similar patterns for almost everything that they are attempting to write. With age and increasing experience with writing, starts a process of internal differentiation of their own written productions under the constraints of minimal number and internal variety: children start producing shorter strings -usually more than two and less than six-of non-repeated letters or simile letters (Ferreiro, 1988). These formal constraints typically appear when children are asked to write single words, but when children attempt to write other kinds of texts -stories, lists or poems-, there is another constraining factor: the type of text children are attempting to write does also affect their way of writing.

3.1 The effect of type of text on children's text layout

Les poèmes on toujours de grandes marges blanches, de grandes marges de silence... 'poems have always white, big margins, big margins of silence...' says Paul Valery. Indeed, texts are artifacts that convey information through linguistic forms and graphic conventions. Although discursive forms can free themselves from a particular physical support part of their meaning is affected.

Research on early writing development has shown that prior of mastering the graphophonemic conventions of the writing system concerning the correspondences between letters and phonological segments children are able to distinguish between different types of texts. The distinctions they make are reflected initially on the graphic layout of their texts. When preschoolers are asked to write shopping lists, they produce something that looks very different from what they produce when they are asked to write newspapers news, advertisements or poems (Pontecorvo & Rossi, this volume; Tolchinsky Landsmann, 1992). Similarly occurs for narratives and descriptions. When 5-to 7-year-olds were asked to write a fairy tale and a description of one of the main elements in the tale their written outputs looked very different. The narratives appear written in long lines of one letter after the other with hardly any internal spacing between them, except for the name of the protagonists, which sometimes appeared with blanks on both sides. But descriptions looked like a list of isolated words (Sandbank, this volume).

Two possible interpretations were advanced for these findings. According to the first they would be a case of iconicity resulting from the effect of previous experience with text layouts of different kinds. It is an interpretation in terms of children's sensitivity to visual information. The reasoning is that in the same extent that children prove to be sensitive to general features of writing (linearity, discretionality, directionality) they are proving to be sensitive to the different layout displayed on shopping lists, poetry or newspapers.

An alternative explanation relates to the kind of linguistic elements that are included in each type of text rather than to the visual appearance of the texts. According to this second interpretation, the segmentation characterizing different types of texts (long lines for narratives, shorter strings for descriptions) would be a result of children attempting to write linguistic constructions that are typical or expected for each type of text. This interpretation is supported by the way children read back their productions. Indeed, when asked to read what they have written, 5-year-olds interpret the long lines with parts of the tale including various sentences or part of sentences. In contrast, when reading back a description they name the different elements in the house using nouns. The say, for example, that there were 'chocolates, candies and cookies'. The different type of text affects therefore the distribution of syntactic categories of words. Descriptions contain more nouns and adjectives and can be reduced to labeling, whereas narratives are built on more complex predication and adverbial. This difference in distribution of syntactic categories of words is the one reflected in children's text layout. For type of texts in which isolated words, mainly nouns, are used, they put strings of letters, usually each on a different line; for utterances including more complex predication they are reluctant to create internal blanks between strings of letters.

3.2 Limits on the effect of text type on text layout

Both interpretations, the one based on visual information and the other one based on the linguistic category of the elements that are typical to each type of texts, are sound and fruitful, they may be even complementary, and they are supported by findings in different languages. Nevertheless, they do not fit Alejandra's way of writing a fable

Alejandra was one of the preschoolers who participated in a study carried out by Cintas (Cintas, Jakubowicz, & Tolchinsky, 1997) to explore the development of graphic words in written Spanish. She is our first counterexample. In this study, Alejandra was asked to re-write a short fable that had been read aloud in school, to the whole group, a few weeks ago. A week later she was asked to write a set of two-word phrases and another set of four-word sentences that were dictated to her. Her way of writing is syllabic alphabetical. As recalled, at this level of writing development children assemble words by mapping letters to syllables and to subsyllabic units but not in a completely systematic way. However, the two-word phrases and the four-word sentences were written *scriptio continua*, that is, without internal segmentation whereas the short story appears as a list of isolated words. Figure 1 presents her written output for the short story.

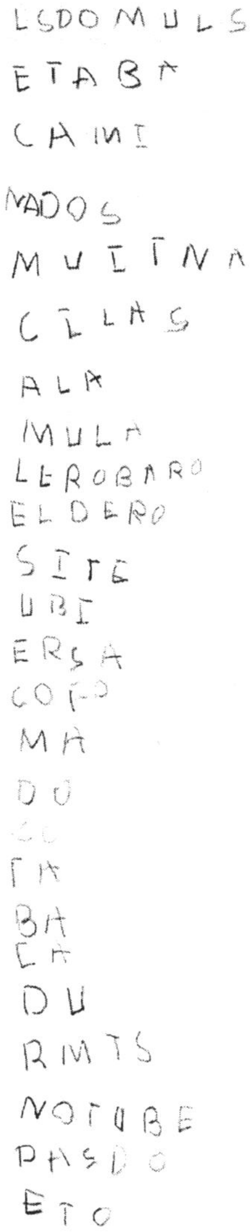

LSDO M U L S

ETA B ^

C A M I

MADO S

M U I T N ^

C I L ^ S

A L ^

M U L ^

L E R O B ^ R O

E L D E R O

S I T E

U B I

E R S A

C O I ^

M ^

D U

^ ^

I ^

B ^

C ^

D U

R M T S

N O I U B E

P ^ S D O

E T O

Figure 1. Alejandra's writing of a fable.

As seen in figure 1, Alejandra's written output does not present the typical layout of stories; rather it looks like a long list of words. In this sense Alejandra way of writing is a counterexample of the general statement we have just made concerning the effect of type of text on children's texts layout. We must look for an explanation that is suitable to account both for the fact that she wrote short sentences without separating between strings of letters, and a story separating into short strings of letters that sometimes coincide with single words but sometimes coincide with parts of words. We think that the explanation can be found at the interaction between Alejandra´s main concern at the particular level of writing development and the specific constraints of the writing task that she is performing. But, before we elaborate on this explanation, it is important to observe in more detail her way of writing as it is illustrated in figure 1.

If we look at her writing, in terms of phonographic correspondences, it is a classical example of syllabic-alphabetic mapping. So, for writing the title (first line on top) *las dos mulas* 'the two mules' she wrote[1] <LSDOMULS> using <LS> for *las*, <DO> for *dos* <MU> for *mu* and <LS> for *las,* without internal spacing. She uses the same type of correspondence throughout the whole text but only two lines, the second and the eight, correspond to spoken words (<ETABA> *estaba* 'was' and <MULA> *mula* 'mule'), the other lines correspond sometimes to verbal phrases, sometimes to prepositions + determiners, and sometimes to parts of words.

It should be also noted that no line contains isolate or repeated letters and very few contain strings of more than five letters. So one is tempted to say that keeping the constraints of minimal number and variety might be one of the factors provoking this kind of segmentation. But why then did she write four-words sentences that contain up to sixteen letters without any kind of internal separation? Based on her way of writing is that she is almost completely focused on working out letter to sound correspondences. At this particular moment the links between the spoken and the written are of central concern for her, in the dictation task the spoken utterance is provided by the experimenter who dictates the phrases. The experimenter's uttering is also monitoring her segmentation, she stops when the experimenter stops dictating. In the task of story writing instead, she has to monitor both letters to sound mapping and segmentation. She has to stop at some point and then continue. This difference may explain why in the dictation task she moves at the next line at the end of each phrase or sentence coinciding with the dictation but in the other task she stops whenever she finished a series of letter to sound correspondence, these detentions are not systematic. The combined effect of her actual concerns and the constraints of the task may explain why the effect of type of text on graphic distribution and separation of strings is momentarily suspended. The case of Alejandra illustrates clearly the need to look at children's productions in a diversity of circumstances and task in order to appreciate the different factors intervening in their writing decisions. Only by looking at her way of writing in the three tasks we could reevaluate the role of the formal constraints that seemed so central when observing just the writing of a story.

---

[1] *Words and letters are in brackets when specifically referring to letters or written forms. So, <lsdomuls> would be used to refer specifically to the written form of the words* las dos mulas *'the two mules'.*

3.3   The effect of word-category and syntactic context on creating blanks

As we have seen, type of text is one of the earliest factors to constraint the external boundaries of texts but the syntactic category of words is one of earliest factors to constraint the separation of strings of elements within text boundaries.

Linguistic theories distinguish at least two categories of words: 'content words' or 'lexical items' are usually opposed to 'function words' or 'grammatical items' (Slobin, 1997, Lyons, 1968). The first denoting 'material content' includes nouns and verbs, and usually adjectives; the second, denoting a 'relation' includes free morphemes such as conjunctions, prepositions and bound morphemes such as affixes marking categories of number, case, tense, and so forth (Sapir, 1958).

Quite a few psycholinguistic studies in Romance languages show that children's creation of blanks between strings of letters is related to this distinction. Clemente (1984), asked children from 5 to 11 years old to write short stories and then to split them up into 'the smallest possible parts'. She found two developmental levels. Children from 5 to 7 years of age try to divide the stories in words; however, they did not produce a blank within *aviaunavez*, 'once upon a time', or *superrito*, 'his little dog' which must be written in Spanish internal blanks: two in the case of *había una vez* 'once upon a time' and one in the case of *su perrito*, 'his little dog'. As a rule, 5 to 7 years olds showed difficulties in separating determiners from names, compound verbs, reflexive pronouns from their host verbs. It is only at a second grade, after the age of 7, that conventional spacing between words is achieved.

Ferreiro and Pontecorvo's study of the development of the separation of words in Italian, Spanish and Portuguese provide support for this claim. They asked second and third graders who already knew the phonographic conventions of their respective languages to write a well known fairy tale (Ferreiro, Pontecorvo, Ribeiro Moreira, & García Hidalgo, 1996). Problems of separation were related to the same kind of elements. Functional elements which are unstressed monosyllables such as *a* 'to', (preposition), *el, la*, 'the', *un la*, (articles), *de* 'of', (preposition), *su* 'his/ her/ its', (possessive), *se* 'it', *le* 'him', (clitic pronouns), *que* 'which' were found as a rule attached (hyposegmented) to the content words (nouns, verbs) they modify.

The authors found a higher frequency of hyposegmentations of the preposition *a* 'to', in comparison to the conjunction *y* 'and'. Similarly, *la* 'the -fem./ her', (article and clitic pronoun) and *el* 'the-masc'/he, (article and personal pronoun) tended to hyposegment to the other graphic elements more often when they were functioning as articles than when functioning as pronominal clitics. This difference is particularly interesting because in the case of *la* the same phonological form is functioning as a determiner 'the –fem', like in *la casa* 'the-fem. house' and as a clitic pronoun like in *la come* '(she/he) eats it-fem.' Therefore, if when attempting to write the same phonological form children tend to separate more or less according to the syntactic function this form performs, this means two important things. On the one hand, it means that children are doing some fine (although unconscious) syntactic distinctions and, on the other hand it means that other factor – in this case syntactic function – besides the functional or content category of the element might be influencing children's decision to attach or separate certain elements.

A recent study by Baez and Cáncenas (1999) with Spanish speaking children found problems of separation up until fourth, fifth and sixth grade (9 to 11 years). Although she worked with a very small sample, she also interpreted these problems in relation to word category.

In order to further assess the effect of category of elements on children's creation of blank spaces and the consistency of the distinction content vs. function words, we designed the already mentioned study (Cintas, Jakubowicz, & Tolchinky, 1997) in which the same child had to write a short text and sentences of differing length. The idea was to determine whether certain categories of elements are consistently separated in every textual environment, or rather certain categories of elements are problematic in one textual environment but not in another, or in one task but not in another.

As said, children had to write a short story that was previously read to them and simple sentences dictated orally. The first task was an open /natural situation of text writing whereas the two other tasks i.e., the dictation tasks, were very controlled. The same syntactic elements were analyzed in the three tasks, and we call them the target region (in italics in the examples). In the dictation tasks half of the sentences included constructions having functional elements (proclitics: e.g., se pinta azul marino, '(3rd person sing) himself painted blue navy'; determiners: e.g., el viento sopla fuerte 'the wind blows strong' and personal pronouns: e.g., Ella pinta cuadros rojos 'she paint(s) pictures red'). The other half included lexical elements (proper nouns: e.g., Luis lee libros tontos 'Luis read(s) books silly', numeral adjectives: e.g., más lluvia hace falta 'more rain (it) is necessary' and adverbs: e.g., hoy lava ropa sucia 'today (s/he) washes cloth dirty'.

Determiners, reflexives and personal pronouns were taken as representatives of function words and compared to adjectives, adverbs and proper names as representatives of content words. In the selection of words number of syllables and gender were controlled. The child's written productions were examined, looking for conventional separation and for different ways of unconventional separation. Children's productions were initially analyzed according to the following ways of unconventional segmentation: hyposegmentation, hypersegmentation in or outside the target region and non-alphabetical or illegible writing[2]. We found similar results to previous studies; the main form of unconventional separation was hyposegmentation. But, as long as hypersegmentation was concern, the frequency of this kind of segmentation was lower than 2% in the total amount of sentences of the dictation task, even having added the responses with both hypersegmentation plus hyposegmentation inside the target region.

In many cases, the part of the word separated corresponds with a possible word, they wrote **la** drones -ladrones- (the-fem, article) 'thieves', **de** fenderle -defenderle- (of-preposition) 'to defend (him)' **es** capar -escapar- (3rd singular person to be) 'to

---

[2]As some scores of unconventional separation were very low (hypersegmentation inside the target region and hyposegmentation outside) we decided to join them and call this kind of segmentation 'other separation'. So we had four main kind of responses: conventional segmentation, hyposegmentation (inside the target region) other separation and non-alphabetical writing.

escape'. However, it was common to find other hypersegmentations in which all the syllables were separated *es ta ba -estaba-* 'was', just the first syllable, ***pa** seaban -paseaban-* '(they) walked', a morpheme *alegre **mente** -alegremente-* 'happily', or groups of letters separated at random, *tra v aj ado -trabajado-* 'worked', *deja nir -dejan ir-* '(they) leave (them) to go'.

In the short story too, hyposegmentation was much more frequent than hypersegmentation, and those texts that presented only a few hypersegmentations were not better written than those with a few hyposegmentations, neither in the quality of composition nor in the lenght. The study showed also two surprising findings. First, in two-words phrases the highest score for conventional separation was obtained for sentences in which the first element was a determiner (*e.g.*, *el viento*, 'the wind'), these were followed by sentences that started with personal pronouns and those that started with proper nouns

Figure 2 displays mean percentage of conventional segmentation and hyposegmentation by category of word in the two-word task[3].

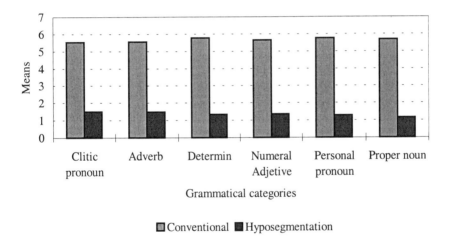

Figure 2. Segmentation in two-word phrases.

As possible to see and against previous findings the highest score was obtained by two functional words, followed in a decreasing order by sentences starting with content-words proper nouns, adjectives and adverbs, and the lowest conventional segmentation score was obtained by sentences starting with a reflexive pronouns. These results show that the typical distinction into lexical and functional elements does not explain the difference found in conventional segmentation.

---

[3] *In order to show better the differences between word categories, we have changed in the graphics the scale range, from 8 (which was the maximum possible score) to 6 in the graphic the maximun obtained score.*

The second surprising finding was that the results obtained in the four-word writing task showed a different pattern but closer to previous studies.

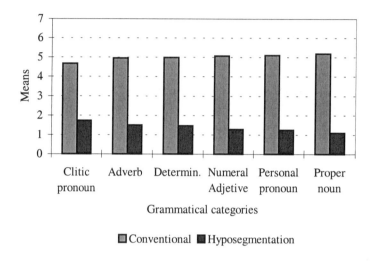

Figure 3. Segmentation in four-word sentences.

In this task, sentences containing proper names as their initial elements obtained the highest score on conventional separation followed by sentences containing personal pronouns. Sentences with reflexive pronouns had the lowest score on conventional separation and the highest on hyposegmentation; exactly the same pattern is repeated in each school year. (There was a main effect of word category $F(5,785) = 11.40$, $p<0.000$ but no interaction). If we look at the two extremes – clitic pronouns and proper names – we should say that the duality *content* vs. *functors* biases the children's use of separation. Indeed, when we compared *functors* – determiners, reflexive pronouns and personal pronouns ($M = 14.75$ $Sd = 10.30$) – versus *content* words – numeral adjectives, adverbs and proper names ($M = 15.20$ $Sd = 10.31$) – we found a significant difference. But a closer look at the mean hyposegmentation score suggests that there are internal differences both among *functors* and among *content* words; *content* words such as adverbs are closer to clitic pronouns than to proper names, and personal pronouns are closer to proper names than to reflexive pronouns. At the same time, determiners (articles) had higher conventional separation scores and lower hyposegmentation scores than reflexive pronouns, despite the fact that both are functional words.

Two conclusions can be drawn from these findings. The first is that there is an effect of length of sentence in children's marking of graphic words. The second is that word category in itself is not enough to explain the difference in this behavior.

In the next section we will deal more specifically with the effect of length but here we address the second conclusion concerning the relative effect of word category.

To interpret the apparently contradictory findings in the two tasks (two-words vs. four-words sentences) we looked at the syntactic context – defined by the category of the element the target elements are modifying. In terms of syntactic environment, determiners and adjectives are *nominal modifiers*, reflexive pronouns and adverbs are *verb modifiers* and proper names and personal pronouns function rather as head of nominal phrases. When the results in the two tasks are compared in terms of syntactic context, elements in the verbal domain (reflexive pronouns and adverbs) differed significantly from elements in the nominal domain (determiners and numerals). Moreover, the fact that both proper names and personal pronouns may form independent phrases and that Spanish is a Pro-drop language and therefore the use of pronouns is always marked makes personal pronouns closer to names than to other functional elements. The conclusion is that more than the category of word *per se*; it is the syntactic environment that seems to affect children's decision to create blanks.

The finding concerning the effect of syntactic contexts is supported by the results in text writing. In this task adverbs obtained the lowest scores both in conventional separation and hyposegmentation, and clitic pronouns had the next lowest conventional separation score but the highest hyposegmentation score. Therefore, the effect of the syntactic context is similar to the one found in the other tasks. Elements in the verbal domain (reflexive pronouns, adverbs) appeared attached to their verbal hosts more frequently than determiners and numerals to the nominal they are specifying. These findings show, therefore, that syntactic context is a relevant factor for explaining children's decisions to create blanks and it might be misleading to consider *word category per se* as the main explanatory factor of children's separation behavior.

3.4 Limits on the effect of syntactic context on creating blanks

As it happened with the constraining effect of type of text on external boundaries, there are individual cases that contradict even this explanation. Arturo a 5-year-old preschooler, one of the participants in Cintas's study provides a nice counterexample to our previous generalization concerning the effect of verbal context to agglutinate clitics and adverbs to their verbal hosts and the relatively detached status of proper names. Arturo, proceeded in exactly the opposite way, attaching proper names to verbs in most two-word phrases and separating reflexive pronouns and determiners from the verbs.

Figure 4. Arturo's writing of two-word phrases.

The figure presents three pairs of two-word phrases. In each pair the uppermost phrase shows the first element (the functional word) detached from the verb whereas the lower down phrase shows the proper name attached to the verb. Arturo, like most children, was not completely consistent but when he was, he did it in the opposite direction. We do not have any sound interpretation of this finding except suggesting once more that whenever individual differences are focussed the typical 'inconsistencies' of transitional knowledge are fore grounded. The participants in our studies are in the *process of acquiring* the conventions of the writing systems they are exposed to. In fact, and in spite of the generalized effect of syntactic context, no child in Cintas's study was completely consistent. That is, no child wrote, for example clitics or determiners always attached to their hosts and proper names consistently separated. On top of the effect of textual environment that provokes grupal trends in children's preferences there are different factors intervening at an individual level. This is the main feature of transitional knowledge in every domain of knowledge. As subjects in the process of acquiring new knowledge, they may advance, retrocede and even produce contradictory moves. Besides, we should recall the particular features of the kind of knowledge children are in process of acquiring. Except for some prototypical elements like proper nouns it is difficult to establish a clear and graspable correlate to graphic separation, therefore it is not surprising that children seem to proceed by hunches and affected by a diversity of factors.

4   THE EFFECT OF LENGTH OF TEXTS ON THE CREATION OF BLANKS

As mentioned before the first surprising finding in Cintas's study was the effect of textual environment. Children's writing of the short story and the two-words phrases and four-words sentence showed a different distribution of conventional segmentation and hyposegmentation despite the inclusion of the same word categories in the different textual environments. The study showed that the amount of conventional marking of graphic words decreases with sentence length. Children produce more conventional separation when writing two word sentences than when writing four word sentences and more conventional separation when writing four words sentences than when writing texts. One possible interpretation of this finding is that when children have fewer marks in front of them they are able to control them better and are less tolerant of lack of spacing. Another, but related, interpretation is that since they are still very occupied with phonographic correspondences they lost track of other needs when they have to write longer texts.

4.1 Limits on the effect of length

To make things more complex, however, Celia's way of marking graphic words contradicts this finding. Out of 48 two-word phrases, she wrote 37 (77%) as one string, without internal spacing. Whereas out of the 48 four-word sentences, she wrote 17 (only 35%) without internal spacing at the target region. Note that for explaining this finding we should resort to the same but reversed reasoning – that since strings are longer the child could not tolerate lack of spacing.

It might be the case that for the effect of length there is no explanation because length does not come alone in language. More words imply a change in structure, in memory load and in our case in elicitation. The sentences were dictated whereas the child wrote the texts from memory. There are here some conflicting variables that require more research in order to understand their role. Nevertheless, sensitivity to textual environments can be taken as a step in learning conventional marking of graphic words. Children are yet in the process of learning the main feature of graphic words, as they are established by printing, their stability. Printed words, current graphic words, are the same irrespectively of textual environment. In learning this convention children must move from linguistically based motives of what should be written separately and what should be written attached to the written language-convention which is not sensitive to context. This process is affected by a number of factors until stability is acquired.

4.2 The effect of kind of handwriting on marking graphic words

So far, we have considered type of text, syntactic context and textual environment as possible sources of motives for marking graphic words. Comparative analysis across languages showed that the kind of handwriting in which children are instructed – cursive linked, or printed – has also an effect on graphic separation. When children are working out the rules of phonographic correspondences printed letters, which are written separated from each other, help them to find more precise correspondences. However, for identifying strings of letters as graphic words, cursive writing seems to be more helpful. Needless to say, this general statement makes sense only for those scripts in which there are two kinds of handwriting. It would be nonsense for Hebrew, for example, where such alternative does not exist.

When comparing Italian, Spanish and Portuguese, three languages in which the two kind of handwriting exist, Ferreiro and her collaborators (1996) found less hyposegmentation in those groups of children that were instructed using cursive linked writing compared to those that were instructed with printed script (Ferreiro, Pontecorvo, Ribeiro Moreira, & Garcia Hidalgo, 1996).

4.2.1   Limits on the effect of handwriting on the creation of blanks

Beatriz, a seven-year-old first grader who participated in Cintas's study contradict this generalization or at least put limits to it. She has almost full command of phonographic correspondences in Spanish but in the three tasks, she tends to hyposegment the target elements. This tendency, however, turns to be particularly accentuated in certain parts of her text.

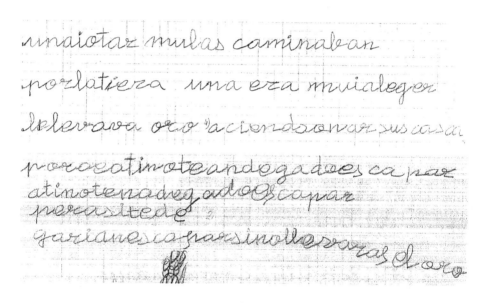

Figure 5. Beatriz' writing of a fable.

As seen on the figure 5, the first lines in her re-writing of the fable present some string with blanks on both sides. But, the three last lines, transcribed bellow, run along the full-page without a single graphic separation.

por qué a ti no te han dejado escapar

why (they) have not let you REFLEXIVE run(away)

<atinotenadregadoescapar>

_a ti no te han dejado escapar

(they) have not let you REFLEXIVE run(away)

porcesitede

porque sí te de

because if (they) do REFLEXIVE let-(uncompleted word,)

garianescaparsinollevaraseloro

-de-jarían escapar si no llevaras el oro

CONDITIONAL run (away) if you were not taking the gold'

The three lines reproduce the words of one of the mules, and for quoted discourse, Beatriz, like some other children, produces more hyposegmentation when quoting than in other parts of the text. May be, in some cases, lack of separation represents better the stream of speech and differentiates between the quotation and the body of the text. Indeed, toddlers and preschoolers have a notion of discourse in terms of a unit that can be transported, transmitted and separated from a wider discourse manifested in their ability to quote. The idea underlying quotation is that a linguistic entity is singled out and reproduced. Only by recognizing an utterance *as such* it can be quoted. Children quote from 3 year of age, particularly in their retelling of narratives. So, in some cases they may resort to lack of spacing to show the different status of quoted speech. Discursive function appears to be an additional possible factor influencing children decision to separate strings of marks.

5   LEARNING FROM COUNTEREXAMPLES

The goal of this overview was to gain a deeper understanding of the multiple factors involved in children creating graphic spacing. We have seen that: word category, syntactic environment, textual environment, kind of handwriting, experience with particular layouts, discursive function of parts of the texts, formal constraints of number and variety of letters, search for phonographic correspondences, each one in turn or in combination may constraint internal chunking of marks. And the list is far from being complete. As we have seen when referring to the few cases of hypersegmentation familiarity with particular graphic words could make a difference Some of these factors were crucial in earlier stages of writing development, and may emerge only in particular circumstances, other may be triggered by the structure of some words but not of others or by the specific constraints of the task, whether it is a task of dictation, re-writing or spontaneous writing.

Obviously each factor interacts with the particular features of the writing system children are exposed to. The effect of hand-writing will be different in those cases in which there are alternative ways of writing (cursive or printed), similarly the effect of word category or syntactic environment may differ for those writing systems in which clitics are indicated by dashes, like in Catalan or in those systems in which determiners are written as affixes of content words, like in Hebrew. From the above description we learn about the complexity of factors influencing any step in learning to write and we are warned against oversimplification in terms of considering just the influence of phonological or morphosyntactic factors.

5.1 Observing writing to unveil the learner implicit linguistic knowledge

One of the main aims of developmental studies on writing was to discover how children build their knowledge about reading and writing, the notion of texts and discourse, the regularities of writing systems and written strings and the phonographic rules of particular systems. There is however, a secondary benefit no less important. Research on the development of writing may function as a window to unveil the linguistic notions that mediate the learning processes without the learner having the capability to verbalize or even to be aware of them.

This claim was clearly illustrated by our findings concerning the notion of syntactic category of words. Obviously, five or six year olds are not able to explain verbally the difference between nouns and reflexive pronouns and yet, through their way of creating blanks between strings researchers are able to infer that the child views nouns and reflexive pronouns as different entities, ones deserving clear boundaries, the other not. The writing activity is a privileged context for assessing levels of knowledge, which are in-between implicit automatic procedures and verbally stayed explanations. Those intermediate levels correspond in a rough sense to what Culioli termed 'epilinguistic' activity (1990) or what Karmiloff Smith (1992) described as a level of knowledge that is implicit for the subject but can be accessed to fulfill certain tasks.

An additional example is provided by previous studies on the relationship between explicit phonological knowledge and writing. When we observe the way in which preschoolers attempt to write unfamiliar words we can easily see that they are able to decompose them into sound components. This is usually the procedure they follow to search for the right letters to correspond to each of the parts of the word they are attempting to write. Observing the writing process it is possible to see the different units of segmentation they are able to manipulate (e.g., syllable, sub-syllabic segments, consonants in isolation). That is, for performing this writing task they are able to analyze the word into syllabic and subsyllabic segments. The same children, however, are unable to perform this analysis outside the task of writing. They fail to do in the context of a metalinguistic tasks the same kind of segmentation they are able to perform *for-writing* (Tolchinsky and Teberosky, 1998).

The construction of the notion of graphic word is particularly revealing of the different aspects of implicit knowledge involved in the act of writing. Observing the circumstances in which children create blanks or leave strings agglutinated we were able to detect that intonational contour, syllabification, word category, syntactic context, knowledge of text layout and discursive function are all aspects of knowledge shaping the notion of graphic words. They are all implicit knowledge components and as such they are unstable, sensitive to changes in context and to individual differences.

Increasing experience with writing mostly through schooling will turn this intuitive and sometimes inconsistent way of creating blanks into the 'institutionalized notion of word. This knowledge, although still a-theoretical, is rather stable and useful enough for most uses of writing. Only a few among the huge amount of practical writers that finish school without particular problems to separate words according to the conventions of the writing system may specialize in linguistics. They are probable the only ones that will attain explicit levels of reflection and theorization. May be, as linguists, some of them will wonder again to find a sound explanation of what exactly is what they have learned to separate while learning to write.

LEARNING THE WRITTEN MORPHOLOGY
OF PLURAL IN WRITTEN FRENCH

MICHEL FAYOL & CORINNE TOTEREAU

Université Blaise Pascal, Clermont Ferrand, France

Abstract. The work presented in this chapter deals with a well defined area of written production: the learning and implementation of French written morphology for noun and adjective plural (–*s*) on the one hand, and for verb plural(-*nt*) on the other. Morphology plays an essential role in written French since most of the written markers have no corresponding pronunciation. Therefore, as we will show in the following chapter, children have to learn the markers and their function without relying on an audible reference.

Key words: spelling of verbs, spelling of adjectives, plural, agreement, generalisation, automatisation, French, learning phases.

1   NUMBER MORPHOLOGY IN ORAL AND WRITTEN FRENCH

Number morphology plays an essential role in the learning and implementation of written French, especially since many written markers have no corresponding pronunciation. In the oral modality, only the determiners for the noun phrase (*le-la/les* [singular *the*/plural *the*'; *un-une/des* '*a/some*'; *ce-cet-cette/ces* '*this/these, that/those*' *etc.*) and auxiliaries for the verb phrase (*a/ont* '*has/have*'; *est/sont* '*is/are*') are subject to a systematic formal variation. By contrast, in writing, almost all the elements of the noun phrase (NP) (determiner, noun, adjective) and verb phrase (VP) (auxiliary, verb) are systematically marked, respectively with –*s* (NP) and –*nt* (VP) (Catach, 1986; Dubois, 1965). This modality difference clearly appears in the following examples:

- oral: singular ->/lap'tit'pulruspikor/ vs. plural ->/lep'tit'pulruspikor/ (only /la/ /le/ difference);
- written modality: singular -> *la petite poule rousse picore* '*the small, red hen pecks*', vs. plural -> *les petites poules rousses picorent* '*the small, red hens peck*'.

This particularity of French has two consequences. On the one hand, French children must acquire the number markers for plural (and also for gender, not dealt with here)

97

L. Tolchinsky (ed.), Developmental Aspects in Learning to Write, 97–107.
© 2001 *Kluwer Academic Publishers. Printed in the Netherlands.*

at the same time they are learning the written language. The reference to oral language is of little use to them. They must discover the specific markers of plurality of the written system and their meaning: *–s* for nouns and adjectives; *–nt* for verbs. Once this discovery has been made, then children have to automatise the implementation of inflections. This automatisation needs regular and frequent writing practice. Single-handed on its own, it does not ensure the correct agreements because of the existence of many homophone words (*timbre 'a stamp/to stamp', fouille 'the searching/to search', ferme 'the farm/to close'*...) which are pronounced alike but are spelled differently depending on their syntactical function (*les timbres/ils timbrent 'the stamps/they stamp'*). The lack of oral cues makes it necessary to resort to morpho-syntactic, syntactic and semantic criteria which are more complex and difficult to mobilize. Little is yet known concerning this type of learning.

On the other hand, the second consequence concerns the implementation of the number markers by adults in written texts. Lucci & Millet (1994) as well as Girolami-Boulinier (1984) have observed frequent omissions of *–s* and *–nt*. These omissions suggest that even educated adults sometimes fail to use known markers which they implement efficiently most of the time. Few studies have investigated the reasons and circumstances favouring the occurrence of such errors. However, sometimes, there are audible variations associated to plurality in nouns – *cheval/chevaux-> horse/horses* – adjectives – *général/généraux->general* – and verbs – *il va/ils vont->he goes/they go*. The presence of audible cues improves the performance of adults in writing tasks (Largy & Fayol, in press).

The studies reported here were conducted in order to determine, first, when and how children identify and use the plural markers of noun and verb. Then they were extended to study the way the automatisation of the use of verbal *–nt* operates. Next, we analyzed how children and adults succeed in differentiating the *–s* and *–nt* markers when they have to inflect homophone words in ambiguous patterns. Finally we studied the learning and use of the number agreement of adjective (*–s*).

2 INTERPRETATION AND PRODUCTION: NOUN (*–S*) AND VERB (*–NT*) PLURALS

A first series of studies has determined when and how 6- to 9-year-old French children, from first to third primary grade, interpret the presence (or absence) of plural markers (*–s*, *–nt*, *–e*) according to whether these markers were combined or not with formal variations that are pronounced for determiners (*le/les* [singular *the*/plural *the*] always audible or not pronounced for pronouns (*il/ils 'he/they'* (Totereau, Thevenin, & Fayol, 1997). Two pictures were presented on a sheet of paper (for example, one with a hen, the other one with at least two hens; or one depicting a child jumping, the other several children jumping). An utterance including either two words (*la poule vs. les poules* for nouns '*the hen / the hens*'); *il saute vs. ils sautent* for verbs '*he jumps / they jump*' or only one word (*poule vs. poules* for nouns '*hen / hens*'; *saute vs. sautent* for verbs '*jumps / jumps*' was presented under the two pictures. The children had to match the utterance with the corresponding picture. They were also presented with production tasks. They were given, orally, a nominal group or a short sentence corresponding to a drawing depicting one (*Il y a une lampe->there is one lamp*) or several objects (*Il y a deux lampes->there are two lamps*), persons or actions (*Ils marchent-> they walk*), and were required to write the words under that drawing. We expected that the presence of audible cues (the *le/les* opposition is audible but not the *il/ils* opposition) and of written cues (the opposition of *il/ils*) would facilitate performance. Results on plural marking showed that:

1) Performance on recognition tasks (matching an utterance with a picture) was significantly better than performance on production tasks. That remained true, even in third grade, but the difference of proportions of correct plural marking between recognition and production decreased with the increase of school levels;

2) Scores on nouns were significantly better than scores on verbs, in recognition as well as in production, for the three primary grades considered.

3) The redundancy of markers (the presence of determiners for nouns and of pronouns for verbs) made recognition easier.

These results suggest two conclusions. First, the comprehension of the meaning of markers does not automatically lead to their use in production. Practice of writing must take place in order to ensure the transition from the knowledge of markers to their implementation. Second, performance on nouns is very high in interpretation tasks as early as first grade (because of the sonorous cue given by the article) and quickly improves in production. By contrast, performance on verbs remains relatively weak in the three considered grades. This difference affecting the noun and verb agreements could be explained by the semantic effect: the noun agreement is semantically based – adding –*s* when there are several objects or persons – whereas the verb agreement, as well as the adjectival agreement (see further), is formal: the fact that several children jump does not lead to a conceptual pluralisation of the action of jumping (Fayol, Thevenin, Jarousse, & Totereau, 1999; Totereau, Fayol, & Barrouillet, submitted).

3   FROM DECLARATIVE KNOWLEDGE OF MARKERS TO AUTOMATIZATION OF THEIR USE

Children can know the form and the meaning of morphological markers without, at the same time, being able to mobilize them systematically when the context requires their production (Totereau, Thevenin, & Fayol, 1997).

This deficiency is probably due to the non-automatisation of the use of these markers. Indeed automatisation makes the activation and the implementation of any given marker fast and unavoidable and considerably reduces the cognitive cost. In other words, we cannot avoid using it. Thus we no longer need to worry about the possibility of markers being used or control their use in a way which is attentionally costly. Attention is relieved of this necessity and can be devoted to other aspects of the task.

In French, the automatic application of agreements – *les* [plural *the*] *chiens* '*dogs*' (determiner noun) *aboient* '*bark*' (NP VP) – leads to success in the majority of cases (see below). This automaticity is necessary so that pupils and adults can devote their attention to dimensions other than the management of orthographic constraints (Fayol, 1999; Kellogg, 1999; McCutchen, 1995). As long as agreements are correctly realized by the application of a rule without, for all that, being automatised, the realization of the agreement remains fragile: a diversion of attention from the realization of the agreement is sufficient to elicit errors. However, when retrieval and implementation are automatic, the agreement becomes systematic with a weak cognitive cost.

The most reliable demonstration of automatisation is the occurrence of expert errors. In a sentence such as *le chien des voisins arrive 'the dog of the neighbours come'*, adults know to agree the verb (*arrive 'come'*) when explicitly asked or when they have to transcribe this sentence when it is dictated to them. However occupying their attention during the transcription is sufficient to elicit errors (from 20 to 30%). These errors consist in making the verb agree with the noun that immediately precedes it (*le chien des voisins arrivent 'the dog of the neighbours come'* where *arrivent* is erroneously inflected with *–nt*) rather than with the subject (Fayol, Largy, & Lemaire, 1994). In this case, automatism induces the error. But that is an expert error, which has a diagnostic value.

Children from 7 to 10 years old can be presented with this same task (Fayol, Hupet, & Largy, 1999). When the agreement is explicitly requested, for example in a completion task, a large majority of children succeed from the third or fourth primary grade (*Le chien des voisins arrive 'the dog of the neighbours comes' / Les chiens du voisin arrivent 'the dogs of the neighbour come' / Les chiens des voisins arrivent 'the dogs of the neighbours come'*). However, if the sentence is dictated and children have to write it in full, they often make errors of non-marking: the verb plural (*-nt*) does not appear (*Les chiens des voisins arrive*). The computation of the agreement (algorithm), which is too costly, could not be implemented because their attention is captured by other aspects of the task. Obviously no error appears with *le chien des voisins arrive' 'the dog of the neighbour comes'* because the lack of an automatic trigger of the agreement makes the occurrence of the *–nt* mark impossible.

In fourth grade, expert errors begin to appear in a way which varies depending on classes and individuals. From now on, the agreement is correctly realized in exercises like *le chien des voisins arriv__ 'the dog of the neighbours com__'* as well as in easy dictations (complete oral presentation of the sentence, followed by its transcription). However when attention is mobilized by a secondary task (pay attention to sounds; count...), the expert errors appear: *le chien des voisins arrivent 'the dog of the neighbours come'* (Fayol, Hupet, & Largy, 1999), in the same way as educated adults.

The results of the first and second series of experiments suggest that there are three phases in the learning of written number morphology. First children identify markers and discover their meaning, discovering the nominal *–s* more easily and earlier than the verb *–nt*. Then the use of rules (algorithms) appears, leading to the production of correct agreements when the time is not limited and the level of difficulty not very high. During this phase, errors become rarer but they continue to appear when the task overloads the attentional capacities or when attention is focused on other aspects, considered more important for the realization of the task. Finally, the phase of expertise comes. It is characterized by the occurrence of rare errors, until now unknown, which result from the automatic activation of morphological markers. These errors occur rarely but systematically even in very educated adults (Fayol & Largy, 1992).

4   OVERGENERALIZATION ERRORS

The development in three phases, such as described here, only partially gives an account of the learning of written morphology beyond the third grade. Indeed, homophony makes the learning more difficult. In French, there are many homophone words which are spelled differently. The most known are *a/à 'has/at', on/ont 'someone/have', son/sont 'his/are'*... Many others pose a problem because their correct transcription needs to take into account the syntactic category of words.

In the sentence *Le postier a des lettres. Il les timbre 'literally, The postman has letters. He them stamps'*, the word *timbre 'stamp'* is clearly a verb and agrees with the pronoun *il*; this agreement is correctly realized in fifth grade. However, when such a sentence is dictated to adults when their attention is attracted by another event during the transcription, most experts tend to write *timbres (stamps,* as in *the stamps)* instead of *timbre (stamps,* as in *he stamps)*. They inflect the verb as a noun (Largy, Fayol, & Lemaire, 1996; Fayol, Largy, Thevenin, & Totereau, 1995). The performed studies showed clearly that these errors occurred especially when the verb (*timbre 'to stamp'*) had a more frequent noun homophone (*le/un timbre 'the/a stamp'*) (this relative frequency is established from the observation of the language corpus). By contrast, these errors remained exceptional with verbs having a rare noun homophone (*trompe, 'trunk'* for example).

How can we explain why educated adults, who know the agreement rule and its implementation perfectly, can make such errors? A plausible hypothesis considers that these adults have two 'routes' for performing the agreement. On the one hand, they know an algorithm corresponding to the implementation of the agreement rule, algorithm that is reliable but relatively slow and cognitively costly. Then it is thus quite easy to disrupt its implementation. On the other hand, they have stocked in memory (as for multiplication tables) associations between words and inflections: such or such word co-occurs massively or in contrary rarely with such or such morphological marker (for example *timbre 'stamp'* with *–s* but *trompe 'to deceive'* with *–nt*). When adults have to write a word, the two routes are simultaneously mobilized. The most fast wins because the writer must treat many difficulties and, in consequence, any problem resolved quickly (eventually erroneously) allows to focus on another task. The most established associations sometimes tend to induce errors even though the writers making them could be able to prevent and/or correct them (Fayol, 1997).

We might think that the prevention and the correction of such errors is easy for educated adults used to read and write. Recent studies (Fayol, Largy, & Ganier, 1997) showed that adults informed of the presence of errors in sentences and having explicitly to detect and correct them either did not perceive them (as in *Il les timbres* [literally, *he them stamps,* as in *the stamps*', or considered correct agreements as erroneous (as in *Il les timbre*, [literally, *he them stamps*]). These data suggest that educated adults not only have a propensity to make errors when they transcribe such configurations, but when realized, these errors become very difficult to detect and to correct. In all likelihood, only a strategic control guided by prior knowledge of configurations which induce errors (Fayol & Monteil, 1994) and resting on an explicit analysis in syntactic categories (grammar) is in a position to allow the anticipation and/or the correction of errors (Nunes, Bryant, & Bindman, 1997).

In order to determine when and how these errors occur, we asked 7 to 11-year-old children, from the second to the fifth primary grade, to complete words preceded by either an article for nouns (*les nuag__*) 'the clouds' or a pronoun for verbs (*ils pilot__*) 'they pilot'. The words were extracted from reading books, so that we could control if the pupils have already encountered them. Two categories of words were selected. On the one hand, we used words that can only be noun (*les nuages* 'the clouds') or verb (*ils mangent* 'they eat'), whatever the syntactic context. On the other, we used words which function either as verbs or nouns depending on the syntactic context (*les timbres* 'the stamps', *ils timbrent* 'they stamp'). Children's performance at the different primary grades makes appear a particular type of development. Firstly (see the first part of this chapter), the absence of plural markers dominates. Secondly, the nominal plural inflection –*s* is systematically used for nouns as well as for verbs. This overgeneralization, due to the use of one mark only (–*s*), lasts no long. Thirdly, on the one hand, –*nt* on verbs but also on nouns (!) occur and, on the other hand, –*s* on some verbs remains. The detailed analysis of corpus reveals that the errors (–*s* on verbs, –*nt* on nouns) affect homophones essentially. In other words, the error probabilities are all the more high that the words can be, depending on the context, nouns or verbs. Furthermore, the tendencies correspond to the adults' one (see above): the words used as verbs in reading books were in a dominant way inflected with –*nt* whereas the words used as nouns were inflected with –*s*. These results suggest the intervention of a process of the direct retrieval of associations between words and morphemes, which leads most often to correct performance (because that corresponds to the most frequent occurrences) but sometimes ends up at errors.

In summary, the learning of written morphology for noun and verb number in French seems to follow a developmental path which is a result of the fact that most of the written markers have no corresponding pronunciation: (1) no detection of markers and of their meaning; (2) detection and interpretation of the nominal –*s*, then of the verb –*nt*; (3) implementation in production of the nominal –*s* and extension (overgeneralization) to verbs (which induces errors) (and to adjectives; which leads to success; see hereafter in this chapter); this implementation probably results from the systematic use of an algorithm corresponding to a simple rule: 'if plural then –*s*'; (4) appearance of the use of –*nt* with overgeneralization on some nouns (which have frequent verb homophones) and disappearance of –*s* on verbs, except with some of them (which have frequent noun homophones). These errors, contrary to the previous ones, no more refer to the dominant use of algorithm (production rule) but to the storage and the direct retrieval in memory of associations between words and inflections. These automatic associations are consecutive to the immersion (implicit learning) by the co-occurrences encountered during reading, what explains their systematic and unconscious characteristic, and then very difficult to prevent. Probably only a retrospective control (Fayol, 1997, Chapter 5) supported by an explicit knowledge of grammar is probably in position to avoid the occurrence of such errors.

5   THE AGREEMENT OF ADJECTIVES IN NUMBER

In French, contrary to some other written systems (*e.g.*, English), the adjectives agree in number (and also in gender) with the noun. This specificity allows to tackle a difficult question: why is the noun plural earlier than the verb plural, even in a language such as English in which markers have a corresponding pronunciation?

As mentioned in the first part of this chapter, the most plausible hypothesis is that the noun plural is semantically based: –*s* is added to mark the plurality of referents. Whether one says *le chien* (singular) or *les chiens* (plural) is simply a function of the number of animals being referred to, and no agreement between sentence elements is encoded in the inflection. On the other hand, the verb plural is formal: the addition of –*nt* does not correspond to a referential plurality (*e.g.*, in *les chiens aboient 'the dogs bark'*, the action of barking is not modified by the presence of several dogs). However, alternative hypotheses can be considered. For example, nouns arc more frequent than verbs: in consequence, the probability to encounter –*s* and to detect it as a plural marker is higher than the probability to encounter –*nt* (verb plural). Then the frequency of occurrence could explain the early use of –*s* rather than of –*nt*. Moreover, the –*s* marker is extremely reliable to signal the plurality: out of 19384 nouns and 10431 adjectives listed by the database Brulex, only 504 and 107, respectively, end in –*s* in the singular form. In other words, the encounter of a final –*s* allows to conclude to plurality with a good certainty. By contrast, many verbs, and in particular the most frequent (*aller 'to go'*, *venir 'to come'*, *être 'to be'*, *avoir 'to have'*, ...), form their plural by a vocalic (*e.g.*, *a/ont 'has/have'*) or consonant (*e.g.*, *est/sont 'is/are'*) change and not by the simple addition of –*nt*. Moreover 2819 words end in –*nt* in the singular form, what gives a lesser reliability to –*nt* than to –*s* as a plurality marker. In brief, –*nt* would be a plurality marker more difficult to detect and use because it is both less frequent and less reliable than –*s*.

The existence of frequency and reliability effects of markers in addition to the semantically based characteristics of plurality makes difficult the determining of the deciding factors, if they exist. However, the agreement of the adjective allows at least partially to dissociate their effects. The agreement of adjectives is no more semantically motivated than the agreement of verbs. On the other hand, it is realized by the addition of –*s*, which is frequent and reliable. In consequence, if the marking of plurality is determined on a semantic basis, then the adjective should be inflected as late as verb. If, in contrary, the formal aspects (frequency and reliability) play a dominant role, then the agreement of adjectives must be realized as early as nouns (Totereau, Fayol, & Barrouillet, submitted).

These alternative predictions were tested by asking 7 to 11-year-old children (from the second to the fifth primary grade) to complete and recall sentences consisting in a noun, an adjective and a verb, either in singular or in plural form. For example, the same child had to add the endings in *la fill__ blond__ parl__ 'the blond girl talks'* and *les chatt__ douc__ ronronn__* *'the gentle cats purr'* whereas another child had to write these same sentences after dictation. More than 3000 inflections were collected, that allowed to bring to the fore three facts. First the proportions of plural non-markings are approximately the same for adjectives and verbs and are significantly higher than for nouns. In other words, the semantically based characteristic of the nominal plural seems to be at the origin of the early marking of plurality. Then adjectives are earlier correctly inflected than verbs. The effect of frequency and reliability of –s arises as well. Finally the verb agreement is often realized erroneously by the addition of –s instead of –nt.

In summary, it is the conjunction of the notional plurality, the frequency and the regularity of marking which leads to the early and systematic use of –s on nouns. The formal aspects play a role as well in the agreement of adjectives: the adjectives, forming their plural by –s, are earlier correctly inflected than verbs. The latter are often pluralized erroneously by the use of –s rather than –nt. These data suggest that adjectives are initially inflected by generalization of the use of –s, which leads to correct marking for adjectives but incorrect for verbs. This learning outline can easily be interpreted in the framework of Anderson's theory (1983, 1993, 1995). In this framework, the acquisition and use of the plural constitute a procedural learning involving rules of the Condition(s) -> Action(s) type. Any rule of this type functions from specified conditions, integrated in working memory, and which, when satisfied, trigger the application of procedures (here adding –s vs. –nt). Initially, as a result of the regularity and the transparency of the relation between semantic plurality, the presence of a final –s, and possibly the influence of teaching (Fayol, Thévenin, Totereau & Jarousse, 1999) children elaborate a production rule of R1 type: if plural then add –s. The generalization of this rule would lead to an agreement which is either correct (adjectives) or incorrect (verbs). Subsequent learning would consist in refining the initial rule by adding new conditions, in particular referring to syntactic features (noun vs. verb) and a new action (adding –nt). Then we would have two rules:

Rule 1: if plural and Noun or Adjective then add –s

Rule 2: if plural and Verb then add –nt

The difficulty encountered by children during learning and by adults when verbs have a noun homophone (or the inverse) is due to the fact that two markers are available (–s and –nt) for one and the same macro-condition: plurality. There is a competition which needs to be resolved in order to take into account and to manage additional conditions.

6   LEARNING AND MANAGEMENT OF NUMBER MARKERS

The agreement phenomena come under a more general problem: the one raised by the acquisition and use of distributed markers. Indeed, a linguistic system can mark a dimension (*e.g.*, number or gender or syntactic function; *e.g.* German) only once by utterance as it is in noun phrases in Dutch: determiners and adjectives are insensitive for number. We could imagine that the plurality might be signalled only on the subject noun. In such a case, the detection and the implementation of the plural would be (relatively) easy. On the other hand, as soon as the presence of a dimension affects several segments of the same utterance, problems of the detection, recognition, comprehension and use of distributed markers (that can differ from one segment to another, see –*s* and –*nt*) arise.

In order to ensure the correct marking of the different constituents of a clause, subjects must first detect the component which governs the agreement, in particular here the number of the subject noun phrase (NP). If the NP is plural, all its variable components (determiner, noun, adjective) must be marked, in general by –*s*. As the plurality of the subject NP commands the plurality of the verb phrase, it must be conveyed on the simple or composed verb. This transport can be realized automatically by proximity and sometimes it induces agreement errors by attraction (Fayol & al., 1994; Largy *et al.*, 1996). A competition between competing markers (–*s* and –*nt*) associated with plurality can also occur (Largy *et al.*, 1996; Totereau, Barrouillet, & Fayol, 1999).

Finally this transport can give rise to the forgetting either of the dimension itself (plurality) or of the corresponding marker (-*nt*). It follows a non-marking. Initially, we studied the possible impact of the forgetting either of the feature [+ plural] or of the marker itself. To do so, we asked 10-year-old children (fourth graders) to write endings of words from a series of sentences, for example *Les camion__ roug__ étai__ sur la route* 'the red trucks were on the road'. The sentences were read to the children (here, *les camions rouges étaient sur la route*). First we tested the impact of distance between the noun governing the agreement and the adjective to be inflected (and at the same time the effect of within and between phrases agreement). For that, the same adjective was put either in post-nominal position (*i.e.*, attributive adjective) or in post-verbal position (complement adjective). For example: *Les trains rapides étaient sur la voie* 'the express trains were on the line' vs. *Les trains étaient rapides sur la voie* 'the trains were express on the line'. Then we studied the possible effect of redundancy. Indeed, we might imagine that the probability of forgetting the plurality which is initially indicated by *Les trains* is all the more high that the plurality is not cued by the oral form of the verb which stands between the noun phrase and the adjective. On the contrary, the probability of forgetting the plurality is all the more weak that the plurality is relieved by intermediate markers between noun and adjective, in particular markers borne by the verb. In this view, adjectives should be more frequently inflected when the information relative to plurality is borne by the verb in the oral modality (this is the case of the present tense – *est vs. sont* 'is/are' but this is not the case for the imperfect tense – *était vs. étaient* 'was/were' which are both pronounced /ete/).

The data collected with fourth graders effectively showed that the non-marking was more frequent with adjectives in post-verbal position than in post-nominal position but mainly in the absence of an audible marker of verb plurality. In sum, the verb marking relieves the information relative to the plurality and contributes to ensure the use of plural inflections on adjectives (Fayol, Totereau, & Maino, 1998).

7   DISCUSSION

The acquisition and use of written morphology for number raise specific problems. These problems stem from several reasons. First, the markers (*-s* and *-nt*) are usually 'silent': children must discover them and adults use them in the written modality, most often without the possibility of using their knowledge on oral (but see Largy & Fayol, in press, for cases where audible cues are present). Second, these markers are distributed selectively to different segments of the sentence. In particular, the noun and adjective components of the noun phrase are inflected with *-s* whereas verbs are inflected with *-nt*. Next, children, like adults, must affect markers to syntactic categories which are suitable and maintain active the information relative to plurality until the transcription of the entire utterance. Third, some words can be either noun or verb (or even adjective). It follows that ambiguities arise, which lead to competitions between markers (*e.g.*, *-s* and *-nt*) for a given inflection. In order to achieve the correct management of agreements, it is necessary to take account of syntactic or semantic information.

The data collected in the different series of experiments showed that the learning of written morphology for number is spread out over a long period and presents many difficulties. Initially, children write words following their phonological form: they use no number marker. Very fast, and more quickly for nouns than for verbs, they detect and interpret the presence of *-s* and *-nt* correctly. However, they need more time to produce these markers. The advisedly recall of these same markers necessary for production is later and more complex than the recognition of these markers in comprehension tasks. The extension of the correct marking varies as a function of syntactic categories; it is earlier and more frequent for nouns than for adjectives and for adjectives than for verbs. The performed studies showed that this hierarchy of difficulty was due to both the semantically motivated characteristic of the plurality and the frequency and reliability of the *-s* and *-nt* markers. Teaching also probably matters but its impact is much more difficult to assess. In France, agreement rules for plural are explicitly and systematically taught from second grade onwards, and exercises are provided to ensure automatisation. At the moment very few data are available concerning the effect of such training (but see Fayol, Thévenin, Jarousse, & Totereau, 1999; Thévenin, Totereau, Fayol, & Jarousse, 1999).

The management of morphological markers distributed throughout an utterance raises particular problems. The more the item, the agreement of which is governed by another item, is far from the latter, the more the frequency of correct agreements decreases, either because of the 'forgetting' of information (*i.e.*, plurality) or because of interferences. The data collected in fourth grade suggest that the redundancy of markers, due in particular to the verb, largely prevents non-marking.

Another difficulty stems from the presence of many homophones that can be, depending on syntactic context, either nouns (*les timbres* 'the stamps') or verbs *(Il les timbre* [literally, *He them stamps'*). These items give rise to frequent errors in educated adults, in particular when they are unable to focus their attention on the required agreement. In those cases, the used marker depends on the relative frequency of the two homophones: if the verb homophone is more frequent than the noun homophone, *−nt* wins; if the noun homophone is more frequent than the verb homophone, *−s* wins, leading to an erroneous agreement. The study of the development of verb agreement reveals that these errors following upon a competition between inflections occur from the third grade, when children have stored in memory regular associations between stems and morphemes. These associations are, at least in certain circumstances, activated faster than the agreement procedure and sometimes they lead to errors (Fayol, Largy, & Ganier, 1997).

The existence of all these difficulties helps us understand that France has elaborated and perpetuates (despite recurring debates about the formal and syntactic driven character of the French spelling of morphology) a learning of grammar spreading until ninth grade. Indeed, children, teenagers and adults need to have an explicit grammar which is able to guide them in the detection and the correction of errors. It is, of course, true that the phenomena described here do not take account of the nature and the frequency of the teaching which is given. Other studies are in progress. Their objective is to study the impact of teaching on learning at different primary grades (Fayol *et al.* 1999; Thévenin *et al.* 1999).

THE POWER OF PLURAL

The acquisition of written morphology of adjectives: Some empirical findings concerning interference of plural nouns on adjectives

GERT RIJLAARSDAM[*/***], MARJOLEIN VAN DORT-SLIJPER[**]
& MICHEL COUZIJN[*]

[*]*Graduate School of Teaching and Learning, University of Amsterdam, The Netherlands;*
[**]*Department of Linguistics, University of Amsterdam, The Netherlands;* [***]*Department of
Communication & Language, Utrecht University, The Netherlands*

Abstract. This chapter reports on developmental processes in written morphology. Focus is on the learning of the rules for written morphology of adjectives in Dutch. In Dutch, this is a simple morphological
rule, mastered rather early in primary school. Agreement rules between noun and adjective – number,
gender – hardly play a role in the Dutch morphological system regarding adjectives. However, during
primary school, the power of plural in adjacent nouns interferes with the correct application of the rule. In
the case of material adjectives (*golden* in *golden chair*) and verbal adjectives (*painted* in *painted chair*),
learning phases are indicated by students' mixing the adjective rule and the noun-plural rule: although the
adjective rule has already been mastered, one may find the occurrence of particular errors at a later stage.
In short, the power of plural in adjacent nouns dominates the spelling of adjectives at a certain moment,
and we take this moment as indicative of a particular learning stage. As an explanation, it may be expected that children invent agreement rules (like in Romance languages) guided as they are by a semantic
awareness of plurality. This could be the case in Dutch, even when no agreement rule between noun and
adjective exists. In the discussion, we hypothesize that the children are distracted by the form-function
relations in Dutch morphemes for plural in nouns and verbs (*–en*), material adjectives (*–en*), and normal
adjectives (*–e*). All these morphemes have different functions, but there is no audible difference. They are
homophone: the n in the *–en* morpheme for plural is not pronounced. When they write *–en* in adjectives,
instead of *–e*, which difference can not be heard in fluent speech, children may want to establish a plural
in the adjective, which does not exist in the Dutch language system.
Key words: spelling of adjectives, plural, generalisation, specification, transfer, developmental stages,
Dutch, English, French, learning phases, interference, regression of learning, written morphology.

L. Tolchinsky (ed.), Developmental Aspects in Learning to Write, 109–132.
© 2001 *Kluwer Academic Publishers. Printed in the Netherlands.*

1   INTRODUCTION

Learning to spell takes a long time and requires much effort from learners and teachers (Fayol & Totereau, this volume). There are rules to acquire, exceptions on rules, and exceptions to exceptions. Learning to spell requires learners to acquire code systems and to implement the complex network of code-sound relations. Different sounds are coded with one grapheme, while at the other hand one sound can be coded with different graphemes. In some cases, graphemes are required while nothing can be heard or is spoken!

Another category of problems children have to tackle is the acquisition of syntactic and morphological rules. Verb, noun and adjective flexion for instance play an important role in learning to spell. Difficulties and complexity depend on the language in question. Native speakers of non-romance languages as English and Dutch, trying to learn a foreign, romance language like French, Spanish, Portuguese or Italian, know how difficult it can be to accept that verb-endings depend on number and person of the subject, and that adjective-endings depend on gender and number. In French, the same morpheme, in most cases not audible, has to be written in many different forms, depending on syntactic features. And, especially in French, a large discrepancy exists between the spoken and the written language. For spoken French, we could say that the language belongs to the less flectional languages. But for written language, French is certainly a flectional language.

Yet, insights in learning processes of rule-based written morphology are scarce. Most studies about acquisition of syntactic and morphological rules are focused on spoken language in young children. Relatively recently, empirical studies and theory building on written morphology have started (Nunes, Bryant, & Bindham, 1997). Among others, current themes in morphology are rule-based versus associanist learning (see Marlsen-Wilson & Tyler, 1998; Kopcke, 1998), learners with language impairments (Bortolini, Leonard, & Caselli, 1998), the acquisition of meaning of suffixes (Nagy, Diakidoy, & Anderson, 1993), subject-verb agreement (Largy, Fayol, & Lemaire, 1996; Hupet, Fayol, & Schelstraete, 1998; Vigliocco & Nicol, 1998; Vigliocco, Butterworth, & Semenza, 1995; Bock & Eberhard, 1993), processes of overregularisations (Marcus, 1995) and overgeneralizations (Fayol, Totereau, & Thevenin, 1996; Totereau, Barrouilet, & Fayol, 1998). The studies reported in this chapter fall in the last class of studies.

In the nineties, Michel Fayol and associates started a research programme on written spelling acquisition, for native speakers of French and English. Later studies by Bryant and associates (Nunes, Bryant, & Bindham, 1997) on English were published. We were inspired and stimulated by these research programmes, and based some of our studies on findings Fayol reported on French and English. Our studies were motivated by practical and scientific reasons.

A practical reason for studying acquisition processes in spelling, is to provide textbook writers with some insights. Little is known about the sequence of acquisition of morphological rules in Dutch written language, although much time is devoted in primary schools on teaching spelling, based on morphological rules in nouns, adjectives and verbs. Textbook writers and teachers cannot rely on theoretical and empirical bases for decisions about what to teach, and when, and in what order. They have to rely on badly documented experiences from teachers and common sense. Sequencing learning matters is based on tradition, which is hard to fight. Although teachers in primary school in the Netherlands know from experience that pupils get confused when they learn to spell verbal adjectives after learning regular adjectives and verbs. Therefore, textbook writers avoid teaching verbal adjectives earlier than verbs.

A scientific reason for studying acquisition sequences is to abstract from language specific particularities by comparing cross-linguistic phenomena fundamentally in order to find general developmental patterns: in which order, at which age are acquisition rules acquired for French and for English, Dutch, *etc.*? To what extent are acquisition rules language-dependent, to what extent language-independent? Studying phenomena in other languages could be inspired by theoretical or methodological reasons. Theoretically interesting for instance is the plural morpheme in nouns, verbs and adjectives, related to the non-audibility of some written morphology, different in various languages (see table 1).

Table 1. Three languages, three systems for plural in nouns, verbs and adjectives.

	French	English	Dutch
Plural Noun	*–s*	*–s*	*–en*
Plural Verb	*–nt*	*–ø*	*–en*
Plural Adjective	*–s*	*–ø*	*–e*
Examples			
Plural Noun	Chaise*s*	Chair*s*	Stoel*en*
Plural Verb	Ils travaille*nt*	They work	Zij werk*en*
Plural Adjective	Grande*s* chaises	Large chairs	Grot*e* stoelen

In French, children have to master two different forms for non-audible plural morphemes (*–nt, –s*). These forms are functionally different: one for nouns, another for verbs. It was proven that these two inaudible forms gave problems of overgeneralisation. Children tend to use the more frequent noun-plural morpheme for verbs (Totereau, Barrouillet, & Fayol, 1998).

In English, children have to learn that in plural nouns, an audible *–s* has to be added. But the same audible *–s* in verbs does not signal plural; in verbs it marks the third person singular ('*he walks*'). So in English, children have one form (*–s*), for two word classes, with different functions.

In Dutch, children learn to add *–en* as plural morpheme in nouns and verbs, while the *–n* in *–en* [ən][1] is not audible[2]. But in Dutch, children have many opportu-

---

[1] *Phonetic transcriptions in this chapter are places within square brackets: [ə].*

nities to learn to write –en while they hear only [ə], because the same form is used for verbs and nouns, with the same function. Three languages, three different language systems, three different learning profiles.

The same holds for adjectives. Compared to English (no flexion in adjectives at all), French and Dutch are more difficult. In French, adjectives agree with the plural noun, with the same inaudible form (–s). In Dutch, children hear the same ending as in plural nouns (–e), but now they have to write –e and not –en, even when the adjacent noun is plural. In French as well as in Dutch, inaudibility plays a role, but in a different way in the two languages. In French, the morphemes for plural in verbs, nouns and adjectives are all inaudible. In this respect, the morphemes are homophone. Children have to rely totally on explicit taught rules for spelling and rules for agreement. When French children make errors, they probably mismatch the rules and the domains of application. In Dutch, the morphemes for plural in noun, verbs and adjectives are also homophone (sound as 'u' in lover[3]). Dutch children can rely partly on sound, but not on agreement rules. When Dutch children make errors, they probably mix sound-grapheme relations, following a self-invented rule:

> 'in plural – nouns and verbs – I have to write en (stoelen, werken) but I hear only the e [stulə, wɛrkə], so when I hear e in an adjective like grote (Eng: large) [xro:tə], I also have to write en in case of plural)'.

Thus different languages cause different problems for spellers. But the developmental process of learning a rule, exploring the domain of application and overgeneralising the rule, and restating, specifying the rule, is found in all these languages as Nunes, Bryant, & Bindman (1997) proved for verbs in English and Totereau, Barrouillet, & Fayol (1998) for nouns and verbs in French. Therefore, cross-linguistic studies might help to reveal underlying cognitive processes. Questions raised in a study on a particular phenomenon in a language, sometimes cannot be studied in the same language, but can be studied in another (see for instance Totereau & Fayol, 1994, 1996). In this chapter, we will present some findings on developmental processes in Dutch morphological spelling of plural in verbs and nouns and relate them to Fayol's findings for French. But the main part of this chapter will be devoted to the spelling of special cases of adjectives in Dutch: material adjectives (golden in golden chairs) and adjectives derived from verbs (painted in painted chairs).

---

[2] *Here we have to nuance this generalisation. The 'n' is not heard in fluent speech, in most regions of the Netherlands. But in some regions, the 'n' is pronounced very clearly (in the North-East and the South-West region for instance. And even in other regions, there are circumstances when the 'n' can be heard, for instance in strongly emphasised speech especially when a word beginning with a vowel follows. The last case corresponds with French: although the –s in plural nouns is not pronounced in general, when a word beginning with a vowel follows, a soft –z can be heard, linking the two separate words. But note that the data we present in this chapter, is collected in regions in the Netherlands where the 'n' is often not pronounced in fluent speech.*
[3] *The pronunciation of this vowel is called 'schwa', explained in the Oxford Concise Dictionary as the indistinctive vowel in the second syllable of 'comma'. The term 'schwa' stems from Hebrew, where it means something like 'emptiness'. The same sound is heard in the second syllables of 'better' and' lover'.*

In the next section, we will demonstrate how learning phases can be distinguished based on the kinds of errors pupils make in their spelling, and on linguistic factors which describe classes of spelling tasks. We will then go into a number of important learning mechanisms for rule-based spelling: generalisation and specification. These two mechanisms may account for the correct application of rules in particular spelling tasks, as well as for the errors pupils make when they make the transition to a new learning phase (by overgeneralisation or underspecification). Two cases of overgeneralisation are presented and empirically demonstrated. The first is the case of Dutch material adjectives, where plural formation may interfere with rules for adjective morphology. The second is the case of Dutch adjectives derived from verbs, in which the spelling of the adjective is disturbed by plural formation and by similarity with the verb from which it was derived. Two troubling factors come to the fore in these two cases: the inaudibility of spelling varieties, and the influence or *power of plural* as an interfering factor. In the discussion section, we will focus on the kinds of problems pupils apparently run into when constructing, applying, and adapting rules for these spelling problems; furthermore, we will present these problems as related to learning phases.

2   CROSS-SECTIONAL STUDIES: INDICATIONS OF LEARNING PHASES

Studies in the acquisition processes of written morphology are usually based on cross-sectional research designs. Tests are assigned to different age groups, and resulting differences in scores are interpreted as phases in acquisition processes: at a certain age, learners make more errors than at a later age. It seems, at first sight, a bit awkward to interpret this data as describing the acquisition data, because nothing is known about the acquisition process itself: different subjects were measured at different ages. A better measurement design that provides real acquisition data is a longitudinal design, even if only one or two cases are studied (see for instance Mervis & Johnson, 1991).

Yet, cross-sectional data can help us – in a global way – to understand at what moment learning is actually taking place. From performance data, we can infer that learners go through a learning phase. We will demonstrate this with data on the plural of nouns in Dutch. First, we will present a short introduction on the Dutch morphological system of plural formation of nouns.

2.1 Plural formation in Dutch nouns: a short introduction

In Dutch, there are two regular productive processes of plural formation of nouns. The first process consists of adding the morpheme *–en* at the singular form of the noun. This process is clearly the most frequent (Geerts, Haeseryn, de Rooij, & Van den Toorn, 1984: 62).

Table 2. Plural in Dutch nouns: Morpheme I: Add –en.

Singular form			Plural form
(Chair)	Stoel	Stoelen	(Chairs)
(Book)	Boek	Boeken	(Books)
(Candle)	Kaars	Kaarsen	(Candles)

The second process requires adding the morpheme *–s* to the singular form of the noun. This is the special case of plural formation, restricted to singular nouns ending on vowels, or in the unstressed phonemes *–el, –er, –em, –en,* in which the *–e* is pronounced as an *e* [ə] in *lover*. This class of singular nouns always consists of more than one syllable.

Table 3. Plural in Dutch nouns: Morpheme II: Add –s.

Singular form			Plural form
(Table)	Tafel	Tafels	(Tables)
(Tower)	Toren	Torens	(Towers)
(Broom)	Bezem	Bezems	(Brooms)
(Gnome)	Kabouter	Kabouters	(Gnomes)

In fluent speech often the *n* of the morpheme *–en* of the plural nouns is not pronounced, and not necessary to pronounce, because the minimal opposition *stoel-stoele* is enough to indicate singular and plural (see footnote 2). Note that one may pronounce the *n* if one wants to, but pronouncing all plural morphemes completely will sound exaggerated. In classroom situations some teachers, teaching the written plural morpheme *–en*, pronounce the *n* for didactic reasons only. Still in most instances there is incomplete audible support for the written morpheme. The plural morpheme *–s*, on the other hand, is always pronounced. This difference in audibility of the two morphemes for plurality will obviously influence the rate of the acquisition of the written morphemes for the plural of nouns.

2.2 Mastery of spelling the plural in Dutch nouns: indicating learning phases

In their study on the acquisition of written plural morphemes of nouns and verbs in French, Totereau, Thevenin, & Fayol (1997) found a positive effect in case the morphemes are put in a context with extra syntactic information, such as articles or numerals in combination with nouns, and nouns or pronouns in combination with verbs. We tested whether the same effect occurs in Dutch. In the test, we inserted items with and without extra syntactic information. In this chapter, we present some of the data just in order to show at which age children master the morpheme for plural (in nouns and verbs), and to present some factors which indicate learning phases. For more detailed information, we refer to Van Dort-Slijper, Rijlaarsdam, & Weel (1998).

In Dutch the definite article *de* can be used with singular and with plural nouns. This definite article does not give any extra syntactic information about number: the children have to infer the number (singular or plural) from the picture that accompanies the item. So we built items with and without extra syntactic information in plural (*de stoelen – twee stoelen*; 'the chairs – two chairs') versus singular (*de stoel*; 'the chair').

Two studies on the acquisition of the written form of the plural morpheme of nouns and verbs (Fayol, Totereau, Thévenin, & Thouilly (1994) for French and Totereau & Fayol (1994, 1996) for English, formed the basis of the study for Dutch. For French, the plural morpheme is silent. Therefore, spellers cannot rely on oral speech. The general trends Fayol *et al.* found, were (1) that the plural of nouns was acquired earlier than the correct spelling of plural in verbs, (2) that recognition of written morphology ('reading') preceded production ('writing'), and (3) that in all stages, syntactic information supports the acquisition. Totereau and Fayol, summarising the results for French, stated (Totereau & Fayol, 1996: 383):

> 'The results showed that recognition was easier than production, for nouns as well for verbs with the 6- and 7-year-olds, and only for verbs with the 8-year-olds. The performance was better for utterances containing a noun than for utterances containing a verb, in production for the 7- and 8-year-olds and in comprehension for the 6- and 7-year-olds. Finally, the redundancy of markers (Article + Noun / Pronoun + Verb) made comprehension easier for the 6- and 7-year-olds. Performance was better when there were two markers rather than only one for the number (singular / plural).'

In French the formation of the plural in nouns and verbs reflects the same rule ('add a silent morpheme', *–nt* in verbs (*ils volent*, 'they fly') and *–s* in nouns (*les chiens*, 'the dogs'). In English, on the contrary, the plural morpheme in nouns is audible *the dogs*), while in the plural of verbs the plural morpheme is equal to zero. It is confusing for children that the *–s*-morpheme in verbs indicates the singular in verbs (3rd person: *she sleeps*). Again, the researchers found that the acquisition of plural formation in nouns precedes the acquisition of plural in verbs, in production as well as in recognition tasks. Although the *–s*-morpheme is audible in the plural of nouns and the singular of verbs (3rd person), one may expect no differences in acquisition to be found in recognition and production.

Indeed, no difference was found when extra information was available; when extra information was absent in verbs, then production scored better than recognition. The researchers attributed this finding to an artefact of the materials.

The study we ran for Dutch combined elements of the study on French (silent morphology) and English (audible support of plural morphology). The formation of plural in nouns has two possible morphemes: audible *–s* (*Appels*; Eng: *Apples*) and semi-audible *–en* (*Stoelen*; 'Chairs') in which the vowel is audible, and the *–n* is not, in fluent speech. Plural formation in verbs is the same as in nouns (*Ik roep, wij* *roepen*; '*I shout, we shout*'). Our data showed the same regularities: recognition preceded production, plural formation of nouns preceded plural formation of verbs, and adding syntactic information about plurality or singularity facilitated recognition and production of the written plural morpheme.

When written morphology is supported by audible observations, then written morphology is easier than when morphology is silent.

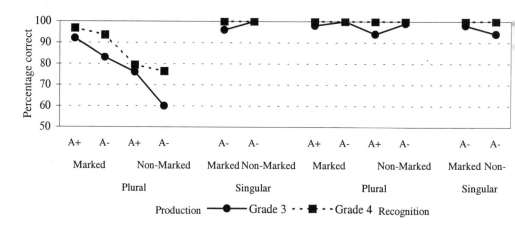

Figure 1. Factors influencing performance on plural morphology in nouns in grade 3 and 4. Effects of audibility (A- / A+), syntactical information (marked/non-marked), number (singular/plural) and task (production/recognition).

Figure 1 shows some of these findings. It contains the percentage correctly spelled plural forms of nouns, broken down for the factors Audibility of Plural Morpheme (plural morpheme –*s* and plural morpheme –*en*), syntactically marked or not, Number (plural or singular) and Task (production or recognition) for two groups (Grades 3 and 4)[4]. It is obvious that both grades mastered the singular forms (recognition and production) and recognition of plural, for both morphemes. Therefore, in these age groups, audibility does not seem to play a role when students have to choose the right spelling from paper. But from the far left in Figure 1, about the production of the plural morpheme, it appears that grade 4 already mastered the correct production, but grade 3 has significantly more difficulties with the inaudible –*en*-morpheme when no syntactic facilitation of number is provided.

The facilitating role of syntactic information is significant. Statistical analyses showed an interaction effect between task and syntactic information besides main effects for Task and Syntactic Information. In Figure 1, there is a clear ceiling effect to be observed on the Recognition task. Within this task, there is no effect of the factor Syntactic Information, whereas in the production tasks, an effect of Syntactic

---

[4] *In the Dutch educational system, grade 1 corresponds with the first year in Kindergarten, children being at the age of four. Thus, in Grade 3 children are about six years old.*

Information is significant. When we compare data of nouns with audible plural endings (*–en*) and non-audible plural endings (*–s*), it appears that no interaction effect of grade and Morpheme Type is observed.

2.3 Factors indicating learning phases

For the choice of factors that could define sequences of acquisition, we try to imagine what choices textbook writers have to make. Therefore, we studied several textbooks for primary schools. Some of the choices were included in studies by Fayol and associates, which gave us the opportunity to relate some of our Dutch observations to phenomena in English and French. It seems that some language-independent factors can be located. Besides age or grade, and task – production tasks are more difficult than recognition tasks – we found influences from four other factors.

Audibility (silent vs. non-silent morphology). In Dutch, as in many languages, children have to learn that written morphology cannot fully rely on spoken language. In Dutch, we have two morphemes indicating the plural formation of nouns –*s* (*appels* (*'apples'*) which is audible as in English, and *–en* (*stoelen* (*'chairs'*), pronounced in Dutch as [stulə]. What children have to learn is that morphosyntactical relationship counts in correct spelling, which overrules audibility of inflection.

Word Class. The correct morphological spelling of the plural suffix of nouns precedes verbs (Van Dort-Slijper, Rijlaarsdam, & Weel, 1998), normal adjectives precede material adjectives (Van Dort-Slijper, Rijlaarsdam, & Ditzel, 1998), which precedes adjectives derived from verbs (Van Dort-Slijper, Rijlaarsdam, & Breedveld, 1999).

Syntactic Information. Extra information that supports the application of the morphological rule facilitates recognition and correct spelling. As Totereau, Thevenin, & Fayol (1996) for French and English, we have found that this facilitating effect occurs in Dutch. When this extra information indicates the number in nouns and verbs, like articles or numerals in combination with nouns, and nouns or pronouns in combination with verbs (see Van Dort-Slijper, Rijlaarsdam, & Weel, 1998), children make fewer errors.

Given-new principle; syntactic markedness. We have found effects of grammatical function and place of the constituent (Van Dort-Slijper, Rijlaarsdam, & Ditzel, 1998) on the performance of the spelling of adjectives. When children are in a learning phase, mastering a spelling rule, they perform better when the problem is stated (1) in the first constituent of the sentence; (2) in the constituent which is not the subject.

These factors, together with task and grade factors, can indicate, alone or in combination, learning phases. As we saw in Figure 1, at the end of Grade 4 (seven-years – old age group), the average score in simple production tasks is about 75%, indicating that this grade has almost mastered the non-audible morpheme of plural in nouns. Using the same production task, in the same grade, same subjects, but adding syntactic information about number (*e.g. two chair—*) the average score is 95%. This implies that this age group is still learning: acquisition is almost completed in certain circumstances, but not in all. Children of this age still need some support about plural in the sentence for spelling nouns correctly. This effect of syntactic supportive information on the scores was found in several cases. We also found this effect in the audible morpheme of plural in nouns (*appel – appels*; '*apple-apples*'): even in completely audible observable morphemes of plural the recognition task is easier than the production task, and a facilitating effect of syntactic information on mastering the spelling is found. In another case, it was shown that children are mastering the written morpheme for singular in the past tense of verbs in Grade 3 in the recognition task, and in Grade 4 in the production task. In Grade 3, an effect of syntactic information was found in the recognition task, in Grade 4 such an effect was established in the production task.

Another indicator of learning is the effect of task: recognition versus production. When performance on both tasks are high and do not differ significantly, mastery is completed; is performance high on both tasks, but still differ significantly, the acquisition process is almost completed. When performance on both tasks is low and not significantly different, the acquisition process had not started. When performance on both tasks is low, but recognition is better than production, acquisition had started. These phenomena were found in several studies.

The most obvious indicator used in developmental studies is the age factor. When the performance in different age groups is low, and not significantly different, we may assume that learning had not started yet. When one of the age groups scored significantly higher, we may infer that learning took place. In this chapter, several of these indicators will be illustrated for the acquisition of spelling rules for adjectives.

3   GENERALISATION AND SPECIFICATION

One of the most intriguing developmental aspects of learning to spell is the sequence of generalisation and specification processes. Children learn a rule ('if condition X, then action Y'), and then have to find out about the domain of application. From time to time, they overgeneralise the domain of application. When they find out, they specify two separate rules for two different domains. When they learn to spell the morpheme of plural in Dutch, they have to resist interference problems. Interference arises when the rule is applied in a wrong situation that *seems* right. In Dutch, children must accommodate the noun-plural rule several times in their learning history. This implies that we can predict errors in a certain stage of acquisition, especially in the spelling of adjectives, as we will illustrate below. In these cases, the plural rule for nouns is applied erroneously to different types of adjectives, guided by the semantic meaning of plural.

It is this process of generalisation, specification and sometimes regression that we deal with in this chapter. We have found that the acquisition of morphological rules for written communication has its ups and downs: sometimes knowledge of newly acquired rules is overgeneralised, and new errors are introduced, for a short time, even in already mastered spelling problems.

A consequent factor involved in new learning seems to be the power of plural of nouns. As you might have noticed from the former sections, one of the first rules learners of Dutch spelling learn, is that the plural of the noun is in most instances indicated by the morpheme –*en,* which is semi-audible: the *e* (pronounced as schwa, see footnote 3) is audible, the *n* is not. Children have to acquire the rule

> 'I have to write *stoelen* (*chairs*), with an *n*, although I cannot hear the *n* at the end'.

Or, formally:

> 'If the noun-to-spell is plural, then add –*en* to the stem, although the *n* will not be heard.'

They have to generalise this rule to other domains, like the plural in verbs (present and past tense), *but not to the domain of adjectives,* which they tend to do when they learn special types of adjectives at a later stage. In principle, three basic types of errors can be made when new rules are introduced, assuming that the rule formation itself is mastered.

1) Regeneration of old rule: the new rule is applied to the target items, but also falsely to already learned items, for instance, the rule for material adjectives if it is also applied to regular adjectives.

2) Incomplete generalisation: the new rule is applied to at least one subclass of the target items, but not to the whole class, for instance, the rule is applied to material adjectives in plural noun phrases, but not to material adjectives in singular noun phrases.

3) Overgeneralisation: the new rule is applied to the target items, but also to other classes of items to which it should not apply, for instance, the rule is applied to material adjectives and erroneously to verbal adjectives.

All combinations of these incomplete specification and generalisation processes can be found. For this chapter we selected data from three studies concerning the interference of the plural of nouns, in learning the flexion of regular or normal adjectives and two special cases of adjectives, *i.c.* material and verbal adjectives (Van Dort-Slijper, Rijlaarsdam, & Weel, 1998; Van Dort-Slijper, Rijlaarsdam, & Ditzel, 1998; Van Dort-Slijper, Rijlaarsdam, & Breedveld, 1999).

In a clear case of interference, material adjectives are spelled better in plural than in singular constituents (albeit on wrong assumptions students construed: 'incomplete generalisation'). We even observed indications of 'regression processes': children introduced errors in regular adjectives, when material adjectives were introduced. For verbal adjectives, it turned out that performance decreased when the noun in the noun phrase was plural ('incomplete generalisation'). Although in Dutch there is no morpheme for plural for adjectives, children tend to develop one, based on the rule for the plural of nouns. That is why we have called this chapter The Power of Plural.

4   OVERGENERALISATION CASE 1: MATERIAL ADJECTIVES

In the former section we laid the basis for the two following studies in which we will present data of interference from morphological knowledge about plural inflexion in nouns into special cases of adjectives: from Grade 4, the plural formation in nouns, even the non-audible morpheme *–en,* is mastered. In the following sections, we try to find phases in the learning process of written morphology, in which children have to readjust the rule they learned:

> 'I have to write the plural on nouns by adding *–en* (*stoel* (sing.) becomes *stoelen* (plural; *'chairs'*), with an *–n* at the end, although I cannot hear the *n* at the end.'

In Dutch, verbs follow the same rule, so children have many opportunities to exercise the rule. Then a problem arises. Flexion in adjectives in Dutch makes no difference between plural and singular: children have to follow just one rule[5]. This problem is mastered quite easily. Then a new problem arises when material adjectives are introduced. A second introduction of Dutch is needed here.

4.1 Adjectival morphemes in noun phrases in Dutch: A short introduction[6]

In Dutch we distinguish two types of adjectives, according to their productive morphological processes (see table 4).

The formation of regular adjectives, used in a noun phrase and placed before the noun (singular or plural) is very simple: adding the morpheme *–e* is sufficient (see table 5). Material adjectives always have more than one syllable. Adding the morpheme *–en* on a noun that names a material forms them (see table 6).

Table 4: Two types of adjectives in Dutch.

Regular adjectives	Material adjectives
Groen (green)	Houten (wooden)
Lekker (delicious)	Katoenen (cotton)
Groot (great)	Koperen (copper)

---

[5] *This is a simplification. For the correct spelling of adjectives, at least one basic rule is to be applied; then some other rules can play a role, related to the spelling of endings of open and closed syllables.*

[6] *Note that we only refer to adjectives in attributional position to nouns; in predicative position (the chair is green) no flexion in Dutch is required (de stoel is groen).*

Table 5: Formation of regular adjectives in noun phrases.

Stem + Morpheme	= Derived Adjective	Phonetic transcription	
Groen + *−e*	= de groen*e* stoel	[də xrunə stul]	(the green chair)
	= de groen*e* stoelen	[də xrunə stulə]	(the green chairs)
Groot + *−e*	= het grot*e* boek	[ət xro:tə buk]	(the large book)
	= de grot*e* boeken	[də xro:tə bukə]	(the large books)

Table 6: Building material adjectives (I).

Basic Noun + Morpheme	= Material Adjective	Phonetic transcription	
Hout + *−en*	= houten	[hɔutə]	(wooden)
Goud + *−en*	= gouden	[xɔudə]	(golden)

Table 7: Building material adjectives (II).

Basic Noun + Morpheme	= Material Adjective	Phonetic Transcription	
Zilver + *−en*	= zilveren	[zɪlvərə]	(silver)
Koper + *−en*	= koperen	[ko:pərə]	(copper)

The *−n* of the morpheme *−en* is normally not pronounced in fluent speech. In classroom situations, teachers teaching children the morpheme of the material adjectives could pronounce the *−n* for didactic reasons. Still most of the time there is not a complete audible support for the morpheme of the material adjective.

Some material nouns end with the syllable *−er*, like *koper* [ko:pər] (copper), a syllable without stress, the *e* is pronounced as a schwa (see footnote 3). The material adjectives made of these nouns by adding *−en* has two syllables at the end without stress.

Not only is the double unstressed syllable a complicating factor, but also the fact that some adults do not pronounce the whole morpheme *−en*. Some of them say: *een zilver horloge* (a silver watch), instead of the correct phrase *een zilveren horloge*. In this case, the audible support for the written morpheme is totally absent. We expect children too will tend to consider the basic word (the noun) to be the inflected adjective. Therefore, we expect this type of material adjectives will give more troubles in the acquisition of the written forms than the material adjectives ending in one unstressed syllable.

4.2 The power of plural: case I

When the spelling of material adjectives is introduced in classes, a problem arises for children: a problem of form and function. One form – the morpheme –*en* – now has two functions instead of one. It indicates the plural in nouns (and verbs) and now also indicates the adjective use of material nouns (*hout-houten*; '*wood-wooden*'). One can easily imagine that children associate the –*en* morpheme in material adjectives with plurality, and again tend to apply the plural rule – erroneously – to regular adjectives: children go through a phase of regression.

Table 8. Differentiation and overgeneralisation.

Phenomenon 1: Number Differentiation in Spelling Material Adjectives

Children spell material adjectives in *plural noun phrases* correctly, which fact does not indicate which rule they applied: the rule for material adjectives, or a erroneously invented rule of number agreement between noun and material adjectives:

De hout*en* schoen*en*   [də hɔutə sxunə] (the wooden shoes)

Drie zilver*en* ring*en*   [dri zɪlvərə rɪŋə] (three silver rings)

Children spell material adjectives in *singular noun phrases* incorrectly, which fact, does not indicate which rule they applied: they might have failed to recognise the adjective as a special case (the material adjective, with another morpheme than a regular adjective, or they might have applied the erroneously invented rule of number agreement between noun and material adjective:

*De houte schoen   [də hɔutə sxun] (the wooden shoe):

instead of   learner fails to recognise *houten* as a mate-

De hout*en* schoen   rial adjective, or erroneously thinks that

                                   adjectives have a plural and a singular form

When children write the same material adjective correctly in plural noun phrases, and incorrectly in singular noun phrases, this could indicate that children apply a non-existing rule of number agreement between noun and material adjective.

Phenomenon 2: Regression of Performance in Spelling Regular Adjectives

Children spell regular adjectives in *plural noun phrases* incorrectly, which indicates that they apply the non-existing rule of number agreement between nouns and adjectives, which they constructed when the spelling of material adjective was introduced:

*De groen*en* schoenen   [də xrunə sxunə] (the green shoes): the *n*

instead of   in groen*en* seems to indicate plural.

De groene schoenen

Two phenomena can be hypothesised (see table 8). The first phenomenon to note is that children will perform better in spelling the morpheme of material adjectives in plural noun phrases than in singular noun phrases. We assume that children may overgeneralise the noun-plural rule to material adjectives, when adjacent to a plural noun. Because, for nouns, children taught themselves that they have to write an *n* in plural forms, although they will not hear them. Then in material adjectives, written with the same morpheme as the plural noun morpheme, they could erroneously redefine the material adjectival morpheme as a plural morpheme, and spell the material adjective correctly, although based on a false rule. If children indeed apply this false rule, then in singular noun phrases, they will write material adjectives erroneously with an –*e*, establishing a non-existing agreement rule of number between noun and material adjective (phenomenon 1).

If this phenomenon is observed, even regression to the flexion of regular adjectives might be the consequence. It is possible that children, after the introduction of the material adjectival morpheme –*en*, overgeneralise the 'invented' agreement rule of number in nouns and material adjectives to regular adjectives, writing *groene* [xrunə] (green) as singular form and the *groenen* [xrunə] as plural form (phenomenon 2).

4.3 The power of plural, Case I: Findings

Two tasks were involved: a production and a recognition task. Both Grades seem to have acquired the spelling of the *regular adjective*. Grade 7 scores about 90%, grade 6 about 80% correct. Production was as good as recognition. Grade 7 scores significantly better. Regarding *material adjectives,* Grade 6 scores about 67% correct, Grade 7 about 71 % (not significantly different); production is as good as recognition. Material adjectives are significantly more difficult to spell, in both grades.

4.3.1 Number agreement rule in material adjectives: Phenomenon 1

Figure 2 shows some of the data. The interaction effect between Morpheme Type and number in nouns is significant (F (1,77) = 24.81; p = .000). The effect of number is significant in Grade 6 for material adjectives (df 38, t = 3.17, p = .003), and for Grade 7 (df 39, t = 3.96, p = . 000).

So indeed we observed the related facts of spelling material adjectives more often correctly in plural noun phrases then in singular noun phrases, in both grades. Probably children differentiate between singular and plural in material adjectives, stimulated by the form of the morpheme of the material adjective (–*en*), which is the same as the noun plural morpheme. This false association leads to errors, except when using material adjectives in plural noun phrases.

4.3.2   Regression: Phenomenon 2

From Figure 2, it seems that phenomenon 2 has also appeared: when the adjacent noun was plural, children in both grades make slightly more errors, by adding a non-existing plural morpheme *–en* to the adjective. However, the effect of number proves not to be significant for both grades in the case of regular adjectives. This implies that children in grade 6 and 7 are not distracted by the plural of nouns when they spell a regular adjective. Although they developed a number agreement rule for material adjectives, they do not transfer this rule backwards to regular adjectives. They are resistant to the overgeneralisation of the noun-plural rule

'write *–en* although you won't hear the *n*.'

They have mastered the spelling of regular adjectives completely, but have difficulties in mastering material adjectives because of the resemblance between plural noun morpheme and the material adjective morpheme.

As conclusion, these findings might have implications for textbook writers. It might imply that teachers and textbooks should start teaching the spelling of material adjectives only in phrases with a noun in singular form in order to avoid the mistake that students see the morpheme *–en* for material adjectives as the same as the morpheme *–en* for the plural in nouns. They have to learn first that material adjectives are written with *–en*, and secondly that this form is uninfluenced by the number of the adjacent noun. Then exercises with plural and singular nouns can follow.

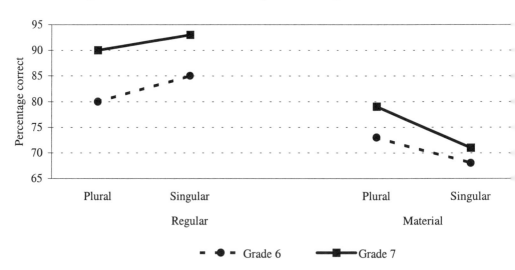

Figure 2. The power of plural. Effect of number in adjacent noun on correct spelling of regular and material adjectives in production task.

5   OVERGENERALISATION CASE 2: ADJECTIVES DERIVED FROM VERBS

Here we introduce another special case of adjective formation in Dutch: adjectives, derived from verbs (Dutch: *de verbrede weg* [də vərbre:də wɛx], *de verlichte weg* [də vərlɪxtə wɛx]; *'the broadened road, the illuminated road'*). In English, these adjectives have flexion (*–ed* morpheme), while in Dutch no special morpheme is used. Verbal adjectives follow the general rule for adjectives: 'add the *–e* morpheme to the stem'. Yet, these verbal adjectives are very difficult to spell in Dutch, because the form of the adjective concurs strongly with the form of the past tense singular of the verb. Different rules have to be applied, resulting in different forms, but these differences in form cannot be heard. In addition, because of the traditional sequence of teaching objects, children in primary schools first learn inflection of the regular adjectives, then the past tense of verbs, and then the verbal adjectives. This sequence could enhance overgeneralisation of the past tense verb form to the adjective form: the better a learner in primary school has acquired the verb formation (past tense) the more difficulties they will experience with writing adjectives derived from verbs correctly.

So at the end of primary schooling, children are confronted with new problems in the spelling of adjectives: verbal adjectives. Note that we explained that plural formation in nouns and verbs follows the same rule: 'add *(e)n* to the stem'. Remember that adjective formation only requires the *–e* morpheme. When children consider verbal adjectives not as adjectives but as verbs, and apply the plural verb rule, they will make mistakes in the spelling of verbal adjectives when the adjacent noun is in plural. The last short introduction on the Dutch language system follows.

5.1   The flexion of adjectives derived from verbs: a short introduction

Although the spelling of each pair on one row in table 9 is different as a consequence of function, the sound is exactly the same. Remember from our short introduction on plural noun formation above, that from the plural morpheme *–en* the *n* is not heard in fluent speech (see in table 9 *Wij verlichtten de weg*; *Wij verbreedden de weg*). Therefore, although the formation rule for adjectives is simple, and was mastered in former grades, a new problem arises. Verbal and adjectival inflexion rules compete with each other. Children put a lot of effort in mastering the complex rules for spelling verbs, especially the past tense formation. And now, verbal adjectives are inserted in the curriculum, and children have to differentiate between the verbal form and the adjective form (*verlichtte(n)* versus *verlichte*).

A second problem is the problem of plural. Because of the verbal stem of the verbal adjective, an old problem can make a re-entree: plural formation of verbs with the *–en* morpheme, erroneously applied on (verbal) adjectives. As can be seen from the table above, number does not affect the adjective. However, in the case of nouns and verbs, the plural is formed in most instances by addition of *–en*, in which the *n* is silent in fluent speech. So when children have acquired the rule for the plural formation of nouns and verbs ('add *–en*'), while they do not hear the *–n*, the danger of applying the same rule to adjectives in plural noun constituents exists (see table 10).

Table 9. Conflicting spelling rules for adjectives and verbs (past tense).

Adjective	Verb, past tense
	Rules
Rule: add *e*	Rule Past tense: add *te/de* Rule for Plural: add *n*
	Examples
De verlich*te* weg [hɛi vərlɪxtə də wɛx] (The illuminated road)	Hij verlich*tte* de weg [hɛi vərlɪxtə də wɛx] (He illuminated the road)
De verlich*te* wegen [wɛi vərlɪxtə də wɛx] (Illuminated roads)	Wij verlich*tten* de weg [wɛi vərlɪxtə də wɛx] (We illuminated the road)
De verbre*de* weg [hɛi vərbre:də də wɛx] (The broadened road)	Hij verbree*dde* the weg [hɛi vərbre:də də wɛx] (he broadened the road)
De verbre*de* wegen [wɛi vərbre:də də wɛx] (The broadened roads)	Wij verbree*dden* the weg [wɛi vərbre:də də wɛx] (We broadened the road)

Table 10. Confusion in plural forms of verbal adjectives: Adjectives do not follow nouns in plural form.

De verlich*te* weg	(the illuminated road)
*De verlich*ten* weg*en*	(the illuminated roads)
De verlich*te* weg*en*	(the illuminated roads)

When children are affected indeed in spelling verbal adjectives by plural formation of verbs, and add the plural morpheme *–en* to verbal adjectives (phenomenon 1 in table 11), this even could affect the spelling of regular adjectives in noun phrases with plural (phenomenon 2 in table 11).

Table 11. *Possible phenomena of interference.*

Phenomenon 1

Applying plural formation on verbal adjectives in case of adjacent plural noun (error)

*De verlichte*n* wegen	Learner adds erroneously a plural *n* in verbal ad-
(the illuminated roads)	jectives, following the rule for verbal/noun plural
*De verbrede*n* wegen	formation
(the broadened roads)	

Phenomenon 2

Regression: Applying plural formation on regular adjectives (error)

*De groenen schoenen	(the green shoes): the *n* in groenen seems to indi-
instead of	cate plural (error).
De groene schoenen	

5.2 The power of plural, Case II: Findings

In this study, we distinguished between five categories of verbal adjectives, assuming different levels of complexity (Van Dort-Slijper, Rijlaarsdam, & Breedveld, 1998). For this chapter, a detailed explanation of the five categories is not necessary: our focus here is on the effect of plural of nouns on verbal and regular adjectives. Here we confine to present the results. It is shown that besides main effects of grade $(F (2, 154) = 7.11, p = . 001)$ and spelling category $(F (4, 151) = 46.70, p = .000)$, an interaction between grade and spelling category is significant $(F (8,151) = 3.66, p = .000)$. Next step is to compare the adjacent categories for each of the three grades. For grade 7 and 8 no significant difference between the scores on spelling category 1 and 2 is found, but the other comparisons confirm the hypothesis for differentiating between the categories: category 1 and 2 > category 3; category 3 > category 4; category 4 > category 5. So for each of these two age grades there is an increasing struggle from category 1 to 5. Grade 6 appears to be insensitive to this pattern: only the difference between spelling category 1 and 2 is significant, in the expected direction. None of the other adjacent pairs shows this pattern. If we drop the restriction of adjacency, then category 1 proves to be easier than the other four categories. So with regards to difficulty, students in grade 6 distinguish only two categories: category 1 ('no problem') versus all other categories.

Quite a remarkable finding is that the scores of the three grades in category 4 and 5 do not significantly differ: obviously the level of difficulty of these categories is the same for the three age grades: the low to moderate scores (30-60% correct) indicates that even grade 7 and 8 are experiencing a learning phase. In the other three categories grade 6 scores lower than grade 7 (category 2) and grade 8 (category 1, 2 and 3).

The most important finding is that indeed an increasing level of difficulty in grade 7 and 8 exists: category 1 equals category 2, category 1 and 2 > category 3;

category 3 > category 4; category 4 > category 5. Grade 6 seems to be insensitive to this pattern. Because of these differences in relative difficulty, we present the data for subsequent analyses including the factor spelling categories.

5.2.1   Phenomenon 1: Overgeneralisation in Verbal Adjectives

Figure 3 shows the data of three grades (grade 6, 7 and 8) on the production task: the percentage of errors for Verbal Adjectives. Errors are those items with –en (indicating a plural) instead of –e. Increasing lines indicate an effect of plural. The most dominant type of lines is a rather steep line, indicating that in Verbal Adjectives errors were made when the adjacent noun was plural. Grade 8 withdraws from this general pattern.

Main effects of grade (F (2, 154) = 6.84, p = .001) and number (F(1, 154) = 7.59, p = .007) were found. The interaction between grade and number is not statistical significant. This implies that the effect of number is the same for each Grade. In addition, an effect of spelling category is observed (F (4, 151) = 17.92, p = .000) and an interaction between number and spelling category (F (4, 151) = 8.90, p = .000), which indicates that the effect of number is different for different categories of adjectives.

Concluding we can say that in the spelling of Verbal Adjectives, the power of plural is observed. Children seem to implement the number agreement rule from the verbal system to verbal adjectives, and implement number agreement in adjectives, although such a rule does not exist in Dutch.

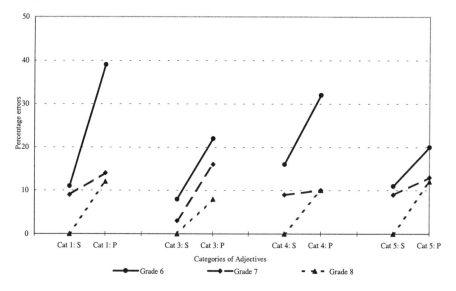

Figure 3. The power of plural. Effects of number in adjacent noun on number of errors in verbal adjectives in production task.

5.2.2   Phenomenon 2: Regression on Regular Adjectives

Figure 4 shows the percentage errors of the three age grades on the production task in Regular Adjectives. Again almost all lines are increasing, indicating an effect of number from the adjacent noun.

An effect of grade (F (2, 154) = 7.76, p = .001) and number (F (1,154) = 53.76, p = .000) is found, as well as an interaction between grade and number (F (2, 154) = 5.09, p = .007): the effect of number varies from grade to grade.

In order to get insight on the effect of number within each of the grades we compared the scores of the plural and singular items per grade per category. No effect is found in category 3 and 5 for any of the three grades. In category 1 and 4 only grade 6 seems to be sensitive to the difference in number. In other words, for regular adjectives, the plural of nouns does not confuse grades 7 and 8. Grade 6 is sensitive to plural, but not in all cases. The power of plural on regular adjectives only plays a role in Grade 6, for two types of adjectives.

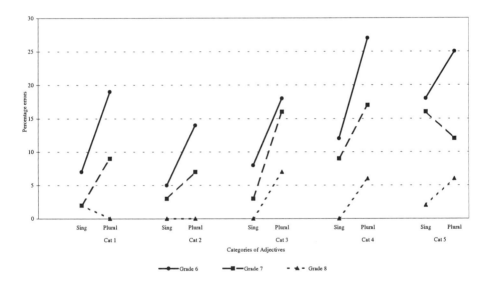

Figure 4. The Power of plural. Effects of number in adjacent noun on number of errors in regular adjectives in production task.

6   GENERAL DISCUSSION

In this chapter, we reported data on interference phenomena in the spelling of adjectives, derived from verbs (verbal adjectives) and material nouns (material adjectives). We tried to find support for our hypothesis that children are affected by the power of plural: they construe a number agreement rule for adjectives, while in Dutch no such rule exists, in spoken nor in written communication.

From time to time, it seems difficult to hang on to the rule of adjective formation in Dutch, which in essence is a very easy rule. Children master the spelling rule at a certain age, and yet, later, in some circumstances, some of them apply plural-formation rules, although such a rule does not exist and is not taught. When the spelling of special cases of adjectives is introduced – material and verbal adjectives – children appear to construe number agreement rules. In the case of material adjectives, this construction is stimulated because the adjectival and plural number morpheme (*–en*) are similar and homophone. In the case of verbal adjectives, the construction is a consequence of the obvious functional relationship between verbs (with plural *–en*) and verbal adjectives. We even reported indications of regression in the case of verbal adjectives: the number in the adjacent noun confused students from Grade 6 in *regular* adjectives, the spelling of which was already mastered.

Children are juggling with different rule systems, and have problems with defining the application domains of the rules. They learn to master a rule for plural formation of nouns and verbs in Dutch, which requires that children accept that they have to write an *n* to indicate the plural, while the *n* is hardly ever heard in normal, fluent speech. Then children learn to master the rule for adjective formation, which is non-sensitive to number. They differentiate between the plural of nouns and verbs on the one hand (*–en),* and adjectives (*–e*) on the other hand, even though no difference in sound is heard, and the *n* in *–en* does not play a decisive role in distinguishing the plural and the singular form of nouns. Compare: *deur* (singular: *'door'*); *de-uren* (plural, *'doors'*) and **deure,* which is incorrectly spelt, but sufficient in spoken and written speech to distinguish the singular and the plural form.

But when new types of adjectives are being mastered, material adjectives and verbal adjectives, the semantics of plural interferes. In material adjectives, children make more mistakes in the singular form, because of the similarity of the plural noun and the material adjective morpheme. In verbal adjectives, they make more errors in the plural form, because they apply verbal morphology instead of adjectival morphology rules. And, as we said before, even regression of the performance on regular adjectives was found.

It seems that children in Dutch, a language without number agreement rules between nouns and adjectives, under some conditions construe a number agreement rule. In this rule, the singular form is the default, the plural the marked form. Therefore, we called the phenomena we described as resulting from the power of plural. But the particular language studied might bias this. In a language in which the plural form is the default, the same effect – establishing a non-existing agreement rule – could be called the power of singular. More important is the developmental perspective: why do children create intermediate agreement rules, when nobody instructs them to create them, and when they are so obviously incorrect? And under which circumstances do they construct these rules? The 'why' question could be answered by referring to the semantics of plural. Jaffré and David (1999: 16) show that French children create plural spellings even when these forms do not exist. From the metalinguistic talk during spelling and revision actions it is clear that children add marks for plural because of the meaning, which can not be heard in spoken language

(French: o*n vend *beaucoups de chose* (They sell *many's) (Note that the –*s* at the end of beaucoup is not audible, and incorrect.). Reference to plurality is an important reason for children to mark words with a plural morpheme; even the plural word does not exist. And words in the proximity of such a word are also reigned by plurality in children's naïve linguistic reasoning (Jaffré & David, 1999:18). The when-question has to do with developmental learning cycles of generalising and differentiating. When new 'near-to-the-old' spelling problems are introduced, at least two learning goals are fought for: mastering the new rule, which at the same time requires a search for redefining the application domain of the older rules.

For us, this clearly illustrates that tradition in sequencing learning matters makes more problems than necessary. We refer to the tradition that exercises with verbal adjectives are offered very late in primary school, after the rules of verbal morphology are taught. Sometimes, the spelling of verbal adjectives is presented as a special case of the spelling of verbs. It is no wonder that some children associate verbal adjectives with verbs. This is unnecessary, while in Dutch the spelling of adjectives has nothing to do with the spelling of verbs. It would be far better if the spelling of verbal adjectives were included in the lessons on adjectives, long before the interfering spelling rules for past tenses are taught.

In this chapter, no attempt was made to separate the acquisition from the schooling effect. Part of the phenomena reported could be attributed to traditional sequencing of learning matters, but most of it belongs to a regular process of learning. Children try to master rules, and try to exploit them: to find the boundaries of the domain of application. New rules ask for a redefinition of the domain of application of the older rule. For Dutch, we found some support for this process for adjectives: it seems that plural of noun influences the spelling of special cases of adjectives very strongly. The question is to what extent this phenomenon is language bound. We do not assume that the power of plural is a special feature of Dutch.

From the studies reported here, we got some indications that the sensitivity to interference is bound by level of development. We found for normal adjectives grades 7 and 8 are not confused by the plural of nouns. Grade 6 is sensitive to plural, but not in all cases. For material adjectives, all three grades were sensitive to the interference of the plural number in adjacent nouns. Neither Grade level 6 nor 7 were sensitive to the plural of the adjacent nouns, when they were spelling regular adjectives. But both grades were sensitive to the interference when spelling material adjectives. Interference indicates a learning phase. From this perspective, signs of interference are positive: they indicate learning. However, the problem for teachers and textbook writers is, how to minimalise the rate of interference, how to anticipate false rule-building, how to prevent stabilising false rules, how to use these interferences in the learning process. The power of plural seems to be everywhere, at least in Dutch: how do you teach children to handle the overwhelming power of plural when they become good spellers?

AUTHORS' NOTE

We thank the anonymous reviewers and the editors for their encouraging and challenging remarks, and Inge Weel (Weel, 1995; Weel, Van Dort-Slijper, & Rijlaarsdam, 1996), Maaike Ditzel (Ditzel 1996; Ditzel, Van Dort-Slijper, & Rijlaarsdam, 1996) and Eva Breedveld (Breedveld, 1997; Rijlaarsdam, Van Dort-Slijper, & Breedveld, 1998) for the effort they put in the studies on which this chapter is based. Special thanks go to Liliana Tolchinsky who inspired us to take the notion of agreement into account when interpreting the underlying processes, which lead to the performances we observed. Ton Koet inserted the phonetic transcriptions, and Laura Rijlaarsdam-Main checked the text linguistically: thanks Ton, thanks Laura!

Correspondence to Gert Rijlaarsdam, Graduate School of Teaching and Learning, University of Amsterdam, Wibautstraat 2-4, 1091 GM Amsterdam, The Netherlands (rijlaars@ilo.uva.nl).

TALKING AND WRITING: HOW DO CHILDREN DE-VELOP SHARED MEANINGS IN THE SCHOOL SET-TING?

PILAR LACASA*, BEATRIZ MARTÍN DEL CAMPO**, & AMALIA REINA*

*University of Cordova, Spain; **University of Castilla-La Mancha, Spain*

Abstract. This study aims to explore how the learning and development of writing take place in the class-room. Adopting a Vygotskian perspective two specific questions form the point of departure of our work. First, we explore the development of writing texts as a social process involving conversations with teach-ers and peers and carried out by the appropriation and recontextualization of other persons' oral texts rather than pure and individual invention; second, we consider how different ways of organizing social relationships are reflected in children's writing processes and products when they learn to write at school. In order to explore the setting of writing teaching in the school context, we acted as participant observers in the classroom where children and their teacher collaborated in a writing workshop. We concentrate here on analyzing the activities of six children (three girls and three boys) who were planning how to write descriptive essays in a group. In this process, we analyze two situations in which the group is de-signing guidelines for writing a descriptive text about two different pictures. The crucial difference be-tween these situations is that in one of them, the participants are six students and their teacher, whereas in the other, the six students are working alone. The video and audio recordings of discussions during col-laboration were transcribed and examined in order to explore 'moment-to-moment social constructions of meaning'. The main objective of this analysis is to identify the kind of conversational activities the stu-dents and the teacher perform in these two situations, and to determine how these activities produce dif-ferent ways of dealing with the joint task of planning an outline. In order to explore the classroom organi-zation we defined a category system that permits us to compare the two situations described above. Re-sults show that there is a striking contrast between the development and learning environments, depend-ing on whether the teacher was present or absent. The challenge for us to explore in further studies is whether the only context in which children can reverse interactional roles with the same intellectual con-tent, *i.e.* giving directions as well as following them and asking questions as well as answering them, is when they are alone with their peers.
Key words: social context, writing development, literacy practices, discourse analysis, adult-child inter-action, writing in the classroom, descriptive texts.

1   INTRODUCTION

This chapter approaches literacy learning and development as a varied and multi-variate phenomenon that takes place in social and cultural contexts. Following Vy-

133

L. Tolchinsky (ed.), Developmental Aspects in Learning to Write, 133–162.
© 2001 *Kluwer Academic Publishers. Printed in the Netherlands.*

gotsky (1978, 1986) this statement has a double meaning (Wells, 1999). *First, development of the individual cannot be understood without taking into account his or her interaction with other people.* In that context, we need to mention a variety of internal development processes that can operate only when the child is learning to write by interacting with people in very different environments; more specifically, learning to write requires the child to develop a more conscious and intentional stance with respect to the realization of meaning activity; from that perspective, we must consider that thought occurs in simultaneous, whole images that do not necessarily coincide with units of language, and that it must therefore be partitioned, recreated, and completed as it is transformed into words (Cazden, 1996). *Secondly, the social environment is itself influenced by the wider culture*, which varies according to the forms and organization of activity practiced and the material and semiotic tools employed; that is, the contexts of writing are shaped by the group norms of differently situated writing communities (Scribner & Cole, 1981). Focusing on the development of writing in the social context, particularly revealing studies have shown that the nature and uses of written language are related to specific and varied social conditions and practices (Moll & Kurland, 1996; Schultz, 2000). In this chapter, we focus on the classroom, where life is organized into hierarchies of positions, which are associated with various kinds of prerogatives that differentiate between teachers and pupils.

Adopting the former perspective, the overall aim of this study is to explore in an open-ended way how children learn to write by composing a text as they work in small groups, paying special attention to how their collaboration is integrated with adult roles. Two other specific questions form the point of departure of our work. First, we explore the development of a written text as a social process involved in conversations and carried out by appropriation and recontextualization of other persons' oral texts rather than pure and individual invention; second, we consider how different ways of organizing social relationships are reflected in children's written processes and products when they learn to write at school. In the sections that follow we focus on a Vygotskian approach to writing and then review research in which adult-child and child-child interactions have been studied in educational settings as a process governed by 'conversational' rules. In the last part of the section we consider the implications of our work for the understanding of the writing process and its relationships with discourse practices, in particular the role played by participants in the situation.

2 WRITING AS A SOCIAL PROCESS: A VYGOTSKIAN PERSPECTIVE

Recent research has approached writing from a social and contextual perspective. Schultz (2000) has recently suggested that the development of writing is related to its social, local and historical context (Goldblatt, 1995); moreover, learning to write is reflective of the classroom curriculum and educational methods employed (Freedman, 1994; Lensmire, 1994a) and is shaped by social interactions (Dyson, 1993; Dyson, 1997; Flower, 1994; Schultz, 1997). This study assumes that children assimilate the social speech and written forms of their culture by means of an active process of transformation, while at the same time assuming greater control over their own activities. Written language is regarded as a historical and cultural accomplishment that facilitates the emergence of a higher form of language than oral language. The interiorization of this new form of language produces higher psychological processes related to abstract thinking processes.

To talk about writing from a Vygotskian perspective involves reflecting on the implications of this linguistic activity, both in the human psychological system and in a variety of fields of human activity. Vygotsky (1987) understood language as something more than an individual capacity; in this perspective, the relevance of language rests on its use as a tool which develops historically in contexts of social interaction, and on how such use produces effects in the interpsychological domain. One of the features of written language is the absence of an interlocutor. This makes writing a more abstract task than talking. Oral language is regulated by a dynamic situation with an interlocutor present, but in written language we have to create the equivalent situation and represent our audience internally. Following Vygotsky, this feature has two important consequences for the development of written language.

First, from a structural point of view, an absent audience produces a change, from dialogic language structures, which create the communication purpose dynamically through an exchange of statements, to monologic structures, in which the motivation to produce the message is neither external nor tacit, but internal and explicit. Vygotsky said that in this sense, monologue is much more difficult than dialogue, and comes later in development (Wertsch, 1991).

Second, from a syntactic and semantic point of view, the absence of an interlocutor creates the need to produce messages that are explicit enough to be self-explanatory. Written messages have to create the communicative context themselves, in order to facilitate audience comprehension. This makes it necessary to elaborate semantic content voluntarily and consciously, and to select syntactic structures carefully; the writer has to take into account the knowledge that she or he shares with the audience.

Written language is therefore a different linguistic process from spoken language, and the difference between them is the same as that between spontaneous, non-voluntary and non-conscious activities on the one hand, and abstract, voluntary and conscious activities on the other (Vygotsky, 1934/1987). However, even oral and written language involve different processes; Vygotskian researchers (Baker-Sennet, Matusov, & Rogoff, 1992; Floriani, 1994; Higgins, Flower, & Petraglia, 1992; Lacasa, Pardo, Herranz-Ybarra, & Martín, 1995) have used the joint planning of texts to study the learning of writing and they assume that dialogue can function as an ideal bridge to assimilate the monological and abstract features of writing. Following these researchers, the aim of this chapter is related to the analysis of the conversations that take place when children plan texts together. The development of writing texts is explored as a social process, involved in conversations and carried out by appropriation and recontextualization of others' oral texts rather than pure and individual invention.

3   WRITING IN THE CLASSROOM WITH TEACHER AND PEERS

In line with Vygotskian perspectives, recent research in educational settings or work places considers writing as part of everyday activities both in school and outside it. For example, Wells (1990; 1999) attempts to unite activity and discourse theories in order to approach classroom activities that can be seen both as goal-directed actions and as processes involving interaction as a central component, all of them including participants and the texts and artifacts that are utilized in carrying out the action. In that context, what are the discursive practices that children appropriate at school while they are learning to write? One of the most common forms of organization within the classroom consists of a teacher and a number of pupils who function as a single, large group. In this situation, control of the pupils' attention is of particular concern to the teacher because, from his or her point of view, if the students are not sufficiently focused, they are quite certainly not learning. Teachers have a number of means of focusing their pupils' attention on the communication processes by which the curriculum is transmitted. These tools include organizing interactions in the context of small groups that include the teacher, and in which he engages in focused interaction with part of the class. These small groups may work unsupervised while the adult works with other groups (Philips, 1983). According to Rogoff (1998), the literature on school restructuring suggests that for children to learn through collaboration requires a rethinking of the role of adults in children's learning and in relation to each other. It is often difficult for teachers to guide rather than to control children's behaviour when they are attempting to move from traditional teacher-controlled whole-class activities to cooperative learning activities. From Rogoff's perspective, children's interactions with peers and with adults can be regarded as involving complementary, multifaceted roles in shared sociocultural activities, rather than contrasting influences. In the sections which follow we focus on two kinds of conceptual and empirical work; first, research on how teachers support pupils working in the classroom, and second, how peers help each other when they create text collectively. Of particular interest for us are those studies that focus on discursive practices and the mutual roles of children and adults in structuring social interactions.

3.1 Working with the teacher: the adult's role

Going into depth on the question of adult-child interaction in the classroom, Rogoff (1998) focuses on various traditions that have addressed the problem of how experts structure novices' engagement in activities (Brown & Palincsar, 1989). According to her, much of this work has focused on the means of support and stimulation that experts provide to novices, using three kinds of methods in particular: scaffolding, Socratic dialogue and tutoring. The concept of scaffolding, which is rooted in the concept of zone of proximal development, is a specific technique that focuses on what experts provide for novices, with individuals as the basic units of analysis. Of special interest in this process is how the tutor's efforts are related contingently to the successes and failures of the novice. Socratic dialogue also involves instructional moves that are oriented to pupils' growing understanding. These techniques include encouraging pupils to specify and evaluate their working hypotheses, suggesting that they should systematically develop hypotheses and counter-examples to test their conclusions. In this technique, the teacher or another student who guides learning supports the use of information by the learner; for example, he or she may continue with an explanation, repeat it or reformulate it. In other words, teachers introduce a collaborative complex of statements as a means of finding out what their students have understood. Finally, tutoring can be characterized by its flexibility of support and shared understanding with the learner. In this context, Rogoff stresses the importance of considering the mutual roles of expert and novice when they collaborate and the relationships and leadership of both adults and children in initiating and managing their shared endeavours.

Several researchers with roots in a psycholinguistic perspective go into some depth on discursive processes as employed in the classroom. More than twenty years ago Mehan (1979) and Sinclair & Coulthard (1975) referred to IRF (Initiation Response Feedback). Cazden (1988) and Mercer (1995), for example, also looked at how often a teacher used questions to which they almost invariably knew the answers, perhaps because they needed to know whether the pupils knew the answers too, and also because by introducing questions they could evaluate pupils' level of knowledge. It is well known, however, that there is some controversy in educational research about the use of this strategy for guiding the construction of knowledge. Wood (1988), for example, argues that teachers' questions often constrain and limit the direction of classroom discussions in quite unfortunate ways. From that perspective, teachers may actually inhibit their pupils' intellectual activity. But there are also opinions that lean in the opposite direction. Cazden (1988), for example, considers that the teacher can offer a model that presents roles for the helper to enact. From that perspective, she suggests that the intellectual value of peer interaction in a classroom will be enhanced when the teacher models a kind of interaction that the children can learn to use with each other.

In any case, disagreement is lessened when the functional dimensions of linguistic tools are considered. For example, Mercer (1995) suggests that teachers might usefully consider other techniques when they are trying to teach. For example, they might try making a declarative, open-ended or provocative statement which invites a rejoinder or disagreement, re-elaboration, perplexity and so on (Edwards, 1992). Similarly, Wood's (1988) own research shows that when teachers use other kinds of conversational strategies, such as offering their own reflective observations, this can encourage pupils to do likewise and can generate longer and more animated responses from pupils. Going in a similar direction, O'Connor & Michaels (1996) note the importance of conditions of entry provided by teachers into speech activities associated with complex thinking and problem solving. They explore those practices that can be related to specific thinking processes; for example, the practices of externalizing one's own reasoning, inquiring into the reasoning of others, or comparing positions and perspectives on a particular issue or problem. At the same time, and within a sociocultural perspective, they assume that particular types of complex thinking follow from repeated experience in taking on various roles and stances within recurring social contexts that support those types of intellectual processes.

They wish to know how students come to appropriate and publicly communicate with providers of evidence, makers of distinctions or checkers of facts. Good teachers see it as their responsibility to provide all children with access to these roles in the context of school learning.

Focusing now on specific work on the adult's role when he or she is teaching writing at school, we refer to the Hansen (1986) approach. From this perspective, the only way in which teachers can help their students to learn to write is to become learners and writers themselves. Teachers who do not write cannot sensitively help others learn to write. Teachers of writing must therefore write themselves, because in that way they will tell their students about their writing problems. At that point we may recall the contributions of Scardamalia & Bereiter (1992) on the subject of how professional writers say they are always learning to write; a writing teacher must thus also be a learner, and students appreciate seeing her/him as an apprentice.

To sum up, on the basis of this earlier theoretical support we wish our work to explore how a teacher supports children when they are jointly elaborating an outline to plan a text in the classroom. More specifically, we focus on how the presence of the teacher creates a specific site that enables children to approach the task and that socializes them into particular ways of speaking and thinking.

3.2 Working with peers: collaborative argumentation

Having considered adult-child collaboration in small groups, we now discuss peer-group collaborative interaction and argumentation. According to Rogoff (1998), several studies report that decision-making that occurs in conjunction with a balanced exploration of differences of perspective among peers is most likely to contribute to children's progress in understanding. She reports that peer interaction facilitates children's learning in the classroom by delineating those aspects of cooperative learning that are involved in successful arrangements. From a general point of view, researchers suggest that cooperation is most useful for learning that involves conceptual change. This type of progress comes via the activity of explaining ideas and resolving controversies through attempts to understand and persuade other people. The conceptual advances that are possible in groups are not an automatic outcome of simply placing peers in contact. Cognitive development is likely to require some members or facilitators of the group to consider alternative concepts and information that fit in with what are regarded as concepts or approaches that are more sophisticated.

Focusing on peer interaction, we are especially interested in interactions related to conversation analysis when discourse is considered as a tool that facilitates collaborative argumentation. From that perspective, the literature reports that decision-making that occurs jointly with a balanced exploration of differences of perspectives among peers is most likely to contribute to children's progress in understanding (Light & Butterworth, 1992; Perret-Clermont, Perret, & Bell, 1991). Higgins, Flower, & Petraglia (1992), for example, exploring how children jointly plan and produce outlines, report that peer discussion help to externalize the writer's thinking and to make pupils' ideas and writing processes more available for scrutiny. Moreover, addressing a peer may give writers an opportunity to articulate their reasoning and perhaps become aware of shortcomings and strategies they did not think of on their own. In any case, even if such interaction can heighten students' awareness of their writing plans and choices, awareness itself may not ensure that students will reflect critically on those choices. From a similar perspective, Kruger & Tomasello (1986) refer to transactive discussion between peers as an important tool to make argumentation easier. This kind of discussion is defined as one in which an individual uses reasoning that operates on the reasoning of the partner or that significantly clarifies his her own ideas. For example, an individual transacts when he or she extends, paraphrases, refines, completes, or criticizes his partner's reasoning. Adopting this perspective, we wish to explore children's conversations when they plan an outline; we are interested in children's collaborative argumentation when all participants have similar status in the group and all have the opportunity to explore ideas within the context of a set of more equal relationships than is possible with adults.

In order to explore how children's status and role in groups are present during their conversation we follow Floriani's (1994) work, in which she examined ways in which group members constructed texts in and via their interactions. From her point of view, text construction shapes and is shaped by what members do and say, and the situated definitions of texts are constructed by members across events. To interact, members must actively monitor their own and others' actions and language, and interpret these interactions in order to select from their repertories possible ways of interacting that meet the local demands of the situation. This dynamic process of oral and written text construction continues throughout the life of the discursive event. View in this way, text is situational and interactionally defined through the interactional history of members within a particular context. Other research has also focused on the roles of children when they work together; for example (Lensmire, 1994a) focused on the ways in which peer culture can be organized into hierarchies of power and status that influence the production of writing in the context of a writing workshop. From his point of view it would be necessary to explore how micropolitics, traditions and values are present in children's contexts when they learn to write.

In any case, we need to consider with Rogoff (1998) that there are some inconsistencies in the results of research that pairs children with partners who are similar or different in their conversational ability. From her point of view the literature on peer argumentation is not yet coherent enough to allow conclusions about what aspects of peer engagement are most important. Nevertheless, it seems that the engagement of partners with each other's thinking is crucial, and this may at least sometimes be facilitated by differences of perspective or expertise.

4   SETTING AND SOURCES OF DATA

The data presented in this chapter come from a broader study of group essay planning processes (Lacasa et al., 1995). We were interested in the process of writing learning and development as it takes place in a natural context. Fieldwork gives the investigator access to the complete natural phenomenon, although in contrast, selected aspects of this phenomenon could be isolated and studied quantitatively in the laboratory (Page, 2000). However, and following Scribner (1976; 1997) we consider the possibility of introducing a degree of intervention in the naturally occurring situation in order to better understand how the social environment, in particular relationships with teacher and peers, is involved in the writing process when children plan a descriptive text by producing an outline.

Two complete classes of eighth graders who attend a school that belongs to one of Madrid's universities participated in the study. We acted as participant observers in the two classrooms, where children and their teacher were collaborating in a writing workshop that formed part of the language class. In the course of six weeks we observed and videotaped their activities once a week for about an hour and a half. We were present in both groups when they were working with the same teacher, who had ten years of teaching experience and was on excellent terms with his pupils. The children at this school are accustomed to working in groups. The tasks were planned by the teacher and the research team.

Two dimensions need to be taken into account here. The first dimension was the classroom setting in which the children participated in two types of situations on an alternating basis: small-group work and large-group work (activities with the entire class). We were especially interested on how children planned their text when working in small groups *(sessions 1, 3 and 5)*. Differences in the situations included the teacher's presence or absence and the goal of writing one group outline or individual outlines (one per student). However, we also wished to create an audience effect, an important dimension of school practice (Bereiter & Scardamalia, 1987; Bereiter & Scardamalia, 1989; Flower, 1994), and as the teacher suggested, when the children worked as part of the large *group (sessions 2, 4 and 6)*, one of the groups read its essays to the rest of the class in order to discuss and correct them. The sequence of activities over the six weeks for each class is shown in Figure 1.

Week	Activity
1	Peer / teacher interaction / group outline
2	Large group / reading and discussion
3	Peer interaction / group outline
4	Large group / reading and discussion
5	Peer interaction / individual outlines
6	Large group / reading and discussion

Figure 1. Classroom activities during the writing workshop when children plan and produce descriptive text.

A second dimension of the task that we need to take into account was the written production. When the children worked in small groups *(sessions 1, 3 and 5)*, they elaborated outlines of a descriptive text and then wrote individual essays. The reason for choosing a descriptive text was that these are very common in Spanish schools and textbooks. Children are trained in language classrooms to produce different kinds of texts according to specific format, for example, descriptive, narrative and so on. As recommended by Bereiter and Scardamalia (1987), we provided the children with an outside support to facilitate their planning and writing of the essays. In this case, the students were given a photograph to describe. The pictures showed an executive, a landscape and a scene. In an earlier study, we showed that differences in descriptive essay quality vary according to age, depending on the stimulus offered; these differences are seen in fourth graders, but not in eighth graders (Martín-del-Campo, Lacasa, Herranz-Ybarra, & Pardo-de-León, 1994). As mentioned above, children worked in the same group during sessions 1, 3 & 5 and the situations were partially counterbalanced among the groups.

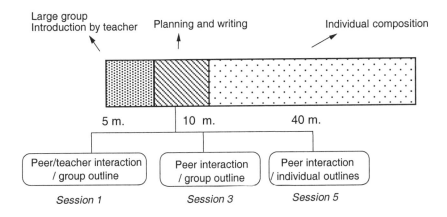

Figure 2. Planning and writing: classroom activities during sessions 1, 3 & 5.

We concentrate here on analyzing the activities of six children (three girls and three boys) when they worked in the small group situations in two settings. The crucial difference between these situations is that in one of them, the participants are six students and their teacher, whereas in the other, the six students are working alone. In this analysis, we found that an important factor in the way students share the meanings of what a guideline and a descriptive text are is the way in which the situations are organized. We have to take into account the possibility that in the situation where students are working with the teacher; he or she is an authority figure, while when the students work alone, they are, in principle, equal partners in the situation, so that they have to negotiate the very organization of the session. These two situations were especially interesting for us according to the results of a previous study (Lacasa *et al.*, 1995), which showed that peer and teacher relationships favor higher levels of planning than the individual situation and they facilitate conceptual planning in addition to content generation. Moreover, it should also be pointed out that, some times, peer interaction situations had been shown to be more favorable than teacher interaction situations when final products were considered, perhaps because when children collaborate in small groups without their teacher, their level of participation is much higher. This was less frequent in groups where the teacher normally organized the activities and children participation decreased. These reasons oriented our research to explore in deep the two situations by adopting a micro-ethnographic perspective that pays attention to discourse processes (Gee & Green, 1998; Jacob, 1988; Jacob, 1997). Finally, we need to point out that we had chosen a specific group considering the specific order in which the two successive settings where introduced: first, children worked with their teacher and second without him; the reason for that choice was related to the possibility of observing models of activity offered by the teacher and assimilated by children.

5   DATA ANALYSIS

The video and audio recordings of discussions during collaboration were transcribed and examined in order to explore 'moment-to-moment social constructions of meaning'. The content of the outlines was also analysed in order to identify relationships between each child's participation during the planning part of the session and their final outline. We will try to explore the differences in the conversational organisation of both situations and reflect on the importance of this factor in this organisation and in the way the outline is constructed within a group. Following Hicks (1996a, 1996b) and Floriani (1994), we use a methodology that combines the study of children's emergent participation in social and discursive activities with the study of their completed texts. Both oral and written qualitative analyses were carried out in order to capture the dynamic nature of text construction by considering 'text' as a written form of language including the oral and visual texts and the social action of members of the group. Central to this view of text construction is an understanding of the ways in which the construction process shapes and is shaped by the actions of members. We thus need to consider what members do in order to participate in this process in socially appropriate ways.

   We take also into account studies of conversation in different institutional settings from the perspective of Conversation Analysis (Atkinson and Drew, 1979; Drew and Heritage, 1992). In this perspective, there is a traditional distinction between formal and informal institutions, based on the influence of participants' social roles on the forms of talk in which they engage (Hutchby & Wooffitt, 1998). In this sense, the kinds of activities that participants can perform on a conversation are ways of 'making an institution'. The analysis developed from this perspective has shown that the social role of participants in institutional conversations has to do with the kind of conversational activities they perform. From this point of view, the notion of 'statement type pre-allocation', proposed by Atkinson and Drew (1979), has some relevance. Following Hutchby and Wooffitt (1998):

> 'Statement type pre-allocation means that participants, on entering the setting, are normatively constrained in the types of statement they may take according to their particular institutional roles. Typically, the format involves chains of question and answer sequences, in which the institutional figure asks the questions and the witness, pupil or interviewee is expected to provide the answers. This format is pre-established, and norma-

tive rules operate which mean that participants can be constrained to stay within the boundaries of the question and answer framework.' (p. 149)

In this sense, the presence of the teacher makes students, and the teacher himself, orienting themselves towards an institutional context, the classroom, in which participants perform specific kinds of conversational activities. As mentioned above, peers working in groups utilise more discussion-oriented conversational activities.

The main objective of this analysis is to identify the kind of conversational activities the students and the teacher perform in both situations, and to determine how these activities produce different ways of confronting a joint task: that of planning an outline. These activities were defined in relation to the role that the *conversational turns* had in the development of the conversation. Conversations were analyzed with the aid of a computer-assisted text analysis program (NUD*IST). This software is designed to manage non-numerical data, and it permits long conversations like those we needed to analyze to be managed.

We closely followed suggestions made by Rogoff (1990) and Wells, Chang, & Blake (1992) in specifying the conditions for the units of analysis. The work of these authors can be summarized in three points: a) individual activities cannot be separated from the context in which they take place; b) activities are organized according to goals and their meaning must be interpreted on the basis of these goals; and c) sentences must be interpreted in the context within which they are stated and in relation to the goals of the subjects participating in conversation.

Our unit of conversation exploration was the individual utterance. In order to define this unit we focus on the contribution of Tomlin, Forrest, Pu, and Kim (1997) to the idea of thematic continuity.

'Despite individual variation in the formulation of definitions and the specific terms defined, there are essentially three basic ideas of what constitutes a clause level theme or topic: 1) the theme is what the sentence is *about*, 2) the theme is the *starting point* of the sentence, and 3) the theme is the *center of attention* for the sentence' (Tomlin *et al.*, 1997: 85)

We also need to remember that, from that perspective, the turns of individual participants during the conversation process may include more than one utterance, especially in the teacher's speech. Utterances were coded by observing the onset of the next message, and by observation of prosodic and non-verbal cues. From this perspective, conversations have been analyzed that consider the participants' framework as a sequence of utterances enacted around a set of schemata in relation to some communicative goal (Givon, 1989; Gumperz, 1981). We assume that in a piece of connected discourse, one referent emerges as central, this being the one dealt with by the propositions in the discourse. This global significance of one referent affects choices made at the clause level; that is, the clause level theme is in some way a local reflection of some higher level unit of discourse, something like a paragraph or episode.

Table 1. Category systems: elements in the instructional conversation.

Common categories founded for the two classroom situations

Category	Definition.
Questions	Statements oriented to asking for a general answer. Moreover, the same person introduces question and answer. On other occasions, questions are introduced as hypotheses.
Answers	Utterances that follow questions and refer to them.
Repetition	Expressions that repeat exactly what was said previously by the same person or another.
Connected Discourse	Utterances complementing a previous one and expressed by another participant. A clear contribution to continuity in the discourse.
Revoicing	A particular kind of re-utterance of a pupil's or teacher's contribution by another participant in the discussion.
Disagreement	Disagreement expressed without introducing any reasons one's own opinion.
Objection	Disagreement expressed by means of arguments.
Statements	Proposals that offer new ideas about the task, providing relevant elements to be included in the outline. Limitation of a specific term or concept in order to follow the conversation.

Specific categories founded in the two classroom situations: Pupils' interaction with the teacher in a small group

Dividing the task	One of the participants organizes the task by introducing several steps in order to elaborate the outline. These utterances may be expressed as orders.
Evaluation	The teacher or one of the students assesses specific contributions from other participants by providing feedback.
Giving Examples	Providing specific contents to be included in the outline or in the final text, related to a more general idea expressed in a previous participant's contribution.
Instructions	The teacher provides direct teaching of a skill or concept in order to elaborate the outline.

Students interaction in small group

Control	Student's utterances oriented to organize the group as a whole or to reorient the conversation in order to achieve agreement between the participants. Attempt to activate the group to begin or to keep on with the task, that is, to focus on writing the outline.
Agreement	Assents to the contribution of another participant.
Justification	Provision of reasons that explain own proposal.
Argumentation	Express not only of disagreement but also provision of reasons for other proposal.
Edition	One of the students practices aloud text's paragraphs, raising intonation intentionally to differentiate a story from a descriptive text.

In order to explore the classroom organization we defined a category system that permits us to compare the two situations described above. In the first, the teacher engages in focused interaction with a part of the class, while in the other, boys and girls interact without the teacher's guidance.

It is important to make it explicit that these categories were defined on the basis of a double criterion: deductively, looking at earlier research on classroom discourse (Cazden, 1988; Edwards & Mercer, 1987; Mercer, 1995; O'Connor & Michaels, 1996), and inductively, focusing on the conversations that actually took place in the two situations observed. This explains why our category system (see Table 2) includes common and specific categories for the two situations and provides an overview of the repertoire of ways of speaking that were identified in the classroom. In other words, even if we begin to explore the two situations using the same category system, not all of the categories appear in both situations; that is, looking at the two settings, specific categories were related to each of them. For example, in this school and this specific setting, when the teacher was present such categories as dividing the task, evaluation and so on, were present; other categories appear only when children were working in group without their teacher; for example, those statements related to the social control of the group or justification of their own proposals. From our point of view, what that could demonstrate would be the relationships between ways of talking and the particular situations in which children collaborate with or without their teacher when they work in a school task. In any case, we consider this study as an exploratory way for understanding collaboration between adults and peers at school, and new studies are needed to go into this topic in more depth.

6   RESULTS: THE WAYS OF TALKING

Two distinct types of analysis were carried out in relation to the two situations: a) we examined conversational activities implicit in both settings and we carried out basic statistical analyses in order to show the differences between them in relation to the kinds of talk used by the participants; b) we performed a qualitative analysis, reflecting the role of these activities in the literacy task, to plan an outline.

Conversational analysis enables us to verify that while there are no major differences in the length of time devoted to drawing up the outlines (teacher 9:26 minutes; group 12:11minutes), the number of turns taken is much greater when the children interact as a group (teacher session: 139 utterances; student session: 310 utterances). Three aspects should be kept in mind in order to understand this data, as shown in Table 1: a) the teacher's turns are much longer since he introduces a variety of ideas in each and the children do not always comment on them; b) it is perhaps more difficult for the entire group to reach agreement when only one outline has been assigned and the teacher is not present because the children's relationships are symmetrical; and c) consideration must be given to the mechanisms underlying the group discussions if we are to understand how changes in conversational content are generated. We wish to explore more deeply the differences between these two settings in order to know how adults' and children's roles are articulated. In fact, we try to examine the dialectic between what is 'inside' the child and what is 'out there' in culture as present during the conversations when children are learning to write in the classroom. To achieve this goal, neither analyses of textual products nor inferential studies of cognitive processes alone are sufficient. Rather, 'thick descriptions' (Geertz, 1973) of overlapping textual contexts need to be merged with detailed interpretive approaches to the individual child when she or he (re)constructs meaning within specific contexts.

Table 2. Teacher and students setting: number of conversational turns. Percentages and frequencies (between brackets).

Participants	Teacher Session	Students' Session
David	6 (9)	22 (69)
Abi	11 (15)	16 (49)
Puy	8 (11)	20 (61)
Julia	9 (12)	19 (58)
Hector	9 (12)	17 (53)
Helena	6 (9)	6 (20)
Teacher	51 (71)	
Total	100 (139)	100 (310)

Looking at our data, we observe that practices can produce a specific environment for writing growth; more specifically, we wish to understand if adult and peer interactions conform to stratified hierarchies of power and status which influence the production of writing in the writing workshop. Figure 3 shows how social interaction as present in the children's and adult's discourses seems to define very different settings. That is, when the teacher was present relationships among participants were mediated by discursive practices where questions, answer and instructions were predominant. In contrast, when children were working by themselves control is the most frequent strategy and some others are predominant, for example, statements, disagreements and revoicing.

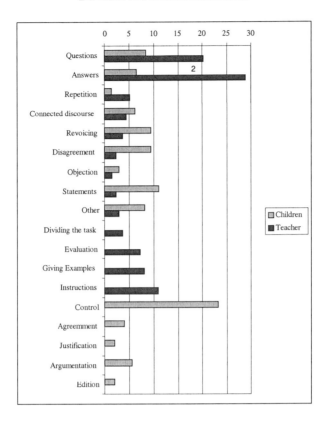

Figure 3. Teacher and students setting. Percentages of the categories defining discursive practices.

Bearing in mind the strategies chosen for dealing with the picture that children were asked to describe (an executive and a landscape), we see some differences when we focus on the conversational content. When the children work with the teacher, the topic of conversation refers sequentially to the essay content and the group stops to make a detailed examination of the physical and psychological characteristics attributed to the character and the setting in which the situation takes place. The conversation then covers the essay characteristics and it ends with a synthesis of how these characteristics can be put into practice when writing. That is, the most of the time is devoted to generating the content and the structure of the final text. When the children work as a group without the teacher, they maintain each topic for a larger number of turns and a longer period. Two major topics are covered in conversation. After an initial approach to the stimulus in which the children limit themselves to naming what is in the picture but without referring to the structure of their final text, they devote almost half the time to relating the scene (a landscape) to the essay to be written, but simply focusing on the content rather than on the structure, as was the case when the teacher was present. They then spend the other half of the session discussing the differences between a story and a description, that is, content and structure are not elaborated together.

6.1 The teacher session

Interaction with the teacher in small groups provides a very interesting orchestration of the group discussion. What we try to show here is how the presence of the teacher creates a specific site for aligning students with each other and with the content of the task involved, while simultaneously socializing them into particular ways of speaking and thinking. The teacher needs to do more than simply make discussion available for students.

Table 3. Pupils interacting with the teacher in a small group. Percentages and frequencies (between brackets).

	Students	Teacher	Total
Questions	7 (10)	13 (18)	20 (28)
Answers	25 (35)	4 (5)	29 (40)
Repetition	2 (3)	3 (4)	5 (7)
Connected discourse	1 (2)	3 (4)	4 (6)
Revoicing	1 (1)	3 (4)	4 (5)
Disagreement	2 (3)		2 (3)
Objection	2 (1)	2 (1)	1 (2)
Statements	1 (1)	1 (2)	2 (3)
Other	3 (4)	1 (2)	3 (4)
Dividing the task	1 (2)	2 (3)	4 (5)
Evaluation	1 (1)	6 (9)	7 (10)
Giving Examples	4 (5)	4 (6)	8 (11)
Instructions		11 (15)	11 (15)
Total	49 (68)	51 (71)	100 (139)

Focusing on Table 3, we observe how the teacher uses certain discourse strategies that do not appear when the teacher is not present. *To give instructions* is one of the most frequent of these (11%) and it is especially important when he tries to organize the children's work at the beginning of the session. From our point of view, this is an example of how constructing knowledge is a process in which power and influence are inevitably exerted, even in very subtle ways.

17. Teacher:	Well, we have to make a guideline, eh,	*Bien, tenemos que hacer un guión,*	INSTRUCTION
	It is important that the whole guideline has a sequence, an order, so that the description that we are going to write	*Eh!, es importante, es importante que todo guión lleve una secuencia, un orden, de modo que la descripción que nosotros vayamos*	INSTRUCTION

could be a little bit systematic	*a hacer sea un poco sistemática.*	
I want you to talk too, O.K.?, because I don't want to guide the whole guideline..	*Quiero que habléis vosotros también, eh?, porque no quiero dirigir yo todo el guión.*	INSTRUCTION
So let me see, eh, what basic things could we discuss, and then we can arrange them?	*Entonces vamos a ver, ¿ese...que cosas elementales podríamos tratar, y después ya las arreglaremos?*	QUESTION

As we can see in this extract, the teacher is establishing the task's goal and its organization giving specific *instructions*. He is, in a sense, designing the situation in advance. In his intervention, the teacher states two main ideas: first, how a guideline has to be in relation to the text that it suppose to guide, and second, how students should participate in the situation. By doing so, the teacher seems to be conscious of his own role in guiding the students' writing activities even while he wants the boys and girls to participate actively. That is, the teacher seems to be interested in helping children to generate and organize ideas when they plan a text all together, but looking at the content of the conversation it is difficult to say that the general ideas coming from the teacher could be assimilated by children and re-elaborated when they write the outline and later, their own text. Adopting a Vygotskian theoretical perspective the question would be how this kind of practice of guidance can contribute to learning and development of writing and more specifically, to create a zone of proximal development where children develop writing as a psychological tool contributing to the development of mental activity (Cazden, 1996; Vygotsky, 1978/1986).

Looking at Table 3 we also notice that other strategies are used by the teacher and that *questions and answers* are the most frequent (*questions*: teacher, 13%; children 7%; *answers*: teacher, 4%; children 25%;). The data also show that it is the teacher who asks the greatest number of questions, and that a large proportion of the answers come from the children, maybe more than one child replies to the teacher. Moreover, sometimes the teacher's questions are supported by teacher's *revoicing* (3%) and/or *evaluation* (6%) as in the following excerpt.

36.Teacher	What else can we say?	*¿Que más cosas podíamos decir?*	QUESTIONS
37.Julia	The environment	*El ambiente*	ANSWERS
38.Teacher	The environment, a bit about what is around him, which surrounds him to the	*El ambiente un poco que le rodea, que rodea al...*	REVOICING
39.Hector	The background	*El fondo*	REVOICING
40.Teacher	But not only that	*Pero no solo*	EVALUATION
41.Julia	First the table and then the flowers	*Primero la mesa y después las flores*	CONNECTED DISCOURSE

| 42.Teacher | In other words, you might say, his immediate environment and then the more distant | *Osea, tú dices, el ambiente cercano y después el lejano* | REVOICING |

But let us focus on how these strategies are used to guide the children's composition of their outlines and how are they reflected in them. In the above conversation, the teacher tries to introduce a new topic and they will begin to talk about the environment (turn 36 and 37). Two aspects may be observed. First, he supports the children's utterances by using the strategy of reformulating them in order to include his own discussion agenda by establishing a new level of abstraction (turn 42). Secondly, his revoicing is oriented towards guiding the children to make the different parts of their descriptions coherent. If we look the children's outlines (Table 4), we see that many of them relate the concept of the introduction to the environment. For example, Elena, Hector and Julia wrote 'Introduction of the environment', David sketches 'Introduction, environment', Puy and Abigail wrote 'Introduction (environment, setting)'. To sum up, what is observed is that children reproduce the teacher's suggestion, even using the same words.

Table 4. Written outlines interacting with the teacher.

David Martín	Hector Sanchez	Julia Ruiz
Outline	Outline	Outline
- Introduction, environment	- Introduction	- Description of environment
- Description	- Description of environment	(Introduction)
- Ending	- Physical and psychological description	-'....Physical and psychological'
	- Title	- Title
Guión	*Guión*	*Guion*
-Introducción, ambiente	*-Introducción*	*- Descripción del ambiente*
-Descripción	*-Descripción del ambiente*	*(introducción)*
-Final	*-Descripción física y psíquica*	*-'... física y psíquica'*
	-Título	*- Título*
María del Puy Pavón	Elena Ostiz	Abigail Sigüenza
- Introduction (environment, setting),	- Introduction to environment's	Outline:
- Description (physical and psychological)	- Description (physical and psychological)	- Introduction (environment, setting),
Title	- Title	- Physical and psychological
		- Title
- Introducción (ambiente, situación)	*- Introducción del ambiente*	*Guión:*
- Descripción (física y psíquica)	*- Descripción (física y síquica)*	*- Introducción (ambiente, situación)*
- Título	*- Título*	*- Física y psíquica*
		- Título

Following the next stages of the conversation, another extract allows us to understand better how the conversation is organized and how the outlines are produced when the teacher is present. In some respects, the teaching process is very similar to the previous one. After asking two questions (turn 54) and revoicing (turn 56) a child's answer, the teacher proposes *an example*, another kind of strategy used by the teacher (4%). By doing so, he tries to organize the children's outlines, differentiating the psychological and physical aspects of the main character.

54. Teacher:	But what can you suggest at this moment? Why is he frowning?	*Pero tú te podrías plantear en el mismo momento: ¿Por qué tiene las arrugas?*	QUESTION
55. Hector:	He's thinking	*Está pensando*	ANSWER
56. Teacher	Well then, because he is thinking,	*Pues porque está pensando,*	REVOICING
	because he has a problem in his company and his character is a bit depressive, so he is very worried. What are you doing here?	*porque le ha surgido un problema en la empresa y su carácter es un poco depresivo, entonces está muy preocupado. ¿Que es lo que estás haciendo?*	EXAMPLE
	You are trying to mix the physical and the psychological a bit. In come cases this is not easy, you won't always manage to mix them, eh, but you can go on observing and can say: look, here I can mix it and here not.	*Estas intentando mezclar un poco lo físico y la psique. En algunas cosas no será fácil, no en todas vas a tener que mezclar, ¿eh?, pero tú lo puedes ir observando y puedes decir: hombre, aquí la mezclo y aquí no.*	DIVIDING THE TASK
	Do you all understand that this is a psychological description?	*¿Todos entendéis lo que es una descripción psíquica?*	EVALUATION

Finally, and trying to make a synthesis of what happen when children and their teacher elaborate the outline, we can re-explore their conversation in order to better understand the teacher's goals. It seems to us that these goals become evident when we look at the conversational strategies he uses. First, even if the teacher answers pupils' questions, his interventions tend to be longer than theirs, and he often includes instructions (turn 17) or examples (turn 56) in what can be interpreted as *a way of orienting students to a specific text model*, even previously defined in the context of the school knowledge (turn 17). Second, sometimes he responds to what students *say* as the basis for what he says next. This strategy can be interpreted as *one way of introducing the pupils' opinions or to connecting with their ideas*. The teacher confirms the pupil's question by amplifying and reformulating the idea, so that he supports their opinions at the same time he extends their knowledge in several ways. Such ways include situating the conversation at a higher level of abstraction (turn 42) and introducing new ideas or opinions related to the main topic (turn 55). Third, *he tries to elicit relevant knowledge from the students* (turn 40), even when we take into account that it is the teacher who decides what kind of knowledge will have meaning in a classroom context. The main problem for us at this point is to decide if all of these strategies help to create a new zone of proximal development for writing, in which children work by complementing and amplifying their ideas (Hicks, 1996; Wells, 1999); new studies need to go into depth on how children appropriate and internalize their teacher's proposals and how these are included in the children's own writing.

6.2   The student session

As with the teacher session, we observe how this one began. Looking at the following excerpt, we soon see that with the aid of questions and answers, children refer to specific and very concrete elements of the picture, in that case a landscape (turns 41 - 43). They then seem to be conscious of the need to focus on the outline elaboration by establishing the conversation at an abstract level as they did when the teacher was present.

41. Puy	(Indicating the photo) Listen, what are these, little houses, or has something been rubbed out?	*(Señalando la foto) Oye,¿ esto que son, ¿casitas o se ha borrado?*	QUESTION
	See how white it is here!	*¡Mira, lo blanco está ahí!*	STATEMENT
42. David	I think it is a village	*Yo creo que es un pueblo*	CONNECTED DISCOURSE
43. Hector	Her are people who are just about to bathe	*Aquí hay personas que están a punto de bañarse.*	STATEMENT
------			
49. David	Come on, let's make the outline	*Venga, vamos a hacer el guión*	CONTROL
50. Puy	Come on, let's make the outline, let's see	*Venga, vamos a hacer el guión, a ver.*	CONTROL
51. Hector	Let's see, was it 'from the general to the particular or from the particular to the general'?	*A ver, '¿de lo general a lo particular o de lo particular a lo general?'*	QUESTION
52. Julia	Ssss	*Ssss*	CONTROL
53. Hector	From the general to the particular	*De lo general a lo particular*	ANSWER
54. Puy	Does it have to be that way?	*¿que tiene que ver eso?*	QUESTION
55. David	Here there is neither general nor particular!	*¡Aquí no hay general ni particular!*	DISAGREEMENT
56. Puy	Yes, that stone is a particular.	*Sí, la piedra ésta es particular.*	ARGUMENT

Reading the above excerpt, we get the feeling that the children introduce some of the strategies used by the teacher when he was developing the outline. It seems to be quite clear that children wish to introduce general principles in order to organize the descriptive text that they will elaborate later on (turn 51). In that sense, when they were working with their teacher they referred to a general principle for organizing their texts by using a statement; in that case, 'a psychological and physical description' of the main character who appeared in the picture. During the peer interaction session, they were presented with a landscape and they may have needed to look for a similar organizational idea that they expressed as 'from general to specific'.

But let us focus on the most frequent strategies used by children when the teacher was not present. These appear in Table 5. We observe that *control (23%)* and *disagreement (9%)* are the categories with the highest number of utterances. From our point of view, both of these categories could be related to the regulation of social relationships among participants. It is likely that such utterances hardly appeared when the teacher was present because it was he who introduced group regulations, not by using explicit norms but by focusing the attention of the children on the classroom task. In relation to the group organization two comments need to be made.

Table 5. Students' interactions in a small group. Percentages and frequencies (between brackets).

Category	David	Abi	Puy	Julia	Hector	Elena	Total
Questions	2 (6)	3 (10)	1 (2)		2 (7)	0 (1)	8 (26)
Answers	1 (4)	1 (2)	1 (4)	2 (5)	2 (5)		6 (20)
Repetition	0 (1)			1 (2)	0 (1)		1 (4)
Connected discourse	1 (3)	0 (1)	2 (6)	2 (6)	1 (2)	0 (1)	6 (19)
Revoicing	1 (3)	1 (3)	4 (11)	3 (9)	1 (2)	0 (1)	9 (29)
Disagreement	4 (11)	1 (3)	1 (4)	2 (5)	1 (2)	1 (4)	9 (29)
Objection	1 (2)	1 (2)	1 (3)	1 (2)			3 (9)
Statements	2 (7)	1 (4)	1 (4)	3 (8)	3 (8)	1 (2)	11 (34)
Other	2 (8)	1 (4)	1 (3)	1 (4)	2 (6)	1 (2)	8 (25)
Control	5 (17)	4 (11)	5 (15)	3 (10)	4 (11)	2 (8)	23 (72)
Agreement	0 (1)	1 (3)		2 (5)	1 (3)		4 (12)
Justification		0 (1)	1 (2)	0 (1)	1 (2)		2 (6)
Argumentation	2 (5)	1 (4)	2 (5)		1 (2)	0 (1)	5 (17)
Edition	0 (1)		1 (2)	0 (1)	1 (2)		2 (6)
Total	22 (69)	15 (48)	20 (61)	19 (58)	17 (53)	7 (20)	100 (310)

First, comparing children working by themselves and with their teacher, we observe that if control is the most frequent category when the teacher is absent, there are others that play an important role (statements, 8%; disagreements, 9% and revoicing, 9%). The main question is how to interpret this data in relation to the development and learning of the writing process. From our point of view, and looking at the examples that will be presented in the following excerpts, children's use of control is usually explicitly oriented to organizing group relationships, sometimes even when they need to solve specific problems in the group and even vote on how to elaborate the outline. Other strategies focus on discussions of how to elaborate the outline, making explicit the children's own opinions, disagreements or revoicing. In contrast, questions and instructions, *i.e.* the discourse strategies used by the teacher, are usually only and clearly related to the writing process example, we can remember how the teacher introduced the children to the outline elaboration. From our point of view, *the problem is if children's reflections on the discourse processes itself are easy in one or the other setting*; Rogoff's (1998) approach to how children's collaboration can contribute to progress in understanding and conceptual change could illuminate this interpretation. That is, looking at the children's outlines it seems to us that when the teacher was present they include many of the teacher's suggestions without too much re-elaboration from the children's own perspective, and we notice that the children even use the teacher's words; in contrast, when they were working with their peers, their outlines seemed to reflect a process very similar to the one that took place in their conversations. For example, and looking at Puy's productions (see tables 4), we observe how she wrote 'Introduction (environment, setting)' and 'Description (physical and psychological)' when the teacher was present; we interpreted this production as a definition of the concepts that would orient the future text. When she worked with her peers, she wrote 'From the most important to less important' and 'Going in depth into the description by using stylistic resources'; from our point of view she was making explicit a much more open process, among other reasons because she did not refer to any explicit content of the future text. We think that symmetrical relationships and open discussions about what ideas need to be introduced in the outline or in the final text, once they have solved the group's organizational problems, could facilitate a reflective process about their own discursive process as present in the writing situation. In any case, new and more specific studies are needed to look at that topic in more depth.

Another interesting aspect of how social relationships are involved in the writing setting is related to the role that some of the children play when they interact with their peers (Lensmire, 1994a; Lensmire, 1994b). That is, we can explore whether hierarchies of power and status can be present in that situation and how these may influence the children's production of outlines. An important topic here would be how different roles were played by individual children. Looking at the number of interventions as a possible index of these roles we found important differences among them. David's (22%) and Puy's (15%) interventions are much more frequent than those coming from Elena (7%). But what was interesting for us was the difference between Puy (11 interventions, 4%) and David (3 interventions, 1%) in the use of revoicing (O'Connor & Michaels, 1996). To return to their outlines we seem to perceive a greater degree of elaboration on the part of Puy than of David; for exam-

ple, when Puy's wrote 'Going in depth into the description by using stylistic resources', David just wrote 'Going in depth'. In other terms, it seems to us that Puy's
influence on the group may have been more important in the elaboration of ideas
than David's, who may have been more involved with organizational problems.

We now focus on other specific categories that appear when children were working without their teacher. One interesting discourse element during the children's
conversations is *statements*, which are also much more frequent in the student group
(11%) than in the teacher situation (1%). At the same time *questions* (8%) and *answers* (6%) are very often used. *Revoicing* also appears very often in the group situation (group; 9%, teacher; 4%) and, as we will show later, it seems to have several
functions in the learning process when children elaborate their outlines; for example,
when concretizing specific topics, going in depth into a question, supporting the
previous idea, and so on. Once again, following Cazden (1988) we relate those data
to a specific kind of discourse that takes place during peer relationships, the *'exploratory talk'*. When they use it, the learners themselves take responsibility for the
adequacy of their thinking. We can interpret these data by suggesting that those elements of discourse facilitate children's argumentation, and this process happens
much more often when the teacher is absent. In that sense, statements and revoicing
appear when all the children are potential creators of the outline and no one dominates the situation from a position of prestige or authority. From another perspective,
and with reference only to the fact of revoicing, we can also interpret these kinds of
utterances in terms of the fact that children, when they are orally expressing ideas
that they will include in the outline, are aware of the necessity to introduce discourse
transformations in order to move from oral to written language.

Looking at some examples, let see how these strategies are present in the children's
conversation and outlines. After the introductory moments when the children were
discussing the first point of their outline, they talk about whether they would write a
story or a description (turns 144, 152). Perhaps they began to be aware of this possibility when, in an earlier session, they discussed the teacher's ideas about the relationships between a descriptive text and a story, a topic that was very often present
in the classroom situation.

144. David:	From here *we cannot invent any story. Since the stones cannot get married, or anything*	*De aquí no nos podemos inventar ninguna historia. Como no sean las, las piedras que se casan o algo*	JUSTIFICATION
-------			
152. Abigail:	*Shall we do it as a story or a description?*	*¿Lo hacemos en forma de historia o de descripción?*	QUESTION
153. Julia:	A description	*De descripción*	ANSWER
154. Puy:	I don't really under-stand. With David talk-ing here....	*No me estoy enterando. Con David aquí hablando...*	CONTROL

.

155. Abigail:	(addresses Puy) Shall we write a simple description or a story?	(se dirige a Puy) ¿Hacemos descripción simple o en historia?	QUESTION
156. Julia:	Description...	Descripción...	ANSWER
157. David:	Simple, simple.	Simple, simple.	CONNECTED DISCOURSE
158. Hector:	As one wishes, as one wishes	Como quiera uno, como quiera uno	STATEMENT
159. David:	(slapping Hector on the back) No, not as one wishes, we have to write an outline	(pegando a Hector) ¡No, como quiera uno no, que tenemos que hacer un guión	OBJECTION
160. Hector:	The description is how one wishes	¡La descripción es como quiera uno!	DISAGREEMENT
161. David:	No, but the description has to follow the outline, nitwit	No, pero es que la descripción hay que seguir el guión, gilipollas.	JUSTIFICATION
162. Abigail:	Of course	Claro	AGREEMENT

Focusing on the above excerpt, we observe how children use discourse strategies to organize both relationships among themselves and the planning process of the written outline. Abigail is the child who organizes the conversation by introducing two *questions* (turns 152 and 155), the second of these amplifying the idea of the first; she was introducing an alternative about how to write, description or story, even defining some characteristics when she refers to a 'simple description'. Other children *answer* this question by citing just one of the options (turns 153 and 156) or by approving Abigail's proposal. In the same excerpt, we also see how the children interwove references to the text and the way they regulated their relationships within the group (turns 159 and 161).

They then reflected in a much more concrete way on how to elaborate a story related to different elements that appeared in the landscape. What is especially interesting for us in the following excerpt is the way in which the children made explicit their concept of a story and, at the same time, how they *agreed and revoiced the ideas of others*. For example, looking at Puy's utterances, we see that for her, a story is a fairy tale that she recites (turns 176, 179 and 181). On the other hand, and looking at the same excerpt, we observe that *children's utterances were supported and complemented by those coming from other children*; for example, Hector followed up Julia's utterance (turns 174 and 175) while David followed Puy's account.

174. Julia:	Description, but a lot about the topic of the mountains	Descripción pero mucho sobre el tema de las montañas	STATEMENT
175. Hector:	I'm going to put in a lot in the story (makes a gesture with his hand as though to	Me voy a meter mucho en la historia (hace un gesto con la mano como de entrar en la	STATEMENT

	enter the photo)	*foto)*	
176. Puy:	'Tell a story that in these mountains…'	*'Cuenta una historia que en estas montañas...'*	EDITION
177.David:	(looking at Puy) '…he lived…' (starts singing)	*(mira a Puy) '...vivía...' (se pone a cantar)*	CONNECTED DISCOURSE
178. Julia:	'In the mountains….'	*'En las montañas...'*	EDITION
179. Puy:	'Tell the story that in these mountains…'	*'Cuenta la leyenda que en estas montañas...'*	EDITION
180. Abigail:	Good, simple description, no?	*Bueno, descripción simple, ¿no?*	QUESTION
181. Puy:	'…grey and dark…'	*'...grises y oscuras'*	EDITION

But a story is not what the children decide to write. After several discussions and disagreements, they finally need to vote to decide whether they will produce a story or a description. The following excerpt is an excellent example of how children regulate their social relationships by establishing different control mechanisms, as expressed in their conversations, and how dependent they are of the writing process. Focusing now on the children's group interactions, we observe that these include a specific category which has the highest number of utterances. This is *control* (23%), and it never appears when the teacher is present. Very similar to this category is another that we call *disagreements*, which are also more frequent when the teacher is absent (teacher situation; 2%, children's group; 9%). From our point of view, both of these categories are related to specific norms that are not always explicit even when they are present and used to regulate relationships between the participants. It is likely that such utterances did not appear when the teacher was present because it was he who introduced social regulations into the classroom relationships.

183. Hector:	Wait a moment, simple description or story, Let's vote. How do you vote, Puy?	*Espera un momento, ¿descripción simple o historia? A votación. Tú que votas, Puy.*	CONTROL
184. Abigail:	Simple description. Except for you, everyone wants a simple description.	*Descripción simple. Menos tú, todo el mundo quiere descripción simple.*	CONTROL
185. Hector:	And how do you know what I want?	*¿Y tú que sabes lo que quiero yo?*	QUESTION
186. Puy:	Simple but good.	*Simple pero buena.*	ANSWER

But after deciding on the format of their text, they still need to concretize the outline and to write it. When we look at the outlines (see Table 6) the concept of 'going into depth' appears.

Table 6. Written outlines when children work by themselves.

Julia Ruiz	Maria del Puy Pavon	Elena Ruiz
Outline 'Simple description'	Outline: 'Simple description'	Outline (simple description)
- From prominent to superfluous	-From most important to less important	- From prominent to inferior
- Going into depth	- Going into depth into the description by using stylistic resources.	- Going into depth
- Title	- Title	- Title
Guión 'Descripción simple'	*Guión: 'Descripción simple'*	*Guión (Descripción simple)*
1. Lo destacado a lo superfluo	*-De lo importante a lo menos importante*	*- De lo destacado a lo inferior*
2. Profundización	*-Profundización en la descripción utilizando recursos estilísticos*	*- profundización*
3. Título	*-Título*	*- título*
David Martín	Abigail Siguenza	Hector Sanchez
Outline: 'Simple description'	Outline: 'Simple description'	Outline (simple description)
- From general to specific (particular)	- From general to specific	- From general or prominent to superficial
- Going into depth	- Going into depth	- Going into depth
- Title	- Title	- Title
Guión: 'Descripción simple'	*Guión: 'Descripción simple'*	*Guión (descripción simple)*
- De lo general a lo particular	*- De lo genera a lo particular*	*- De lo general o destacado a lo superficial*
- Profundización	*- Profundización*	*- Profundización*
- Título	*- Título*	*- Título*

Looking at the following conversation we observe the way in which they decide on one of the points included in the 'outline'. We notice that even though Julia had stated this idea (turn 194) children forgot it until she revoiced it (196) and, finally, they discussed considering it as one of the main topics of the outline. Let us transcribe their discussion.

194. Julia:	We could write '… in greater detail'	*Podemos poner ' … profundización'*	STATEMENT
96. Puy:	More detail in a description…	*Profundización en una descripción...*	REVOICED
281. Abigail:	More detail (starts writing) All right? All	*Profundizar (se pone a escribir. ¿vale? ¿Vale?)*	REPETITION

right?

282. Hector:	No	*No*	DISAGREEMENT
283. Abigail:	Hector, the stylistic resources are contained in the description, in case you didn't know	*Hector, los recursos estilísticos van dentro de la descripción, por si no lo sabes.*	ARGUMENTATION
284. Hector:	I know	*Ya lo se*	AGREEMENT
285. Abigail:	Well then!	*¡Pues entonces!*	CONNECTED DISCOURSE
286. Helena:	It's just that in a section you are not going to put: 'the stylistic resources' and that's it	*Es que en un apartado no vas a poner: 'los recursos estilísticos, punto'*	JUSTIFICATION
287. Julia:	We'll put 'in greater detail', and everything goes in there	*Ponemos profundización, que ahí entra todo*	STATEMENT
288. David:	(writing) In greater detail	*(escribiendo) Profundización*	REPETITION
289. Puy:	I've put 'Greater detail using stylistic resources'	*Yo he puesto: 'profundización utilizando recursos estilísticos'*	JUSTIFICATION
290. David:	Well, it's not like that	*Pues no es así*	DISAGREEMENT
291. Julia:	Well, it's all the same.	*Bueno, da igual*	CONNECTED DISCOURSE

Reading the above transcript we observe how the children were discussing the meaning of the words because some of them, particularly Abigail, seemed to be aware that they needed to write the outline in terms of general rather than concrete ideas (turns 281, 283). From the point of view of this girl, 'going into depth' seemed to be a general idea that included other concepts, for example the fact that they needed to include 'stylistic resources'. In contrast, Puy included the two ideas in the same turn (turn 289). At the same time, children were expressing disagreement among themselves (turns 282, 289).

From our point of view, and even considering that we have just compared conversations in two groups, children's small-group interaction without the teacher in the classroom seems to give students a wider range of opportunities for presenting and discussing their own ideas than when the teacher is present. We believe that our data support those referred to by other researchers (for example, Mercer, 1995) who explore the students' angle on classroom conversations. Three important points need to be emphasized. First, conversations among peers are closer to a debating model than those they have with the teacher present; here we saw how the children presented their positions in relation to the outline that they were writing, accounted for them and agreed or disagreed. Second, references to writing were not always inter-woven with the process of control of social relationships, but when they were, it was not easy for the children to come to agreement; they often argued roughly, in a way that they would not have done if the teacher had been present. Finally, it seems to us that children do not play identical roles when interacting with their peers. By ob-serving the conversations transcribed in the previous excerpts we found that Abigail was usually organizing the relationships within the group, but particularly guiding the other children in the process of writing the outline. It is difficult to know whether she had learned this role when she interacted with her teacher. More research is re-quired to study this question in depth.

7   CONCLUSIONS

We began this chapter by discussing how writing learning and development can be explored from a Vygotskian perspective that emphasizes how individual develop-ment cannot be understood without taking into account interactions with other peo-ple; moreover, the social environment is itself influenced by a wide culture that var-ies according to the forms and organization of labor activity. This approach seems to us specially interesting as a means of examining the development of writing be-cause, according to Vygotsky, what is important for the teaching of writing is the set of transformations by which inner speech and thought are generated from social ex-perience (Cazden, 1996). If the source of inner speech is the shared social activity of the child, then classrooms must be language-rich communities in which teachers create new zones of proximal development for their students. Taking this as our starting point and focusing on how children learn to write in the classroom, we ex-plored how teacher and students compose an outline, working together in small groups. *We were particularly interested in the question of how students' collabora-tion is integrated with adult roles.* We explore how interaction in the classroom takes on specific characteristics because, and even recognizing differences among these institutional settings, schools are very often organized into hierarchies of posi-tions that are associated with different kind of prerogatives that distinguish teachers and students. After exploring the activities of six children working as a group as they planned a descriptive essay, and considering what happened when the teacher was either present or absent in the group, we can advance the following conclusions.

In very general terms, we can say that the social organization of the group is clearly different, depending on whether or not the teacher is present. Our data have shown that the teacher's participation as expressed in discourse is much more fre-quent than the pupils' interventions. Moreover, the teacher's discourses presented specific characteristics that did not appear when children interact with each other. The main question here is how different dimensions of the two classrooms' settings, as they are expressed in conversations, were interwoven with the processes of teaching and learning writing. From our point of view, when children work with their teacher an external model of the written production seems to be present throughout the session, when a specific outline was proposed by the teacher and that needed to be elaborated according to very clear instructions related to the final text structure.

In contrast, when students were working by themselves, the content and structure of the outline seemed to be generated by the group, even if the children created the impression of taking into account specific patterns given by the teacher in the previous session. But let us be more precise about the differences between the two situations and how both of them can create different zones of proximal development for learning to write.

When the teacher was present elements of the instructional conversations showed that the teacher's questions and children's answers are the most important communicative strategy among the participants. Furthermore, the teacher organized the session both socially and intellectually. For example, he decided what were the main topics of the conversation, even by introducing more abstract ideas that might be regarded as a synthesis. From our point of view these strategies contribute to the introduction a model for the children's texts that was mostly created by the teacher. Moreover, when we focus on the children's own outlines we observe that they included specific points for the future text just the teacher's ideas, even using the same words.

In contrast, the pupils enjoyed a more open and extended discussion when the teacher was not present that can contribute to the generation of a shared model for the future text. We think that this joint activity offered them opportunities for practicing and developing ways of reasoning with language, in addition to other discourse strategies that they do not use during the teacher session. Some interesting questions are raised when we observe peer interaction: Did the children disagree? Did they ask each other questions? Did they share knowledge relevant to the task? Did they seem to have a common understanding of what the task was about? In very general terms we can answer yes to all these questions, but we need to recognize that such use of discourse was related to social and intellectual conflicts that were not always easy to solve. On the other hand, the data show that some of the strategies for approaching the task of writing the outline that they used when the teacher was interacting with them were also present when they worked by themselves; for example, they discussed how to introduce 'general principles' that is, 'abstract utterances'; in the outline oriented in order to organize the final text. To round off these pages we should like to say, perhaps as the most general of our conclusions, that the construction of knowledge is not a homogeneous process, and that more research is needed to explore the process in more depth.

From our point of view, there is a striking contrast between learning environments, depending on whether the teacher was present or absent. The teacher gives directions and the children carry them out; he asks questions and children answer them, frequently with only a word or a phrase. Students almost never give directions to the teacher and rarely even ask questions. The challenge for us to explore in further studies is whether the only context in which children can reverse these interactional roles with the same intellectual content, giving directions as well as following them, and asking questions as well as answering them, is when they are alone with their peers.

AUTHOR'S NOTE

Thanks to editors and anonymous reviewers for their interesting and helpful comments. Address for correspondence: Pilar Lacasa, p.lacasa@uah.es, Universidad de Alcalá Licenciatura en Psicopedagogía Aulario María de Guzmán San Cirilo s/n 28801 Alcalá de Henares, Spain.

WRITTEN ENGLISH, WORD-PROCESSORS, AND MEANING-MAKING

A semiotic perspective on the development of adult students' academic writing

MARY SCOTT

University of London, Institute of Education, United Kingdom

Abstract. This chapter rests on three propositions: (1) writing development is a matter of learning how to exploit the possibilities which written English offers as a resource for making meaning; (2) writing in the social sciences in higher education requires the construction of argument, which in turn depends on the exploitation of particular aspects of written English; (3) technology enters the meaning-making process through the kinds of meaning it affords. These propositions provide the rationale and context of a project which addressed two questions: (1) Do 'non-native speaker' students see the word-processor's properties as affecting their meaning-making in written English in their essays or dissertations? (2) To what extent do the printouts of students' word-processed texts indicate not only an exploitation of the meaning-making resources of written English but also a use of the word-processor's facilities as semiotic resources?
Key words: written English, word processors, academic writing, semiotic perspective.

1   INTRODUCTION: DEVELOPMENT FROM A SEMIOTIC PERSPECTIVE

This chapter adopts a particular approach to 'development' – an approach which is encapsulated in Kress' (1996) statement that 'development' has an 'intimate connection with the possibilities of systems of representation' such as language, image or gesture (p. 237). When placed within the context of Kress' overarching argument, this statement can be elaborated in the following way: in a pedagogic environment 'development' is a matter of learning how to exploit systems of representation (of

L. Tolchinsky (ed.), Developmental Aspects in Learning to Write, 163–186.
© 2001 *Kluwer Academic Publishers. Printed in the Netherlands.*

which language is the most obvious example) as resources for making meaning in response to the demands of particular tasks.

This semiotic focus on development does not, however, imply a model of pedagogy in which the teacher simply transmits her knowledge to the student – a model which Kress detects in educational discourse that refers to learners 'acquiring' language ready-made. For Kress 'acquisition' edits out the fact that meaning-making is always implicated in individuals' 'social and cultural histories and present positions, … their affective dispositions, their interests …'. From this perspective meaning-making necessarily involves the individual in a making or remaking, to a greater or lesser extent, of systems of representation. As Kress (1996: 236) puts it: 'Individual users of language – or any other human system of representation – are users and (re)makers of that system of representation'.

Kress' emphasis on the (re)making of systems of representation has strongly influenced my view of my role as a university teacher who seeks to foster the development of her postgraduate students' academic writing in English, and is mindful of the fact that many of these students are 'non-native speakers' (NNS) of English. Firstly, following Kress, I place the individual learner and her meanings centre stage. Secondly, I perceive a synonymy between cognition and the individual's (re)making of written English as a system of representation. In Kress' words: 'the individual's semiotic work is cognitive work' (1996: 237).

Building on these two themes from Kress, I arrive at a particular theoretical position regarding the development of NNS students' writing in English within the contexts of postgraduate education – a position which shifts the focus from inner mental processes and measurements of linguistic proficiency to the individual student's perceptions of the possibilities of written English as a semiotic resource. From this perspective, pedagogy ceases to be seen as primarily dependent on general stages of cognitive or linguistic development. The pedagogic emphasis is placed instead on enlarging the individual student's awareness of written English as a resource for making meaning in the student's particular field of study.

In keeping with Kress' emphasis on the users of systems of representation as (re)makers of those systems, I also regard attention to individual students' current perceptions as indispensable if I am to succeed in moving students on in their learning how to mean in the medium of English in their essays and dissertations. In short I would argue that Clay's (1996) observation that children enter the 'complex activity' of writing from many different starting points is as true, if not truer, of the adult learning to be a successful writer at university, since as Clay (1996) puts it: 'Descriptions of average/typical/normal achievement or sequences for learning are always surrounded by error, generate their own exceptions, and do not necessarily constrain what can be true of individuals' (p.207).

A corollary of this view of development is that I see myself as an interpreter of students' meanings and of the extent of their awareness of the 'possibilities of systems of representation', but an interpreter who seeks to be alive to other possible interpretations. To put it another way, I attempt to lend students my consciousness, offering not assertions but hypotheses and alternatives for discussion. This aim finds its theoretical summation in Vygotsky's writings (trans. & ed. Kozulin, 1986). It represents an intention to identify and collaborate with the individual student's zone of proximal development (ZPD) or, to borrow Doris Lessing's (1972) metaphor, to find the cracks through which the new may flood.

2   WRITTEN ENGLISH AS A SEMIOTIC RESOURCE

The focus on pedagogy which I have outlined above provides the studies reported in this chapter with their primary rationale. However, a question that the comments above are likely to provoke is, of course: what are the characteristics of written English when it is used as a resource for meaning-making in academic writing?

In linguistics (see Ventola, 1996), 'lexical density' (Halliday, 1989) tends to be presented as the primary characteristic of academic writing. 'Lexical density' is achieved primarily by nominalization (the objectifying of processes by the replacement of verbs with abstract noun forms). This leads to a compactness and compression of content. As Halliday (1989) observes, lexical density is a matter of how 'closely packed the information is' (p. 66). Taking the metaphoric implications of 'closely packed' further, I arrive at a view of the text as a container into which a great deal of content has been compressed. Another characteristic which is commonly ascribed to 'good' academic prose and which also implies the metaphor of text-as-container (but in this case a transparent container) is 'clarity'. (See Lakoff & Johnson, 1980).

'Lexical density' and the metaphors it spawns are, of course, related to a view of academic writing as a form of meaning-making that is primarily concerned with conceptual abstractions. In other words, academic writing is associated with a particular conception of rationality in which language is merely a container of, or conduit for, objective meanings. However, this view of academic writing actually neglects an aspect of written argument which is emphasised in the Social Sciences in UK universities, especially at the postgraduate level, viz., 'argument' as constituted primarily by the adoption of an individually distinctive focus (See Scott, 1999). Such a focus, particularly if nuanced, tends to require the exploitation of the prosodic aspects of written English. A text needs, in short, to give the impression of meanings in the process of being made, debated and engaged, and not simply displayed. It is here that rhythm and the creation of a 'voice' in the text become important. As Kane (1988) points out, 'good rhythm' both reinforces meaning and gives words 'nuances they might not otherwise have' (p.166). Kane also reminds us that, while there is inevitably a subjective element in rhythm, with even experienced readers differing in what they 'hear' as they read silently, rhythm is not simply a matter of individual perception: 'writers can...regulate what their readers hear; not completely, but within fairly clear limits' (p.166).

Rhythm as a semiotic resource tends to be neglected, however, in study skills guides aimed at student writers. For example, the 'introduction, body and conclusion' of an essay clearly spatialise the text by analogy with a physical object with visible parts. Even 'flow' is related not to rhythm but to a view of a text as an object or physical structure in which the parts are attached to each other by means of cohesive devices (*e.g.* Swales & Feak, 1994). The importance of punctuation to rhythm (see Halliday, 1989; Kane, 1988) is also overlooked, its function being seen as only grammatical or logical.

I have concentrated so far on written English as a semiotic resource without taking into account the technical means used to generate written texts. In now seeking to remedy that oversight I am indebted to Kress and van Leeuwen (1996) who have shown me that 'technology enters fundamentally into the semiotic process through the kinds of meanings which it facilitates or favours' (p. 233). In other words, the 'tools' we use and the surfaces on which we use them, whether pen, ink and paper or word-processor with screen, keys, mouse, and facilities such as a choice of fonts, are not mere tools or surfaces since 'modes of inscription' and surfaces carry meanings. New technologies thus afford new semiotic resources which combine with other systems of representation traditionally associated with semiosis to give meaning its materiality in the form of, for example, a written text, drawing, or sculpture.

In elaborating this perspective, Kress and van Leeuwen (1996) ask a question of importance to this chapter. Their question is: 'Is a written text the same object or a different one when written with pen and ink or with a word-processor?' In introducing their own answers to that question they point out that most linguists would reply: 'No question. It is the same text'. To Kress and van Leeuwen (1996), however, 'the material expression of a text is always significant', *i.e.* it carries meanings (p. 231). They amplify that statement in the following words:

> Texts are material objects which result from a variety of representational practices that make use of a variety of signifying systems each of which contributes to the meaning of the text in its own particular way.... We are interested, therefore in the surfaces on which inscriptions are made (paper, rock, plastic, textile, wood, etc), in the substances with which inscriptions are made (ink, gold, paint, light, etc) and in the tools used for making the inscriptions (chisel, pen, brush, pencils, stylus, etc) (p.231).

Kress and van Leeuwen (1996) have led me to ask questions of my own. As in most universities, my students are now expected to word-process their essays and theses. This means that their texts move finally from one surface (the screen) to another (the page). My questions are thus: (i) Do my students see the word-processor's properties as affecting in some way their meaning-making in written English in their academic essays or dissertations? (ii) To what extent do the printouts of students' word-processed texts indicate not only an exploitation of the meaning-making resources of written English (*e.g.* lexis, syntax, rhythm) but also a use of the word-processor's facilities as semiotic resources?

These are large and complex questions. In the next parts of this chapter I describe my initial attempts to obtain answers. I begin with a small-scale study which involved some of my own students.

3   SETTING THE SCENE

The 17 students on whom my study is based were all 'international' students (*i.e.* they came from countries outside the United Kingdom). All were 'non-native speakers' (NNS) of English. They were also all graduates who were following doctoral or master's degree programmes in Education. One of the requirements for admission to such programmes is several years' experience as a practitioner in the field of education. This means that the students I teach tend to be older than postgraduates at other institutions where graduates may be admitted to a master's course immediately after completing their first degrees. The students to whom my study refers ranged in age from 27 to 45 which is an age spread that is typical of many of the groups I teach. Of particular relevance to the study is the fact that, as undergraduates, the participants had all written essays by hand or, less frequently, on a typewriter, but were now composing on the computer screen. In other words, although they were accustomed in most cases to using the computer to word-process non-academic texts such as letters, they had not previously produced academic texts on the word-processor. Sharples (1999) points out that the movement 'from page to screen' (Snyder, 1998) gradually changes the way we compose. Contrasting his own experience as an undergraduate, when revisions meant laboriously rewriting whole sections or the whole of an essay, with the comparative ease in redrafting which the word-processor affords, he concludes that he has now become a 'brick-layer', *i.e.* someone who polishes a text piece by piece. The focus of my study is very different, however. As the questions which I listed above indicate, my interest is in the word-processor not as a facilitating tool but as a resource for meaning-making and thus I am primarily concerned with how students who have made the transition from composing on the page to composing on the screen (and back to the page) now perceive and use the word-processor's properties – use them, that is, in combination with the semiotic resources that written English is traditionally seen to afford (*e.g.* lexis, syntax, punctuation).

3.1 Collecting and recording the data

My small-scale study can be broadly categorized as 'action research', that is, research undertaken by a practitioner (or practitioners) with the aim of bringing about some kind of change (Cohen & Manion, 1994). The raw data became available to me in the course of my day-to-day teaching, and relate to my perception of my role as that of a reflective practitioner. The data are of two kinds:(i) oral comments students had made, in individual tutorials or seminars, when asked about their perceptions of the effect of the use of the computer on their production of academic texts; (ii) samples of the students' writing. In all, 17 students' comments were written down. (I inserted punctuation which corresponded to the oral units of sense, and gave each student a pseudonym.) The comments varied in length, ranging from 5 or 6 words in a small number of cases to over 30 in a few instances. Since I was interested in the kinds of assumption which the comments suggested, and not in statistical frequencies, I concentrated on interpreting the comments, seeking to identify the range of positions represented in them. What emerged were pointers in directions that need to be further explored in future research.

4 THE STUDENTS' COMMENTS

As indicated earlier, the students were unaccustomed to using the word processor to produce academic essays or theses. Their past experience had been of pen, ink and paper or, in a few cases, of typewriter and paper. However, as already mentioned, academic texts produced on the word-processor are finally printed on paper. In fact, most of the students said that they made a number of printouts as they drafted their texts on screen. A student's comment that 'it is easier to read, to get the sense and coherence of the whole from the printed version', met with general agreement in a seminar. In short, the students' comments suggested that in their use of the word-processor the students aimed, consciously or intuitively, to bring their texts as close as possible to an idea of academic writing which preceded their writing on screen, *i.e.* to an idea of what was required that related to their past experience as student writers. The majority of the comments thus indicated the ways in which the word-processor was seen to help or hinder the realisation of the students' individual views of an academic text. When I attended to the students' choice of words, and to the metaphors housed within them, I then saw that the view of a text as a container of meaning, to which I referred earlier, was implicit in most of the comments. So, too, was the assumption that language is, or should ideally be, a conduit for the writer's meanings and that those meanings should not be superficial. This was the case no matter whether the students regarded the word-processor as helping them to compose or not. For example, Pemlo, who found composing on screen a problem, commented as follows:

> When I compose on the screen it does look good – too good.... Sometimes I end up feeling that I have written something really good when I haven't.... I haven't got into the topic.

Here 'really good' writing is treated as under threat from the superficially pleasing which can keep the writer on the surface of a topic. When this view was expressed in a seminar a number of students said it matched their experience.

Katerini, on the other hand, described the effect of composing on screen in words which suggested that the computer spatialised and objectified her meanings so that they became like objects at a distance – objects which could then be changed. In her comment (which was echoed by others) language is by implication a conduit for her thoughts.

> It [the computer] makes my thoughts visible. They are out there, over there. I can think about them: Is this what I really mean? I can make a change, scroll back, read and see the effect of the change immediately.

This primary concern with meaning was also apparent in the large number of comments (10) which referred to paragraphing as a problem when the writer was composing on screen. Each of these comments implied that seeing their texts on the computer screen tended to deflect the writers' attention from the paragraph as a unit of meaning. For example:

> On the computer a paragraph is a block of text. It is easy to forget it's an idea.

> My paragraphs become a matter of size, number of lines on the screen. I think, I have written a lot, lets have a new paragraph. Of course that is the same with a page but it seems more difficult on a computer to know where to start a new paragraph.

> Because the screen moves as I write I lose all sense of paragraphs .... I just have a continuous text; ideas get jumbled.

Only two of the comments which I collected referred to the temporal dimensions of written English. Rosa commented on the rhythms that the use of the keyboard 'can't capture':

> The computer is over there, at a distance.... I use my hands and see words and sentences appear. I feel rather remote from what I am writing so I always do my first draft with pen and paper...I write very quickly; there is a rhythm that the keyboard can't capture. I stop hearing and feeling it when I try to compose on the screen.

Christina also referred to the difficulty of hearing and feeling written English when using the computer, and linked the problem to her tendency to read only with the eye when word-processing:

> A sentence can look good, not too long, grammar and spelling, OK; I have to be careful to try to hear it .... not to read it only with my eye. Then it doesn't sound right..... If I write by hand I hear the sentence more. It is easy to think a sentence is right if you only see it.

As only these two students had mentioned rhythm, which Kane (1988) and Halliday (1989) regard as an important semiotic resource, I put the following question to all the students in a seminar: 'Do you hear what you write in English?'. A Greek student, Athene, immediately understood the relevance of the question but replied, like the 13 members of the group who spoke languages with alphabetic scripts: 'Yes, but not as much as in my language'. She recognised that some of her errors and uncertainties at the level of the sentence were connected to her failure to hear the tune on the screen or page; for example, her not being able to decide where to put connectors like 'however', 'in fact', or 'on the other hand', or whether to write 'he was recently informed' or 'he was informed recently'. To the four Chinese-speaking students, on the other hand, my question was incomprehensible. They did not understand the paradox of a silently 'heard' text. One commented: 'But you mustn't hear it. You mustn't subvocalise'. This kind of response is not surprising from students whose first language is logographic and tonal. Furthermore, in their earlier learning of English greater emphasis had been placed on writing and silent reading or chanting in unison than on individual speech or on listening. Consequently these students tended to bring to writing a disposition which led them to compose sentences by grammatical rule only, whereas the students familiar from childhood with alphabetic scripts had developed some awareness that written language has temporal aspects – that, as Olson (1994) points out, alphabetic scripts provide models, however distorted, of speech.

4.1 Summary and evaluation

I have singled out those trends in the students' comments which have a bearing on my question: Do my students see the word-processor's properties as affecting in some way their meaning-making in English in academic essays or theses? As the comments which I have quoted indicate, the distancing effect of keyboard and screen was a dominant theme. That effect was viewed positively by Katerini who saw her thoughts externalised, but negatively by Rosa and Christina who felt that a distanced visuality in place of the close physical engagement of hand-held pen with paper made it difficult for them to 'hear' their texts. The aesthetic appeal of the visual text on the screen was regarded by Pemlo as a barrier to in-depth thinking, while the comments on the difficulty of paragraphing suggested that the writers either felt controlled by the size of the screen space or by the screen's automatic accommodation of additional lines of text. Only one student referred to the choice of fonts which the word-processor affords. Unlike the students I have quoted or referred to above, she did not link presentation to meaning. She saw a change of fonts as a means of creating a visually pleasing document. It is perhaps significant that she had a background in graphic design.

5   ANALYSIS OF SAMPLES OF STUDENT WRITING PRODUCED ON THE WORD-PROCESSOR

The students' comments on how they perceived the word-processor's properties as affecting their writing do not, of course, tell us anything about the texts which the students produced. That is the topic to which I now turn. My focus is encapsulated in the question which I formulated earlier, viz.: To what extent do the print-outs of students' word-processed texts indicate not only an exploitation of the meaning-making resources of written English (*e.g.* lexis, syntax, rhythm) but also a use of the word-processor's facilities as semiotic resources?

I have selected three sample texts which are representative in different ways of the kinds of academic texts which my NNS students produce. In each case I first comment on the extent to which the student has used the characteristics of written academic English to make meaning. I focus in particular on the students' texts as illustrative of the spatial and temporal features of written English which I earlier related to the properties of academic argument. I then consider what evidence there is across the three texts of the use of the word-processor's facilities as meaning-making resources.

5.1 Katerini's text

I begin with a sample text which illustrates the effective use of the semiotic resources of written English in the realisation of academic argument. The paragraph below is from a draft of Katerini's master's degree dissertation. Katerini's topic is the use of literature in TEFL/TESL contexts.

The potential contribution of literature to language learning

Brumfit and Carter (1986, p. 15) explain the distinctive role of literature. Literature, though not mundane, can provide learners with 'real' opportunities for language use and can encourage genuine performance. Kramsch (1993) also writes of literature as able to provide varied and stimulating contexts in which the learner can escape the predictable routines and oversimplified speech transactions that have been encouraged by functional approaches to language teaching. 'Literature can be not a script but a prompt' (Kramsch, 1993, p.70).

This paragraph follows a section in which Katerini presented objections to the use of literature in the teaching of ESL and EFL. She concluded that section by looking ahead to her preferred view, which the paragraph above then introduces. In stating that preferred view Katerini develops an argument which emphasises the conceptual. No matter whether the verbs are in the active or the passive voice, most of the agents are abstractions or generalizations ('literature'; 'functional approaches to language teaching'; 'the learner'). Verbs such as 'encourage' and 'can provide' constitute grammatical metaphors (Halliday, 1989) in that their function is relational (*i.e.* they define what literature represents) and not material, while 'escape' suggests a mental process or condition and not a physical action. In other words, the verbs are of the kind associated with academic argument (Knapp, 1992).

However, the excerpt also represents the aspect of academic argument in the Social Sciences to which I referred earlier, viz., the impression of an individual 'voice' actively engaging with ideas. Katerini's awareness of the importance of 'voice' is visible in the change she has now made to an earlier draft which she had given me. In that earlier draft she had written: 'Literature can provide learners with "real" opportunities for language use and can encourage genuine performance though literature is not mundane ...'. Now she keeps the basic sense but changes the word order: 'Literature, though not mundane, can provide learners with "real" opportunities for language use and can encourage genuine performance'. With this new phrasing, which is reinforced by the punctuation (as indicated above), Katerini refers back to the preceding part of her chapter in which she had put the arguments against the use of literature, and so introduces the 'voice' of counter-argument.

The impression of a voice in the text is also achieved at the beginning of the long third sentence in which the use of 'also' makes a link both rhythmically and logically to the preceding sentences: 'Kramschalso writes of literature...'. However, the structure of this sentence rests mainly on the difference between formal written argument and informal spoken argument. In written argument passages that require reading with the eye co-exist with those where a 'voice' gives emphasis. In its length and absence of commas, which is in accordance with the conventional rules of grammar relating to such kinds of relative and noun clauses, the third sentence appeals to the eye rather than the ear. 'Voice' can, however, be 'heard' again in the succinct concluding quotation in which an emphatic contrast is signalled by 'not' and 'but'—'Literature can be not a script but a prompt' – a contrast that serves to sum up and make Katerini's point.

5.2 *Christina's text*

The following excerpt is from the first draft of Christina's master's degree dissertation on approaches to writing in English language teaching. I have reproduced the excerpt exactly as it appeared in her text indicating in square brackets the spaces between sentences.

Approaches to Writing

Greek teachers do not let the students write an essay at an early age. [three spaces]
Of course, only letting students write essays at a later age makes the teachers' task
easier – they do not need to do so many corrections. [single space] Meanings would
be clearer. [three spaces] But is writing made easier for students in that way? [three
spaces] I doubt it.[three spaces] Students would get less practice.[three spaces] Does
practice make perfect then? [three spaces] Burgess (1973) does not seem to think
so.[single space] Burgess is sure we would not be able to develop children's writing
through practice.

This paragraph conveys to me a sense of the speaking voice; *i.e.* it invites a reading
that supplies patterns of stress and intonation – a silent reading with the ear and not
just the eye. This effect is created, for example, by the implicit address to the reader
in 'of course', and in the use of question and answer. This impression of the writer
in the guise of a speaker participating in a debate is strengthened for me by Christina's use of personal subjects (*e.g.* 'Greek teachers'; 'I'; 'Burgess') with active
verbs, in place of the nominalisations of 'lexical density' (Halliday, 1989) that are
characteristic of academic argument's concern with the conceptual, and especially
by her choice of verbs of opinion such as 'think', and 'doubt'. These features of her
text suggest to me that Christina has not grasped the kinds of meaning she needs to
engage with. Unlike Katerini's, her arguments do not relate to ideas. Instead of the
'approaches' (*i.e.* theories) referred to in her title, she offers opinions and beliefs.
Her demonstration of the possibilities of written English are appropriate to that orientation but it is an orientation that indicates a misconception of what is required in
an MA dissertation in Education.

5.3 Monica's text

The next excerpt is from a draft of Monica's dissertation. Monica regards the word-
processor as helping her to structure her ideas. However, the excerpt indicates a fundamental problem. Monica writes:

In this chapter, it will be argued that the unified state of the German Empire was
constructed politically and culturally along Prussian lines. The Empire was framed
on the model and within the institutional pattern of the 'militaristic, paternalistic,
authoritarian and quasi-feudal Prussian state machine (1). This pattern exhibited the
Prussian desire for the unification of German states under Prussian hegemony and
within Prussian political and cultural traditions.

Furthermore it will be argued that political and social reforms in the process of state
formation were undertaken 'from above' by a small number of leading statesmen
and high-ranking bureaucrats. Aristocratic German bureaucrats in particular deliber-
ately attempted to maintain their influence within a new political structure as well as
many feudalistic aspects of German society. The bureaucracy was powerful socially
as well as politically in Germany

It is clear that Monica is strongly aware of those conventions of academic writing which I earlier described metaphorically as 'spatial'. The primary grammatical forms are nominalizations and a number of verbs are in the passive voice. What is immediately most striking, though, is how concretely spatial her text is. The paragraphing visually comprises two blocks of text of equal size. This impression of a careful, symmetrical, spatial arrangement is reinforced by the fact that each paragraph contains three sentences. Furthermore, within each paragraph the sentences are of approximately the same length except for the final sentence of the second paragraph. The almost identical opening phrases: 'in this chapter it will be argued'; 'furthermore it will be argued' add to the impression of structural parallelism.

This careful structuring of the paragraphs corresponds to the kinds of meaning being made. Monica has laid the components of her 'argument' side by side but the phrasing of the sentences which follow the first sentence of each paragraph (*e.g.* 'the Empire was framed on the model....; 'aristocratic German bureaucrats....') suggests facts and not a particular focus. The final sentence of the second paragraph is shorter than the others – a variation in length which could have been used to bring an argument to a conclusion. In Monica's text, however, it serves rather to add another fact, almost as an afterthought: 'The bureaucracy was powerful socially as well as politically in Germany'.

The punctuation of the excerpt reinforces the impression of a text as a visual and spatial arrangement of facts rather than a nuanced argument. Punctuation is noticeably absent where it could help to give emphasis and focus. For example, the addition of commas in 'on the model, and within the institutional pattern, of ....' could lend emphasis both to 'model' and to 'institutional pattern'.

6   THE STUDENTS' TEXTS AS 'MATERIAL OBJECTS'

The characteristics of written academic texts, which I have used above as criteria, are, of course, independent of whether or not a text is produced with pen and paper or on a typewriter or word-processor and paper. I now consider the three texts which I have discussed from a different perspective, *i.e.* as 'material objects' produced on the word-processor. I begin with some general observations that apply to all three texts before considering differences across the texts.

It might be argued that a word-processed essay or thesis chapter differs little as a material object from the typed essays and chapters which students submitted to their tutors in the past. However, I would claim that there are differences in surfaces and in 'modes of inscription' (Kress & van Leeuwen, 1996) which herald different emphases and meanings. Firstly, the quality of the paper tends to be different. I have before me a number of typed essays from the past. The essays are on flimsier paper than the computer paper which my students use. Where the typists used underlinings for headings and usually had a choice of only lower or upper case the word-processor now enables my students to vary font sizes, and to use 'bold' or 'italics' in place of underlinings. Furthermore, several of the typed essays which I am looking at show the use of correcting fluid; in contrast, corrections that were made to the word-processed texts reproduced above are now invisible to the reader. I may seem to be simply stating the obvious and the trivial. I would, claim, however, that these kinds of difference are significant. The boundaries between student writer and professional writer are now overtly blurred. The word-processor's facilities enable the production of an essay or thesis which is visually indistinguishable from published academic texts such as journal articles or chapters in books. A question this raises and which calls for future exploration is: What effect, if any, might this have on students' development as writers?

Returning to the excerpts reproduced above, I note that Katerini, Christina and Monica have made particular choices from the range of options that the word-processor offers; choices which suggest that the surface of an academic text must not detract from the content represented. I refer to the use of a plain, unembellished font, of black and white to the exclusion of colour, and, in Monica's and Katerini's texts, to the choice of 'bold' for headings.

Each of the three students has, however, also used the word-processor's properties to reinforce the particular semiotic resources of written English which they have drawn on and which, as I have shown earlier, suggest different conceptions of how to write argument.

Christina was one of the two students who had referred to the temporal aspects of writing: 'I have to try to hear it ... not to read only with my eye'. Her text suggests, however, that she has over-compensated for what she perceives as the screen's invitation to concentrate on the 'look' of a text. In an effort to 'hear' her text, and to help her reader to 'hear' it, she has used spacing in a novel way, a way that emphasises the speech-like qualities of her writing. The longer spaces between some sentences isolate those sentences; they can thus be said to function in this context like pauses for dramatic effect; they place emphasis on certain sentences, especially the questions and their answers.

Christina's choice of italics for a heading is unconventional. *'Approaches to Writing'* seems to imply a concern with the aesthetics of presentation. Perhaps also, in view of its unconventionality, the italicised heading represents Christina's way of leaving her individual mark. It can then be said to be in keeping with the emphasis in her text on personal opinion as expressed, for example, in 'I doubt it' and in the prose rhythms which create such a strong impression of her speaking to the reader.

When viewed on the word-processor, Monica's text occupies a full screen. It then takes on the form of a strongly framed visual composition comprising two symmetrical blocks of text. This leads me to conclude that whereas Christina was reacting against the visual and spatial properties of the computer screen Monica was dominated by them. Her 'arguments' are impersonal arrangements of facts and her use of the word-processor visually reinforces that conception of argument.

Katerini had referred to the word-processor as enabling her to see her thoughts: 'it makes my thoughts visible'. That visibility is apparent in her text in her use of a semiotic resource which the word-processor makes available, viz., bold type for a heading: **'The potential contribution of literature to language learning'**. The type combines with Katerini's linguistic choices to make explicit the central focus of the paragraph. However, Katerini said she had to produce numerous printouts in order to 'hear' the flow of her ideas.

My analyses do, of course, ignore the question of the quality of the content of the students' texts. This is in line with my primary focus which is on argument as the realisation in written English of an individually distinctive focus in an engagement with ideas. Katerini clearly held such a view and could assess in what ways the word-processor helped and did not help her to textualise it. Christina and Monica, on the other hand, made assumptions about argument which did not conform to what is expected at postgraduate level in studies of Education. Those assumptions were reflected in the different affordances which they found in the word-processor's properties.

7   CONCLUSION

There is, of course, no single solution to NNS student difficulties in producing written argument in English. However, I have found that giving class time to the analysis of excerpts like those above can help students, especially students like Christina and Monica, in their development as writers of argument. Such whole-class sessions need, of course, to be supplemented by one-to-one tutorial discussions of samples of each student's own writing.

Considering a text as a material object is a new focus which interests all my students. More importantly, it offers me, the teacher, a concrete, clearly visible, basis for a discussion of the kinds of meanings being made by individual students. As I have tried to demonstrate in this chapter, it is but a short step from the 'look' of a student text to conceptions of academic argument, and to how presentational conventions might reinforce the kind of meaning-making that is expected.

This chapter has also touched on two issues of broader significance. One of those issues is the inadequacy of descriptions of written English, and especially of academic argument, which appear in course books (*e.g.* Swales & Feak, 1994) designed for international students. The importance of rhythm and the creation of a speaking voice in a text is neglected. Perceptions of the word-processor's role in the composition of texts is the second issue on which this chapter touches. My analyses of students' texts have led me to question the view of the word-processor as simply a useful tool which facilitates emendations and insertions and ensures a text that looks readable. While this chapter has taken only a few tentative steps towards a view of the word-processor's properties as semiotic resources, and more extensive research is clearly needed in this area, I hope I have stimulated an interest in presentation as an aspect of meaning.

I draw this chapter to its conclusion by opening it up to speculation and even fantasy. The criteria of a good essay or dissertation have changed over time and are likely to change in the future. (See Russell, 1991). What role will the word-processor play in that process of change? Will voice recognition software mean, for example, that temporal, speech-like dimensions of language become more acceptable in academic papers? Will we move towards Christina's style with a corresponding change in our conceptions of academic argument? I have no answers, only possibilities for consideration, but that is, after all, the intended tenor of the whole chapter.

Considering a text as a material object is a new focus which interests all my students. More importantly, it offers me, the teacher, a concrete way into discussing the kinds of meanings being made by individual students: as I have tried to demonstrate in this chapter, it is but a short step from the 'look' of a student text to conceptions of academic argument and to the reasons why the presentational conventions of academic texts are as they are, *i.e.* to how the conventions reinforce the kind of meaning making that is expected.

In relating 'development' to meaning-making in academic writing this chapter has touched on two issues of broader significance. One of those issues is the inadequacy of descriptions of written English, and especially of academic argument, which appear in study skills guides for nonnative speakers of English (*e.g.* Swales & Feak, 1994). These descriptions ignore the temporal aspects of written academic argument. The second issue concerns perceptions of the word-processor's potential semiotic role. The studies I have reported in this chapter and especially my analyses of students' texts have led me to question the view of the computer as simply a useful tool which facilitates emendations and insertions and ensures a text that looks readable. While this chapter has taken only a few tentative steps towards a view of the word-processor's properties as semiotic resources, and more extensive research is clearly needed in this area, I hope I have stimulated an interest in presentation as an aspect of meaning.

I draw this chapter to its conclusion by opening it up to speculation and even fantasy. The criteria of a good essay or dissertation or thesis have changed over time and are likely to change in the future (See Russell, 1991). What role will the word-processor play in that process of change? Will voice recognition software mean, for example, that temporal, speech-like dimensions of language become more acceptable in academic papers? Will we move towards Christina's style with a corresponding change in our conceptions of academic argument? I have no answers, only possibilities for consideration, but that has, after all, been the tenor of this whole chapter.

AUTHOR'S NOTE

Address for correspondence: CCS Institute for Education, University of London, 20 Bedford Way, London WC1H OAL, England.

REFERENCES

Adam, J. M., & Petitjean, A. (1989). *Le Texte Descriptif.* [The descriptive text] France: Nathan.

Anderson, J.R. (1983). *The architecture of cognition.* New York: Academic Press.

Anderson, J.R. (1993). *Rules of mind.* Hillsdale, NJ: Erlbaum.

Anderson, J.R. (1995). *Learning and Memory. An integrated approach.* NewYork: John Wiley & Sons.

Atkinson, J. M., & Drew, P. (1979). *Order in court: the organization of verbal interaction in judicial settings.* London: Macmillan.

Baez, M., & Cárcenas V. (1999). *Segmentación y escritura. Dos estudios sobre adquisición.* [Segmentation and writing. Two studies on acquisition] Rosario: Homo Sapiens

Baker Sennet, J., Matusov, E., & Rogoff, B. (1992). Sociocultural processes of creative planning in children's playcrafting. In P. Light & G. Butterworth (eds.), *Context and cognition: Ways of learning and knowing.* Hertfordshire, England: Harvester Wheatsheaf. (pp. 93-114).

Bereiter, C., & Scardamalia, M. (1987). *The psychology of written composition.* Hillsdale, N.J: Lawrence Erlbaum Associates.

Bereiter, C., & Scardamalia, M. (1989). Intentional learning as a goal of instruction. In L. Resnick (ed.), *Knowing, Learning and Instruction. Essays in Honor of Robert Glaser.* Hillsdale, N.J: Lawrence Erlbaum Associates. (pp. 361-392)

Berman, R. (1997). Narrative theory and narrative development: the Labovian impact. *Journal of Narrative and Life History, 5,* 4, 285-313.

Berry, D.C., & Dienes, Z. (1993). *Implicit learning: Theoretical and empirical issues.* Hillsdale, N.J: Lawrence Erlbaum Associates

Bissex, G. L. (1980). *Gnys At Wrk.* Cambridge: Harvard University Press.

Blanche Benveniste, C. (1997). The units of written and oral language. In C. Pontecorvo (eds.), *Writing development: An interdisciplinary view.* Amsterdam: John Benjamin

Blanche Benveniste, C., & Chervel, A. (1970). *L'Orthographe.* Paris: Maspero.[The Orthography].

Bock, K., & Eberhard, K.M. (1993). Meaning, sound and syntax in English number agreement. *Language and Cognitive Processes, 8* (1), 57-99.

Bockheimer, J. (1998). The rise of the literacy episteme. Redefining Literacy. *Newsletter of the language, Literacy and Mind Research Group,* OISE, Toronto: University of Toronto.

Bombi, A.S., & Marotti, A. (1998). Bugie, errori e scherzi (Lies, Mistakes, and Jokes). *Psicologia Generale, 1,* 122-134.

Bortolini, U., Leonard, L.B., & Caselli, M.C. (1998). Specific language impairment in Italian and English: Evaluating alternative accounts of grammatical deficits. *Language and Cognitive Processes, 13* (1), 120.

Breedveld, E. (1997). *De spelling van het bijvoeglijk naamwoord dat is afgeleid van het voltooid deelwoord. Over de invloed van het woordbeeld van de verleden tijd en van het bijbehorende zelfstandig naamwoord in een meervoud op en.* [The spelling of adjectives derived from verbs. About the influence of the past tense of verbs and the adjacent noun in plural with the plural –en morpheme]. Amsterdam: Department of Dutch Linguistics. [unplished MAthesis].

Brown, A. L., & Palincsar, A. S. (1989). Guided, cooperative learning and individual knowledge acquisition. In L. B. Resnick (ed.), *Knowing, Learning and Instruction.* Hillsdale, N.J: Lawrence Erlbaum Associates (pp. 393 452).

Brumfit, C., & Carter, R. (eds.). (1986). *Literature and language teaching.* Oxford: Oxford University Press.

Bryant, P. E., Nunes, T., & Snaith, R. (2000). Children learn untaught rule of spelling. *Nature, 403,*157-158.

Bugarski, R. (1993). Graphic relativity and Linguistic constructs. In R. Scholes (ed.), *Literacy and language analysis.* Hillsdalle,NJ:LEA (pp. 518).

Camps, A., & Milian, M. (vol. eds.) (2000). *Metalinguistic activity in learning to write.* Vol. 6 in G. Rijlaarsdam & E. Espéret, Studies in Writing. Amsterdam: Amsterdam University Press.

Catach, N. (1986). *L'orthographe française.* Paris: Nathan.

Catach, N. (1989). *Les délires de l'orthographe.* Paris: Plon.

Cazden, C. B. (1988). *Classroom discourse. The language of teaching and learning.* London: Routledge & Kegan Paul.

Cazden, C. B. (1996). Selective traditions: readings of Vygotsky in writing pedagogy. In D. Hicks (ed.), *Discourse, learning, and schooling* Cambridge, MA: Cambridge University Press (pp. 164 -185)..

Cintas, C., Jakubowicz, C., and Tolchinky, L., (1997). *Morphosyntactic knowldge in the acquisition of writing.* Special Interest Group on Writing (Barcelona). European Association for Research on Learning and Instruction (EARLI).

Cintas, C., Jakubowicz, C., and Tolchinky, L., (1997). *Separation between words in early written Spanish.* Paper presented at the VIII European Conference on developmental Psychology. Rennes, France.

Clark, A. (1999). *Estar Ahi.* [Being there]. Barcelona: Paidos.

Clark, R., & Ivanic, R. (1997). *The Politics of Writing.* London & New York: Routledge

Clay, M. M. (1996). Accommodating diversity in early learning. In D. R. Olson & N. Torrance (eds.), *The handbook of education and human development: New models of learning, teaching and schooling.* Oxford & Cambridge, Mass.:Blackwell Publishers (pp 202-224).

Clemente, A. R. (1984). La segmentación de textos. El comportamineto evolutivo [Segmentation of texts. Develomental patterns]. *Infancia y Aprendizaje, 26,* 77-86.

Cohen, L., & Manion, L. (1994). *Research methods in education* (4th ed.). London: Croom Helm.

Coulmas, F. (1989). *The Writing Systems of the World.* Oxford: Blackwell.

Chan L., & Nunes T. (this volume). Explicit Teaching and Implicit Learning of Chinese Character.

Chan, L., & Louie, L. (1992). Developmental trend of Chinese preschool children in drawing and writing. *Journal of Research in Childhood Education, 6(2),* 93-99.

Chen, Y. P., & Allport, A. (1995). Attention and Lexical Decomposition in Chinese Word Recognition: Conjunctions of Form and Position Guide Selective Attention. *Visual Cognition, 2,* 235 – 268.

Culioli, A. (1990) *Pour une linguistique de l'énonciation.* Tome 1. Paris: Ophrys.

Chan, L., & Nunes, T. (1998). Children's understanding of the Formal and Functional Characteristics of Written Chinese. *Applied Psycholinguistics, 19,* 115 – 131.

Chen, Y. P., Allport, A., & Marshall, J.C. (1996). What are the functional orthographic units in Chinese word recognition: The stroke or the stroke pattern? *Quarterly Journal of Experimental Psychology Section A Human Experimental Psychology, 49(4),* 1024-1043.

Eberhard, K.M. (1997). The marked effect of number on subject-verb agreement. *Journal of Memory and Language, 36* (2), 147-164.

Fang, S. P., & Wu, P. (1989). Illusory Conjunctions in the Perception of Chinese Characters. *Journal of Experimental Psychology: Human Perception and Performance, 15* (3), 434 – 447.

Ditzel, M. (1996). *De schriftelijke verwervingsvolgorde van het morfeem 'en' bij stofadjectieven en het morfeem 'e' by 'normale' adjectieven.* [The sequence of acquisition of written morphology of Material and 'Regular' Adjectives]. University of Amsterdam: Unpublished MA. thesis.

Ditzel, M., Van Dort-Slijper, M., & Rijlaarsdam, G. (1996). Overgeneralisation in agreement: A special case in adjectives in Dutch. A. Camps, M. Castelló, M. Milian, P. Monné, J. Rodriguez Illera Luis, & L. Tolchinsky. *Abstracts. 1996 European Writing Conferences.* Barcelona, October 23-25, 1996: 61.

Dort-Slijper, M. van, Rijlaarsdam, G., & Weel, I. (1998). De verwerving van morfologische regels in schrift. Over de schriftelijke verwerving van het meervoudsmorfeem –en in zelfstandige naamwoorden en werkwoorden. [The acquisition of morphological rules in written language. About the acquisition of the plural morpheme –en in nouns and verbs] *Toegepaste Taalwetenschap in Artikelen, 59* (2), 67-87.

Dort-Slijper, M. Van, Rijlaarsdam, G., & Ditzel, M. (1998). De verwerving van morfologische regels in schrift (II). Over de schriftelijke beheersing van het morfeem –en in stoffelijke bijvoeglijke naamwoorden. [The acquisition of morphological rules in written language. About the acquisition of the morpheme –en in material adjectives] *Toegepaste Taalwetenschap in artikelen, 60,* 3,87-101.

Dort-Slijper, M. Van, Rijlaarsdam G., & Breedveld, E. (1999). De verwerving van morfologische regels in schrift (III): de verbuiging van bijvoeglijke naamwoorden, afgeleid van werkwoorden. [The acquisition of morphological rules in written language. The inflection of verbal adjectives] *Tijdschrift voor Toegepaste Taalwetenschap in Artikelen, 61* (1), 97-110.

Drew, P., & Heritage, J. C. (1992). *Talk at work: interaction in institutional settings.* Cambridge: Cambridge University Press.

Dubois, J. (1965). *Grammaire structurale du Français: Nom et pronom.* Paris: Larousse.

Dyson, A. H. (1993). *Social Worlds of children learning to write.* New York & London: Teachers College, Columbia University.

Dyson, A. H. (1997). *Writing Superheroes: Contemporary Childhood, Popular Culture, and Classroom Literacy.* New York: Teachers College Press.

Edwards, A. D. (1992). Teacher talk and pupil competence. In K. Norman (ed.), *Thinking voices: The work of the National Oracy project*. London: Hodder & Stoughton. (pp. 235-236).

Edwards, D., & Mercer, N. (1987). *Common knowledge. The development of understanding in the classroom*. London: Methuen.

Fayol, M., & Largy, P. (1992). Une approche fonctionnelle de l'orthographe grammaticale. *Langue Française, 95*, 80-98.

Fayol, M., & Monteil, J.M. (1994). Stratégies d'apprentissage / apprentissage de stratégies. *Revue Française de Pédagogie, 106*, 91-110.

Fayol, M. (1997). *Des idées au texte: psychologie cognitive de la production verbale, orale et écrite*. Paris: Presses Universitaires de France.

Fayol, M. (1999). From online management problems to strategies in written composition. In M. Torrance & G. Jeffery (ed.), *The cognitive demands of writing*. Amsterdam: Amsterdam University Press.

Fayol, M., Hupet, M., & Largy, P. (1999). The acquisition of subject-verb agreement in written French: from novices to experts' errors. *Reading and Writing, 11*, 153-174

Fayol, M., Largy, P., & Ganier, F. (1997). Le traitement de l'accord sujet verbe en Français écrit: le cas des configurations pronom1 pronom2 verbe. *Verbum, 12*, 103-120.

Fayol, M., Largy, P., & Lemaire, P. (1994). When cognitive overload enhances subject-verb agreement errors. A study in French written language. *Quarterly Journal of Experimental Psychology, 47*, 437-464.

Fayol, M., Largy, P., Thevenin, M.G., & Totereau, C. (1995). Gestion et acquisition de la morphologie écrite. *Glossa, 46-47*, 30-39.

Fayol, M., Thevenin, M.G., Jarousse, J.P., & Totereau, C. (1999). From learning to teaching to learning French written morphology. In T. Nunes (ed.), *Integrating research and practice in literacy*. Amsterdam: Kluwer.

Fayol, M., Totereau, C., & Maino, O. (1998). The impact of redundancy on the agreement of adjectives, a study in written French. Paper presented at the Meeting of the S.I.G. Writing, E.A.R.L.I., Poitiers, France, July 24.

Fayol, M., Totereau, C., & Thevenin, M.G. (1996). Acquiring French written morphology: A case of inflection overgeneralization. *International Journal of Psychology, 31* (34), 42-21.

Fayol, M., Totereau, C., Thevenin, M.G., & Thouilly, C.(1994). Acquisition et mise en oeuvre des marques écrites du pluriel. [The aquisition of written signs for plural]. In *Horizons linguistiques, psychologiques: Horizons neuropsychologiques, médicaux*. Isbergues: L'Ortho Edition. (pp.31-49).

Ferreiro, E. (1997). *Alfabetizacion*. [Literacy] Madrid: Siglo XXI Editores.

Ferreiro, E.(1981). La posibilidad de la escritura de la negaciòn y la falsedad. *Cuadernos de Investigaciòn Educativa, 4*, Departamento de Investigaciones Educativas, Mexico D.F.

Ferreiro, E. & Pontecorvo, C. (1996). Los límites entre las palabras. E. Ferreiro, C. Pontecorvo, N. Ribeiro Moreira & I. García Hidalgo (eds.). *Caperucita Roja Aprende a Escribir* [Little Read Ring Hood learns to write]. Barcelona: Gedisa. (pp. 4571).

Ferreiro, E., & Pontecorvo, C. (1999). Managing the written text: the beginning of punctuation in children's writing. *Learning and Instruction, 9*, 543-564.

Ferreiro, E., & Teberosky, A. (1979). *Los sistemas de escritura en el desarrollo del niño*. México, Siglo XXI (Literacy before schooling, 1982, London New York: Heinemann).

Ferreiro, E. (1978). What is written in a written sentence? A developmental answer. *Journal of Education, 160*, 4, 25-39.

Ferreiro, E. (1988). L'écriture avant la lettre. In H. Sinclair (ed.), *La production de notations chez le jeune enfant: langage, nombre, rythmes et melodies*. Paris: Press Universitaire de France

Ferreiro, E. (1994). Two Literacy Histories: A possible dialogue between children and their ancestors in D. Keller Cohen (ed), *Literacy: interdisciplinary conversations*, Chesskill: New Jersey, Hampton Press, Inc. (pp. 115-128)

Flores d' Arcais, G. B. (1992). Graphemic, phonological and semantic activation processes during the recognition of Chinese characters. In H. C. Chen, & O. J. L. Tzeng (eds.), *Language Processing in Chinese*. Amsterdam: Elsevier Science Publishers.

Flores d' Arcais, G. B., Saito, H., & Kawakami, M. (1995). Phonological and semantic activation in reading kanji characters. *Journal of Experimental Psychology: Learning, Memory, and Cognition, 21*, 34-42.

Floriani, A. (1994). Negotiating what counts: Roles and relationships, texts and contents, content amd meaning. *Linguistics and Education, 5(3 / 4)*, 231-240.

Flower, L. (1994). *The construction of negociated meaning. A social cognitive theory of writing.* Illinois: Southern Illinois University Press.

Franks, J. J., & Bransford, J. D. (1971). Abstraction of visual patterns. *Journal of Experimental Psychology, 90* (1), 65-74.

Freedman, S. (1994). *Exchanging writing, exchanging culture: Lessons in school reform from the United States and Great Britain.* Cambridge, MA: Harvard University Press.

Gee, J. P., & Green, J. L. (1998). Discourse analysis, learning and social practice: A methodological study. *Review of Research in Education, 23,* 119-171.

Geerts, G., Haeseryn, W., Rooij, J. de, &Toorn, M.C. van den (ed..) (1984). *Algemene Nederlandse spraakkunst.* [General Dutch Grammar] Groningen: Wolters-Noordhoff.

Geertz, J. P. (1973). *The interpretation of cultures.* New York: Basic Books.

Gibson, E. J., Osser, H., & Pick, A. (1963). A study in the development of graphemephoneme correspondences. *Journal of Verbal Learning and Verbal Behaviour, 2,* 142-146.

Gibson, E. J., Pick, A., Osser, H., & Hammond, M. (1962). The role of graphemephoneme correspondence in the perception of words. *American Journal of Psychology, 75,* 554-570.

Gibson, E., & Levin, H. (1975). *Psychology of Reading.* Cambridge: MIT Press.

Gillis, S., & Ravid, D. (1999). Differential effects of phonology and morphology in children's orthographic systems: a cross-linguistic study of Hebrew and Dutch. In E. Clark (Ed.), *The proceedings of the 31ˢᵗ annual child language research forum.* Stanford: Center for the study of language and information.

Girolami Boulinier, A. (1984). *Les niveaux actuels dans la pratique du langage oral et écrit.* Paris: Masson.

Givon, T. (1989). *Mind, code and context. Essays in Pragmatics.* Hillsdale, N.J.: Lawrence Erlbaum Associates.

Goldblatt, E. C. (1995). *Round my way: Authority and double consciousness in three urban high school writers.* Pittsburgh: University of Pittsburgh Press.

Goldfajn, T. (1998). *Temporality and the Biblical Hebrew Verb.* Oxford: Clarendon Press.

Golinkoff, R. (1974). Children's discrimination of English spelling patterns with redundant auditory information. Paper presented to the American Educational Research Association, February, 1974; in Gibson, E., & Levin, H. (1975). *Psychology of Reading.* Cambridge: MIT Press.

Gomez, R. L. (1997). Transfer and complexity in artificial grammar learning. *Cognitive Psychology, 33,* 154-207.

Goodman Y. (1990). *How children construct literacy.* Newark, Delaware: International Reading Association.

Goodman, Y. (1984). The development of initial literacy. In H. Goelman, A. Olberg, & F. Smith (eds.), *Awakening to literacy.* Exeter, NH: Heinemann Educational.

Goody, J. and Watt, I. (1963). The consequences of literacy. *Comparative Studies in Society and History, 5,* 340-345.

Gumperz, J. J. (1981). Conversational inference and classroom learning. In J. L. Green & C. Wallat (eds.), *Ethnography and Language* (pp. 3-24). Norwood: New Jersey: Ablex Publishing Corporation.

Halliday, M.A.K. (1989). *Spoken and Written Language.* Oxford, England: Oxford University Press. 2nd edition.

Hansen, J. (1986). Learners work together. In T. E. Raphael (ed.), *The contexts of School Based Literacy.* New York: Random House (pp. 181-190).

Harste, J.C. Woodward, V.A., & Burke, C.L. (1984). *Language Stories & Literacy Lessons.* N.H.: Heinemann Educational Books.

Havelock, E. (1963). *Preface to Plato.* Cambridge, Mass.

Havelock, E. (1986). *The Muse Learns to Write: Reflections on Orality and Literacy from Antiquity to the Present.* New Haven: Yale University Press

Hicks, D. (1996a). Contextual inquiries: a discourse oriented study of classroom learning. In D. Hicks (ed.), *Discourse, learning, and schooling.* Cambridge, MA: Cambridge University Press. (pp. 104-144)

Hicks, D. (1996b). Learning as a prosaic act. *Mind, Culture and Activity, 3(2),* 102-118.

Higgins, L., Flower, L., & Petraglia, J. (1992). Planning text together. The role of critical reflection in student collaboration. *Written Communication, 9(1),* 3-47.

Hildreth, G. (1936). Developmental sequence in name writing. *Child Development, 7*, 291 – 303.

Ho, C. S., & Bryant, P. E. (1997). Phonological skills are important in learning to read Chinese. *Developmental Psychology, 33*, 956-951.

Ho, C. S., & Bryant, P. E. (1999). Phonological awareness and visual skills can predict success in learning to read Chinese and English: A crosscultural research with two longitudinal studies (submitted).

Holt, P. O'B., & Williams, N. (Eds). (1992). *Computers and Writing: State of the Art.* Oxford, England: Intellect Books. Dordrecht, The Netherlands: Kluwer Academic Publishers

Hoosain, R. (1992). Psychological Reality of the Word in Chinese. In H. C. Chen & O. J. L. Tzeng (eds.), *Language Processing in Chinese.* Amsterdam: Elsevier Science Publishers B.V.

Hupet, M., Fayol, M., & Schelstraete, M.A. (1998). Effect of semantic variables on the subjectverb agreement processes in writing. *British Journal of Psychology, 89*, 59-75.

Ibrahim, A. (1994). L'alphabetisation dans un contexte diglossique arabe. In U. Frith, G. L· di, M. Egli and CA. Zuber (eds.), *Contexts of Literacy* Vol. III. Nice: ESF Network on Written Language and Literacy, 23-35.

Jacob, E. (1988). Clarifying qualitative research: A focus on traditions. *Educational Research* (February), 16-24.

Jacob, E. (1997). Context and cognition: Implications for educational innovators and anthropologists. *Anthropology and Education Quarterly, 28*(1), 3 -21.

Jaffré, J-P., & David, J. (1999). Le nombre: essai d'analyse génétique. *Langue Française, 124,* 7-22.

Kane, T.S. (1988). *The new Oxford guide to writing.* New York & Oxford: Oxford University Press.

Karmiloff Smith, A. (1992). *Beyond Modularity.* Cambridge, MA: MIT Press

Kato Y., Ueda A., Ozaki K., & Mukaigawa Y. (1999). Japanese Preschoolers' Theories about the 'Hiragana' System of Writing. To appear in *Linguistics and Education.*

Kellogg, R.T. (1999). Components of working memory in text production. In M. Torrance & G. Jeffery (ed.), *The cognitive demands of writing.* Amsterdam: Amsterdam University Press.

Knapp, P. (1992). *Literacy and learning program: Resource book.* North Parramatta, NSW: Literacy and Learning Program.

Kopcke, K.M. (1998). The acquisition of plural marking in english and German revisited: schemata versus rules. *Journal of Child Language, 25* (2), 293-319.

Kramsch, C. (1993*). Context and culture in language teaching.* Oxford: Oxford University Press

Kress, G. (1996). Writing and learning to write. In D. R. Olson & N. Torrance (eds.), *The handbook of education and human development: new models of learning, teaching and schooling.* Oxford & Cambridge, Mass.: Blackwell Publishers, p. 185.

Kress, G. (1998). Visual and verbal modes of representation in electronically mediated communication: the potentials of new forms of text. In I.Snyder (ed.), *Page to Screen. Taking literacy into the electronic age.* London & New York: Routledge.

Kress, G. (1996). Making Signs and Making Subjects: The English curriculum and social futures London: Institute of Education

Kress, G., & van Leeuwen, T. (1996). *Reading images: The Grammar of visual design.* London & New York: Routledge.

Kruger, A. C., & Tomasello, M. (1986). Transactive discussions with peers and adults. *Developmental Psychology, 22(5),* 681685.

Lacasa, P., Pardo, P., Herranz Ybarra, P., & Martín, B. (1995). Textos y contexto social: Aprendiendo a planificar en un taller de escritura. *Infancia y Aprendizaje, 69-70,* 157-182.

Lakoff, G., & Johnson, M. (1980). *Metaphors we live by.* Chicago & London.

Lavine, L. (1977). Differentiona of letterlike forms in prereading children. *Developmental Psychology, 23,* 89-94.

Largy, P., Fayol, M., & Lemaire, P. (1996). The homophone effect in written French: the case of verb-noun inflection errors. *Language and cognitive processes, 11* (3), 217-255.

Lensmire, T. J. (1994a). *When children write: Critical revisions of the writing workshop.* New York: Teacher College Press.

Lensmire, T. J. (1994b). Writing workshop as carnival: reflections on an alternative learning environment. *Harvard Educational Review, 64,* 371-391.

Leroi-Gourham (1964/65). *La geste et la parole.*

Lessing, D. (1972). *The Golden Notebook* (New ed.). London: Paladin. (Original work published 1962).

Levi Strauss, C. (1962). *La pensèe sauvage.* Paris: Plon

Levin I., Ravid, D., & Rappaport, S. (In press). Developing morphological awareness and learning to write: A two way street. In T. Nunes (ed.), *Literacy in theory and practice*. Amsterdam: Kluwer.

Light, P., & Butterworth, G. (eds.). (1992). *Context and cognition*. New York: Harvester Wheatsheaf.

Linnel, P. (1982). *The written language bias in linguistics*. Linköping:University of Linköping Studies on Communication.

Liu, I. M., Chuang, C.J., & Wang, S. C. (1975). *Frequency count of 40,000 Chinese Words*. Taipei: Lucky Books.

Lucci, V., & Millet, A (1994). *L'orthographe de tous les jours*. Paris: Champion.

Ludwig, O. 1983. *Writing in Focus*. Berlin: Walter de Gruyter

Lyons, J. (1968). *Introduction to Theoretical Linguistics*. Cambridge: Cambridge University Press.

Manguel, A. (1995). *A History of reading*. London: Flamingo

Marcus, G.F. (1995). Children's overregularizations of English plurals. A quantitative analysis. *Journal of Child Language, 22* (2), 447-459.

MarslenWilson, W., & Tyler, L.K. (1998). Rules, representations and the English past tense. *Trends in cognitive sciences, 2 (11)*, 428-435.

Martín del Campo, B., Lacasa, P., Herranz Ybarra, P., & Pardo de León, P. (1994). *How do Children Produce Descriptive Texts at School? The Role of Content, Structure and Linguistic Markings*. Paper presented at the 23rd International Congress of Applied Psychology, organized by 'Colegio Oficial de Psicólogos', Madrid, July 1994.

McCutchen, D. (1995). Cognitive processes in children's writing: developmental and individual differences. *Issues in Education, 1*, 123-160.

Mehan, H. (1979). *Learning lessons*. Cambridge, Mass: Harvard University Press.

Mercer, N. (1995). *The guided construction of knowledge. Talk among teachers and learners*. Clevedon, UK: Multilingual Matters.

Mervis, C.B., & Johnson, K.E. (1991). Acquistion of the plural morpheme A case study. *Developmental psychology, 27* (2), 222-235.

Michalowski, P., (1994). Writing and Literacy in Early States: A Mesopotamianist Perspective in D.Keller Cohen (ed), *Literacy: interdisciplinary conversations*, Chesskill: New Jersey, Hampton Press, Inc. (p.49-70).

Moll, L., & Kurland, B. F. (1996). Biliteracy development in classrooms. In D. Hicks (ed.), *Discourse, learning, and schooling*. Cambridge, MA: Cambridge University Press. (pp. 220-246)

Moreira, N. R., & Pontecorvo, C. (1996). Chapeuzinho/Capuceto. As variações gráficas e a norma ortográfica (Chapeuzinho/Caperuceto: Grafic and orthografic variations): In E. Ferreio, C, Pontecorvo, N. R. Moreira, & I. G. Hidalgo (eds.), *Capeuzinho Vermelho aprende a escrever* [Little Red Riding Hood learns how to write] Saõ Paulo, Brazil: Ática. pp. 78-122).

Nagy, W.E., Daikidoy, I., & Anderson, R.C (1993). Acquisition of morphology Learning the contribution of sufixes to the meanings of derivatives. *Journal of Reading Behavior, 25* (2), 155-170.

Nunberg, G. 1990. *The linguistics of punctuation*. Stanford, CA: Center for the study of language.

Nunes, T., Bryant, P., & Bindman, M. (1997). Spelling and grammarthe necsed move. In C. Perfetti, M. Fayol & L. Rieben (eds.), *Learning to spell*. Hillsdale. Mahwah, NJ: L.E.A.

Nunes, T., Bryant, P. E., & Bindman, M. R. (1997a). Morphological spelling strategies: Developmental stages and processes. *Developmental Psychology, 33*, 637-649.

Nunes, T., Bryant, P. E., & Bindman, M. R. (1997b). Learning to spell regular and irregular verbs. *Reading and Writing: An Interdisciplinary Journal, 9*, 427-449.

O'Connor, M. C., & Michaels, S. (1996). Shifting participant framework: orchestrating thinking practices in group discussion. In D. Hicks (ed.), *Discourse, learning and schooling*. Cambridge, MA: Cambridge University Press (pp. 63-103).

Olson D.R. (1996). The written representation of negation, Paper presented at the invited syposium *Literacy, knowledge and mind* at Vygotsky Piaget Centennial, IInd Conference for Sociocultural Research, University of Geneva, September 1115, 1996.

Olson D.R., Homer (1996). Children's concepts of words. Montreal: International Congress of Psychology.

Olson, D. (1994). *The World on Paper: The conceptual and cognitive implications of writing and reading*. Cambridge, England: Cambridge University Press.

Olson, D. R., & Bruner, J. S. (1996). Folk Psychology and Folk Pedagogy. In D. R. Olson & N. Torrance (eds.), *The Handbook of Education and Human Development* (pp. 927).

Page, R. N. (2000). Future directions in qualitative research. *Harvard Educational Review, 70*(1), 100-108.

Parkes, M. B (1992). *Pause and effect An introduction to the history of punctuation in the West.* Hats, UK, Scolar Press.

Perera, K. (1984). *Children's Writing and Reading.* London: Blackwell.

Perfetti, C. A. (1997). The psycholinguistics of spelling and reading. In C. A. Perfetti, L. Rieben & M. Fayol (eds.), *Learning to Spell. Research, theory, and practice across languages,* pp. 2138. Hillsdale, N.J: Lawrence Erlbaum Associates.

Perret Clermont, A.N., Perret, J. F., & Bell, N. (1991). The social construction of meaning and cognitive activity in elementary school children. In L. B. Resnick, J. M. Levine, & S. D. Teasley (eds.), *Shared cognition: thinking as social practice.* Washington, DC: American Psychological Association (pp. 41-63).

Philips, S. U. (1983). *The invisible culture. Communication in classroom and community on the Warm Springs Indian Reservation.* Prospect Heights, IL: Waveland Press.

Piolat, A. (1988). Le retour sur la texte dans l'activitè rèdactionnelle précoce [Going back over one's text in early writing]. *European Journal of Psychology of Education, 4,* 449-459.

Pontecorvo C. (1995). Iconicity in Children First Written Text. In R.Simone (ed), *Iconicity in Language.* Amsterdam:John Benjamins.

Pontecorvo C., Orsolini M. Burge B., & Resnick L.B. (ed). 1996 *Children's Early Text Construction.* Hillsdale, N.J: Lawrence Erlbaum Associates.

Pontecorvo C., & Zucchermaglio C. (1988). Modes of differentiation in children's writing construction. *European Journal of Psychology of Education, 3* (4), 371-384.

Pontecorvo, C., & Morani, R. M. (1996). Looking for stylistic features in children's composing stories: products and processes. In C. Pontecorvo, M. Orsolini, M. Burge & L. Resnik (eds.). *Children's Early Text Construction.* Hillsdale, N.J: Lawrence Erlbaum Associates (pp. 229-259).

Pontecorvo, C. (ed.). (1997). *Writing Development.* Amsterdam: John Benjamins.

Pontecorvo, C. and Rossi, F. (this volume). Absence, negation, impossibility and falsity in children's first writings

Pontecorvo, C., Orsolini, M., Burge, B., Resnick, L.B. (eds). (1996). *Children's Early Text Construction.* Hillsdale, N.J: Lawrence Erlbaum Associates.

Ravid, D. (in press). Representation of morphological unity in the development of Hebrew spelling. *Reading and Writing.*

Ravid, D., & Tolchinsky, L. (in press). Developing linguistic literacy: A comprehensive model. *Journal of child language.*

Read, Ch. 1973. Children's Judgement of Phonetic Similarities in Relation to English Spelling. *Language Learning, 23,* 17-38.

Reichler Beguelin (1990). La notion de 'mot' en latin et dans d'autres langues indoeuropéenes anciennes. In Fruyt, M, and Reichler Beguelin, MJ. *Modeles Linguistiques, 12 (1)* 2246.

Reichler Beguelin, MJ (1992). Perception du mot graphiquedans quelques systémés syllabiques el alphabétiques. *Lalies, 10,* 144-211.

Rijlaarsdam, G., Van Dort-Slijper, M., & Breedveld, E. (1998). About the acquisition of the morphology of adjectives, derived from verbs. An Empirical Study on influential factors. Presentation in Symposium 'A crosslingusitic approach to written morphology. Conference Writing and Learning to Write at the dawn of the 21st Century. Special Interest Group Writing of EARLI, Poitiers 24 July 1998. Astracts p. 85.

Rogoff, B. (1990). *Apprenticeship in thinking. Cognitive development in social context.* New York: Oxford University Press.

Rogoff, B. (1998). Cognition as a collaborative process. In D. Kuhn & R. S. Siegler (eds.), *Cognition, Perception and Language.* (Vol. 2) New York: Wiley (pp. 679 - 744).

Rosinski, R. R., & Wheeler, K. E. (1972). Children's use of orthographic structure in word discrimination. *Psychonomic Science, 26,* 97-98.

Russell, D. (1991). *Writing in the academic disciplines, 1870/1990: A curricular history.* Carbondale & Edwardsville: Southern Illinois University Press

Sandbank, A. (this volume). On The Interplay Of Genre And Writing Conventions In Early Text Writing

184

Sandbank, A. (1999). Foundations of literacy. In R. A. Aisenman (ed.). *Working Papers in Developing Literacy across Genres, Modalities, and Languages* Tel Aviv: Tel Aviv University Press (pp. 237-247)..

Sapir, E. (1958). The grammarian and his language. In D. G. Mandelbaum (ed.)*Selected writings of Edward Sapir in language, culture ands personality.* Berckley/Los Angeles: University of California Press. [First published 1924]. (pp. 150-159).

Saussure, F. de, (1987). Curso de lingüística general [Cours of general linguistics]. Madrid: Alianza Editorial. [First published 1916.]

Scardamalia, M., & Bereiter, C. (1992). Dos modelos explicativos de los procesos de composición escrita. *Infancia y Aprendizaje, 58*, 43-64.

Scarlett, C. M. (1989). *Children's Understanding of Written Language before Formal Teaching Instruction.* Unpublished Master dissertation. University of London.

Scott, M. (1999). Agency and subjectivity in student writing. In C. Jones, J. Turner & B. Street (eds.), *Students writing in the university: Cultural and epistemological issues.* Amsterdam: John Benjamins (pp 171-191).

Scribner, S. (1976/1997). Situating the experiment in crosscultural reseach. In E. Tobach, R. J. Falmage, M. B. Parlee, L. M. Martin, & A. Scribner (eds.), *Selected writings of Silvia Scribner.* Cambridge, UK: Cambridge University Press (pp. 94-105).

Scribner, S., & Cole, M. (1981). *The psychology of literacy.* Cambridge, MA.: Harvard University Press.

Scholes, R. (1993). *Literacy and language analysis.* Hillsdale, N.J: Lawrence Erlbaum Associates

Schultz, K. (1997). Do you want to be in my story?: Collaborative writing in an urban elementary school classroom. *Journal of Literacy Research, 29*, 253 - 287.

Schultz, K. (2000). Society's child: Social context and writing development. *Educational Psychologist, 35*(1), 51-62.

Seidenberg, M. S. (1985). The time course of phonological code activation in two writing systems. *Cognition, 19*, 130.

Sharples, M. (1999*). How we write: Writing as creative design.* London & New York: Routledge.

Sinclair, J. M., & Coulthard, R. M. (1975). *Towards an analysis of discourse: The English used by teachers and pupils.* London: Oxford University Press.

Sirat, C. 1994. Handwriting and the Writing Hand. In W. C. Watt (ed.), *Writing Systems and Cognition.* Dordrecht: Kluwer.

Slobin, D. (1997).The origins of grammaticizable notions: Beyond the individual mind. In D. Slobin (ed.), *The crosslinguistic study of language acquisition.* Vol. 5. Hillsdale, N.J: Lawrence Erlbaum Associates. (pp. 265-323).

Snyder, I. (Ed.). (1998). *Page to Screen. Taking literacy into the electronic age.* London & New York: Routledge.

Snyder, I. (1998). *Hypertext: The electronic labyrinth.* Melbourne, Australia: Melbourne University Press.

Sulzby, E. (1986). Children's elicitation and use of metalinguistic knowledge about word during literacy interactions. In D. B. Yaden, Jr. & Sh. Templeton (eds.). *Metaliguistic Awareness and Beginning Literacy.* Portsmouth: Heinemann Educational Books (pp. 219-233).

Sulzby, E. (1992). Writing and reading organization. In W. H. Teale & E. Sulzby (eds.). *Emergent Literacy.* Norwood, N.J.: Ablex. (pp. 219-233).

Sulzby, E. (1996). Roles of oral and written language as children approach conventional literacy. In C. Pontecorvo, M. Orsolini,, M. Burge, & L. Resnik (Eds) *Children's Early Text Construction.* Hillsdale, N.J: Lawrence Erlbaum Associates (pp. 25-47).

Swales, J.M., & Feak, C.B. (1994). *Academic Wriitng for Graduate Students: A course for nonnative speakers of English.* Ann Arbor: University of Michigan Press.

Taft, M., & Zhu, X. (1995). The representation of bound morphemes in the lexicon: A Chinese study. In L. B. Feldman (ed.), *Morphological Aspects of Language Processing,.* Hillsdale, (NJ): Lawrence Erlbaum (pp. 293-216).

Teale, W. L., & Sulzby, E. (1986). *Emergent Literacy: Writing and Reading.* NJ: Ablex.

Thévenin, M.G, Totereau, C., Fayol, M., & Jarousse, J.P. (1999). L'apprentissage/enseignement de la morphologie écrite du nombre en français. *Revue Française de Pédagogie, n°126*, 39-52.

Todorov, T. (1977). *The Poetics of Prose.* Ithaca, New York: Coronell University Press.

Tolchinsky Landsmann L., (1988). Form and meaning in the development of writing. *European Journal of Psychology of Education, 4*, 385-398.

Tolchinsky Landsmann L., Levin I. (1987). Writing in four to six years old: Representation of phonetic similarities and differences. *Journal of Child Language, 14*, 127-144.

Tolchinsky Landsmann, L., & Karmiloff Smith, A. (1992). Children's understanding of notations as domain of knowledge versus referential communicative tools. *Cognitive Development, 7*, 287-300.

Tolchinsky Landsmann, L. (1990). La reproducción de relatos en niños entre cinco y siete años: organización sintáctica y funciones narrativas [Storyreproduction in five to seven year olds: Syntactic organization and narrative functions]. *Anuario de Psicología, 47.* 65-88.

Tolchinsky Landsmann, L. (1996). Three Accounts of Literacy and the role of the environment. In C. Pontecorvo, M. Orsolini, M. Burge & L. Resnik (eds.). *Children's Early Text Construction.* Hillsdale, N.J: Lawrence Erlbaum Associates (pp. 99-101).

Tolchinsky Landsmann, L. 1990. Early Writing Development: Evidence from Different Orthographic Systems. In M. Spoelders (ed.), *Literacy Acquisition.* (pp. 223-239).

Tolchinsky, L. (1991). Lenguaje, escritura y conocimiento lingüístico. (Language, writing, and linguistic knowledge), In M. Siguán (ed), La enseñanza de la lengua (Language teaching). Barcelona, ICEUniversidad de BarcelonaHorsori.

Tolchinsky, L. (1992). *El aprendizaje del lenguaje escrito: procesos evolutivos e implicaciones didacticas.* [Learning written language: developmental processes and educational implications]. Barcelona: Anthropos.

Tolchinsky, L., & Teberosky, A. (1998). The Development of Word Segmentation and Writing in Two Scripts. *Cognitive Development, 13*, 121.

Tolchinsky, L., Teberosky, A. (1997). Explicit Word Segmentation and writing in Hebrew and Spanish. In C. Pontecorvo (ed), *Writing Development.* Amsterdam: John Benjamins.(pp.77-99).

Tolchinsky Landsman, L., & Levin, I. (1985). Writing in preschoolers: An age related analysis. *Applied Psycholinguistics, 6*, 319 – 339.

Tolchinsky, L. (in press). *The child's path to writing and numbers.* Mahwah NJ.: Lawrence Erlbaum Associates.

Tomlin, R. S., Forrest, L. P., Pu, M. M., & K.Kim, M. (1997). Discourse semantics. In T. A. VanDijk (ed.), *Discourse as structure and process. Vol. 1. Discourse Studies: A multidisciplinary introduction.* London: Sage (pp. 63-111).

Totereau, C., & Fayol, M. (1996). The acquisition of number inflections in written language. In: Rijlaarsdam, G., Van den Bergh, H. & Couzijn, M. (eds.). *Theories, Models and Methodology in Writing Research.* Amsterdam: Amsterdam University Press (pp. 381-397).

Totereau, C., & Fayol, M. (1994). *The acquisition of number inflections in written English.* Technical Report. Université de Bourgogne: Dijon.

Totereau, C., Barrouillet, P., & Fayol, M. (1999). Overgeneralizations of number inflections in the learning of written French. The case of nouns and verbs. *British Journal of Developmental Psychology, 16*, 447-464.

Totereau, C., Fayol, M., & Barrouillet, P. (submitted). The acquisition of noun, adjective and verb inflections for number in written French.

Totereau, C., Thevenin, M. G., & Fayol, M. (1997). The development of the use and understanding of number morphology in written French. In Rieben, L., Fayol, M. & Perfetti, C. (eds.). *Learning to Spell.* Hillsdale, NJ: Lawrence Erlbaum Associates.

Untersteiner, A., (1959). *I presocratici* [The presocratic philosophers], Torino: Einaudi.

Vackeck, J. (1932/1988). *Written language revisited.* (P.A. Luelsdorf, Ed.) Amsterdam & Philadelphia: John Benjamin.

Veneziano, E. (1992). Ganando pericia con la edad: Una aproximación constructivista a la adquisición inicial del lenguaje [Getting expert in the old: A constructivist approach to early language acquisition]. *Substratum, 1*, 79-101.

Ventola, E. (1996). Packing and unpacking of information in academic texts. In E. Ventola & A. Mauranen (eds.), *Academic writing: intercultural and textual issues* Amsterdam & Philadelphia: John Benjamins (pp 153-194).

Vigliocco, G., & Nicol, J. (1998). Separating hierarchical relations and word order in language production: is proximity concord syntactic or linear? *Cognition, 68* (1), 13-29.

Vigliocco, G., Butterworth, B., & Semenza, C. (1995). Constructing subject verb agreement in speech the role of semantic and morphological factors. *Journal of Memory and Language, 34 (2),* 186-215.

186

Volterra, V. (1972). Il no: prime fasi dello sviluppo della negazione nel linguaggio infantile, (First phases in the use of negation in children's language development). *Archivio di psicologia, neurologia e psichiatria, 33,* 16-53.

Vygotsky, L. S. (1934/1987). *Thought and language.* (Newly revised and edited by A. Kozulin.) Cambridge, Mass.: MIT Press.

Vygotsky, L. S. (1978/1986). *Mind in Society. The Development of Higher Psychological Processes.* Edited by M. Cole, V. John Steiner, S. Scribner, E. Souberman. Harvard, Mass: Harvard University Press.

Vygotsky, L. S. (1987). *The collected works of L.S. Vygotsky. Volume 1. Problems of General Psychology.* Edited by R. W. Rieber & A. S. Carton. Translation Norris Minick. New York: Plenum Press.

Weel, Inge M. (1995). *De schriftelijke verwervingsvolgorde van meervoudsmoffemene van zeltstandige naamwoorden en enkelvouds en meervoudsmorfemen van werkwoorden. Over de invloed van auditieve waarneembaarheid, woordsoort en extra syntactische informatie.* [The sequence of acquisition of written plural morphemes of nouns and written singular and plural morphemes of verbs. About the influence of audibility, word type and syntactical information.] University of Amsterdam: MAThesis.

Weel, I., Van Dort-Slijper, M., & Rijlaarsdam, G. (1996). The acquisition of plural morphology in noun and verb inflectionns for number in written Dutch (1996). In Camps, A, Castelló, M., Millian, M., Monné, P., Rodriguez Illera, J.L. & Tolchinsky, L.(1996). *Abstracts. 1996 European Writing Conferences.* Barcelona, October 2325, 1996.p. 6061.

Wells, G. (1990). Talk about text: Where literacy is learned and taught. *Curriculum Inquiry, 20(4),* 369-405.

Wells, G. (1999). *Dialogic inquiry. Towards a sociocultural practice and theory of education.* Cambridge UK: Cambridge University Press.

Wells, G., Chang, G. L., & Blake, M. (eds.). (1992). *Language and learning: learners, teachers and researchers at work. Vol 4. Collaborative research.* Toronto: OISE, Joint Centre for Teacher Development.

Wertsch, J. V. (1985). *Vygotsky and the Social Formation of Mind.* Cambridge, Massachusetts & London, England: Harvard University Press.

Wertsch, J. W. (1991). *Voices of the Mind. A Sociocultural Approach to Mediated Action.* Cambridge, MA.

Wood, D. (1988). *How children think & learn.* Oxford: Blackwell.

Zecker, L.B. (1996). Early development in written language: Children's emergent knowledge of genre specific characteristics. Reading and Writing, 8, 1, 525.

Zhou, Y. K. (1980). *Precise guide to pronunciation with Chinese phonological roots.* Jilin People's Publishing. [in Chinese]

Zhu, Y. P. (1987). *Analysis of cuing functions of the phonetic in modern China.* East China Normal University. [in Chinese]

Zucchermaglio, C., & Scheuer, N. (1996). Children dictating a story: Is together better? In C. Pontecorvo, M. Orsolini; M. Burge & L. Resnick (eds.). *Children's Early Text Construction* Hillsdale, N.J: Lawrence Erlbaum Associates (pp. 83-99).

NAME INDEX

SUBJECT INDEX

Studies in Writing

7. P. Tynjälä et al. (eds.): *Writing as a Learning Tool*. 2001
    ISBN HB 0-7923-6877-0; PB 0-7923-6914-9
8. L. Tolchinsky (ed.): *Developmental Aspects in Learning to Write*. 2001
    ISBN HB 0-7923-6979-3; PB 0-7923-7063-5

For Volumes 1 – 6 please contact Amsterdam University Press, at www.aup.nl

KLUWER ACADEMIC PUBLISHERS – DORDRECHT / BOSTON / LONDON